Learning and Teaching with Maps

This book explains how children and young people read, understand and interpret maps and how teaching with maps can be more effective. Learning about maps has never been so important for children and young people. The rapid growth of internet mapping, digital atlases and Geographical Information Systems demands new skills alongside traditional ones such as locating places and using a map to find the way.

Learning and Teaching with Maps describes how children make meaning with maps, including large scale plans, topographic and thematic maps, globes and maps of the world. Using evidence from psychology, geography and education it describes how children understand scale, coordinates, symbols, contours and place names and identifies common learning difficulties. New perspectives are provided on children's understanding of small scale and atlas maps as well as recent evidence for young people's use of Geographical Information Systems. The text is extensively illustrated with examples of maps, including those made by children themselves using conventional materials as well as computer software.

The book describes how teachers can plan a curriculum to ensure balance and progression and suggests workable classroom activities for children from the early years of primary school to the middle of secondary education. Particular attention is paid to how learning with maps can contribute to children's developing literacy and numeracy skills. The book draws on the author's unique experience of teaching in primary and secondary schools, teacher training and extensive research and development in educational cartography.

Patrick Wiegand is Reader in Geography Education at the University of Leeds and Chair of the Cartography and Children Commission of the International Cartographic Association.

REFERENCE

ONLY

Learning and Teaching with Maps

Patrick Wiegand

Routledge
Taylor & Francis Group

LONDON AND NEW YORK

First published 2006 by Routledge
2 Park Square, Milton Park, Abingdon, Oxon OX14 4RN

Simultaneously published in the USA and Canada
by Routledge
270 Madison Avenue, New York, NY 10016

Routledge is an imprint of the Taylor & Francis Group

Typeset in Galliard by Graphicraft Limited, Hong Kong
Printed and bound in Great Britain by TJ International Ltd, Padstow, Cornwall

British Library Cataloguing in Publication Data
A catalogue record for this book is available from the British Library

Library of Congress Cataloging in Publication Data
A catalog record for this book has been requested

ISBN10: 0–415–31209–4 (hbk)
ISBN10: 0–415–31210–8 (pbk)
ISBN13: 9–78–0–415–31209–7 (hbk)
ISBN13: 9–78–0–415–31210–3 (pbk)

Contents

List of colour plates   viii
List of figures   ix
Acknowledgements   xi

1   **Introduction**   1

    Research in cartography and children 2

PART 1
Understanding maps   5

2   **Cartography and geo-information science**   7

    The 'cartographic revolution' 8
    How maps work 9

3   **How children learn with maps**   12

    Is map learning innate? 12
    Map learning as the personal construction of knowledge 13
    Map learning as the social construction of knowledge 20
    Perspectives from an information processing approach 22

4   **Models, aerial photographs and large scale plans**   26

    Understanding that models can represent space 26
    Understanding that aerial photographs can represent space 27
    Understanding that maps can represent space 29
    Using maps to find a location 30
    Understanding the map's alignment and viewing angle 33
    Understanding scale 34
    Using coordinates 36
    Understanding symbols and text on large scale maps 37

5   **Using maps to find the way**   39

   A life skill we don't teach 39
   Using maps to identify a route 40
   Navigating small spaces 41
   Navigating in the real world 42

6   Children's neighbourhood maps   45

   Recreating the view from above 45
   Children's maps of their home area 45
   Assessing children's maps 46
   Using mapping software 50

7   Understanding topographic and thematic maps   51

   Some learning difficulties with scale 51
   Generalisation 53
   Understanding conventional symbols on topographic maps 53
   Visualising relief 55
   Contours 59
   Reading and understanding text on small scale maps 61
   Understanding picture maps 62
   Understanding thematic maps 63

8   World maps, globes and atlases   67

   Understanding the Earth 67
   Development of world place knowledge 69
   Children's maps of the world 69
   Map projections 74
   Understanding the spherical Earth 77
   Children's maps of their own country 79
   Understanding nested spatial hierarchies 80
   School atlases 83
   Electronic atlases 85

PART 2
Better teaching with maps   89

9   Planning a map and GIScience curriculum   91

   Map skills 91
   Progression 92
   Evaluating map teaching strategies 96
   Gender differences 97
   Maps and special users 98

10   Practical map activities: up to age 7   100

Direct and indirect environmental experience 100
Learning with models, photographs and large scale plans 102
Learning with atlases and globes 104

11   Practical map activities: age 7 to 11   106

Developing map numeracy 106
Developing map literacy 109
Learning with large scale maps 110
Map making 112
Learning with atlases and globes 114

12   Practical map activities: age 11 to 14   116

Map numeracy 116
Map literacy 118
Developing map and atlas skills 119
Learning to use GISystems 121
Beyond age 14 122

13   Making better maps for children   124

Putting maps on the page 124
Graticules and grids 127
Showing scale information 128
How much detail to show? 128
Symbology and legends 128
Supporting map reading through type 130
Labelling geographical names 133

14   Conclusion   136

Appendix   139
Bibliography   141
Index   152

Colour plates

Colour plates between pages 50 and 51

Plate 1   A map of the world by Miss Vevers, Leeds Ladies College, 1880 (from the author's collection)

Plate 2a   Character appraisal of the village of Hebden using *ArcView* GIS, 2005: age of building survey

Plate 2b   Character appraisal of the village of Hebden using *ArcView* GIS, 2005: building materials survey

Plate 2c   Character appraisal of the village of Hebden using *ArcView* GIS, 2005: topographic context

Plate 3   Point, line and area symbols combine with text to make a topographic map

Plate 4   Visual variables used in map symbology

Plate 5   Coordinate game devised by Blades and Spencer

Plate 6   A village study using *Local Studies*

Plate 7   Children's electronic map making using *Textease*

Plate 8   Picture maps provide a 'sense of place'

Plate 9a   *ArcView* GIS project on the quality of life in Brazil: illiteracy

Plate 9b   *ArcView* GIS project on the quality of life in Brazil: participation in higher education

Plate 10   Atlas map legend from *Atlas Rodinoznanie*

Plate 11   Project on regional variations in Italy using *AEGIS 3*

Figures

3.1	Model used in Piaget's 'Three Mountains' experiment	16
3.2	Model landscape used in Laurendeau and Pinard's 'localisation of geographical positions' test	16
3.3	Flowchart of human information processing	22
3.4	Thematic point symbol map showing manufacturing industry	23
4.1	Experimental space and equipment used by Bluestein and Acredolo	30
4.2	Layout used by Blades and Spencer for a map-using task	31
4.3	Scale error in reconstructing a layout	35
4.4	Street maps pose particular challenges for young map readers	38
5.1	Subjective and objective frameworks of spatial relations	40
5.2	A portion of the Leeds Picture Map	43
6.1	Journey from home to school maps	49
7.1	Some alternative scale representations	52
7.2a	Digital Elevation Model (DEM) of Reno, Nevada, from the north	56
7.2b	The same view rotated so that it is seen from the south	56
7.3	Mapping relief in 2D using a sandbox	57
7.4	Hierarchy of children's 2D representations of relief	58
7.5	Map used to test secondary school students' interpretation of contours	60
7.6	Crop and livestock production in Africa: a thematic point symbol map	64
7.7	Children's interpretation of proportional circle legends	65
8.1	Children's conceptions of the Earth as a cosmic body	68
8.2	Typical development of the 'known world' of childhood from a UK perspective	70
8.3	Children's free recall sketch maps of the world	71
8.4	Some contrasting map projections	75
8.5a	Earthquake and volcano project using *ArcVoyager*: Robinson projection	76
8.5b	Earthquake and volcano project using *ArcVoyager*: View of the Earth from space	77
8.6	Drawing land masses on a spherical surface	78
8.7	Free recall map of the British Isles drawn by a girl, aged 10 years	79
8.8	Materials used by Jahoda (1962) for exploring children's thinking about nested spatial hierarchy	81
8.9	Relative locations of Reno and San Diego	82
8.10	Hierarchical coding of spatial relations	83
8.11	Relative locations of Edinburgh and Madrid	84

8.12	Contrasting approaches to sheet lines for Europe	85
10.1	Oblique view playbase with model vehicles	103
11.1	'Colour the left boots red and the right boots green'	107
11.2	A teacher-produced map of Australia showing a British Isles scale comparitor	109
11.3	'Match the building to the correct plan'	111
13.1	Some alternative page layouts for the maps of the United Kingdom	125
13.2	Figure-ground differentiation and the use of a locator	126
13.3	Supporting students' use of coordinates	127
13.4	Contrasting hierarchies of settlement symbols	129
13.5	Land height legend from the *Oxford Primary Atlas*	130
13.6	Sample of school atlas type from the *Oxford Student Atlas*	131
13.7	Background affects legibility of type	132
13.8	Some contrasting positions of type for point symbols	133
13.9	Some contrasting positions of type for linear symbols	133
13.10	Some contrasting positions of type for areas	134

Acknowledgements

I would like to acknowledge assistance from the following friends and colleagues. Carolyn Anderson, Head of Cartography, and Karen Brittin, Cartographic Editor, at Oxford University Press (OUP), together with Eunice Gill, formerly of OUP, have taught me a great deal about the practical business of making atlases. I have also learned much from Adrian Smith's skilful page design and knowledge of typography. Tracey Learoyd, Cartographic Technician at OUP, drew many of the figures for this book, some of which are adapted from OUP material. I am most grateful to her and to the Publishing Director (Schoolbooks), Denise Cripps, for supporting this project. I would especially like to thank Oxford University Press for permission to reproduce extracts from several Oxford atlases with which it has been such a great pleasure to be involved.

Some of the work described in this book was undertaken whilst I held a Leverhulme Research Fellowship in GIS in Education. I am grateful to Jackie Anderson, former (and founding) Chair of the Cartography and Children Commission of the International Cartographic Association and to other members of the Commission for providing many opportunities to talk about children and maps. I have benefited greatly from the work of Mark Blades, David Boardman, Henry Castner, Simon Catling, Roger Downs, Lyn Liben, Herbert Sandford, Christopher Spencer and Joseph Stoltman. Alberta Auringer Wood very kindly sent me biographical information about Barbara Bartz Petchenik who, sadly, I never met and Henry Castner very helpfully located microfilm copies of some of her unpublished work. These helped to fill in some gaps in my knowledge about someone whose work I have long admired. Joseph Kerski (United States Geological Survey), Roger and Anita Palmer (GIS Educational Technology Consultants) and Charlie Fitzpatrick (ESRI) 'got me going' with GIS. Several of the research projects described in this book were undertaken with the assistance of Bernadette Stiell. Rob Robson and his colleagues at Tadcaster Grammar School made me welcome and enabled me to pursue several studies with students at the school. Janet Coles provided substantial assistance in the preparation of the bibliography. Sally Beveridge was, as ever, encouraging and supportive throughout the entire project.

I am grateful to the following people who have allowed me to reproduce or make reference to their work: Temenoujka Bandrova, Anna Bartholomew, Mark Blades, Diana Freeman, Joseph Kerski, David Owen, Tony Ramsay, Christopher Spencer.

Plate 3 From the *Oxford Student Atlas*, copyright © 2002 Oxford University Press, reproduced by permission of Oxford University Press.

Plate 5 I am grateful to Mark Blades and Christopher Spencer of the University of Sheffield for allowing me to reproduce this version of the materials used for their coordinates experiment (Blades and Spencer, 1989a).

Plate 6 Local Studies. Reproduced by permission of Soft Teach Educational.

Plate 7 David Owen and the Register of Research in Primary Geography. Aerial image © Getmapping plc. *Textease* is published by Softease.

Plate 8 Map by Digital Wisdom Publishing; illustrations by Ray Grinaway, James McKinnon, Claudia Saraceni, Michael Saunders, Rode Westblade and Ann Winterbotham from *The Reader's Digest Children's Atlas of the World* © Weldon Owen Pty Ltd.

Plate 9 ArcView Graphical User Interface is the intellectual property of ESRI and is used herein with permission. Copyright © 1992–1996 ESRI.

Plate 10 From *Atlas Rodinoznanie*. Reproduced by permission of Dr Temenoujka Bandrova and Data Map Europe, Sofia, Bulgaria.

Plate 11 The Italy worksheet is part of the *AEGIS 3* interactive mapping (GIS) package for schools. © AU Enterprises Ltd. For information about *AEGIS 3* refer to www.advisory-unit.ork.uk

Figure 3.1 From Piaget, J. and Inhelder, B. (1956) *The Child's Conception of Space*, London: Routledge, reproduced by permission of Taylor and Francis.

Figure 3.2 Reprinted from *The Development of the Concept of Space in the Child* by M. Laurendeau and A. Pinard. By permission of International Universities Press Inc. Copyright 1970 by IUP.

Figure 3.4 From the *Oxford School Atlas*, copyright © 1997 Oxford University Press, reproduced by permission of Oxford University Press.

Figure 4.1 Reprinted with permission of the Society for Research in Child Development.

Figure 4.2 From *The Journal of Genetic Psychology*, 150: 5–18, 1990. Reprinted with permission of the Helen Dwight Reid Educational Foundation. Published by Heldref Publications, 1319 Eighteenth St., NW, Washington, DC 20036–1802. Copyright © 1990.

Figure 4.3 From Uttal (1994), reproduced from the *British Journal of Developmental Psychology*, © The British Psychological Society.

Figure 5.2 © James Brown Designs 2004. email: james@bbbrown15.freeserve.co.uk Updated from 1932 OS map by local survey. No part of this map may be copied without a licence from the publisher.

Figure 7.1d From the *Oxford Junior Atlas*, copyright © 1996 Oxford University Press.

Figure 7.1e From the *Oxford Primary Atlas*, copyright © 2004 Oxford University Press, reproduced by permission of Oxford University Press.

Figure 7.2 DEM and DOQ courtesy United States Geological Survey. I am grateful to Dr Joseph Kerski of the USGS for supplying these figures.

Figure 7.3 Photograph, Patrick Wiegand.

Figure 7.4 Adapted from Wiegand, P. and Stiell, B. (1997b) 'Children's relief maps of model landscapes', *British Educational Research Journal*, 23: 179–92.

Figure 7.5 Reproduced from Boardman (1989: 324) with permission of The Geographical Association.

Figure 7.6 Adapted from *The Oxford Practical Atlas*, 2003, copyright © 2004 Oxford University Press, reproduced by permission of Oxford University Press.

Figure 7.8 From Wiegand, P. and Stiell, B. (1997b) 'Children's relief maps of model landscapes', *British Educational Research Journal*, 23: 179–92. Reproduced by permission of Taylor and Francis. www.tandf.co.uk/journals

Figure 8.1 Adapted from Nussbaum, J. (1979) 'Children's conceptions of the Earth as a cosmic body: a cross age study', *Science Education*, 63: 83–93; Nussbaum, J. (1985) 'The Earth as a cosmic body', in R. Driver, E. Guesne and A. Tiberghien (eds) *Children's Ideas in Science*, Milton Keynes: Open University Press; Nussbaum, J. and Novak, J.D. (1976) 'An assessment of children's conceptions of the Earth utilizing structured interviews', *Science Education*, 60: 535–50.

Figure 8.3 Reproduced with permission from *International Research in Geographical and Environmental Education*, 4, 1995, pp. 19–28.

Figure 8.5 *ArcView* Graphical User Interface is the intellectual property of ESRI and is used herein with permission. Copyright © 1999 ESRI.

Figure 8.6 Photograph Patrick Wiegand.

Figure 8.7 From *The Cartographic Journal*, 34, 1, pp. 13–21, published by Maney Publishing on behalf of the British Cartographic Society (BCS) and reproduced by permission of the BCS.

Figure 8.10 Adapted from McNamara, T.P. (1986) 'Mental representations of spatial relations', *Cognitive Psychology*, 18: 87–121, Copyright 1986, with permission from Elsevier.

Figure 8.12a From the *Oxford Student Atlas*, copyright © 2002 Oxford University Press, reproduced by permission of Oxford University Press.

Figure 10.1 Photograph Patrick Wiegand. Map playbase by Sport and Playbase Ltd.

Figure 11.1 From Wiegand, P., *Oxford Junior Map Skills*, copyright © 1998, Oxford University Press, reproduced by permission of Oxford University Press.

Figure 11.3 From Wiegand, P., *Oxford Junior Map Skills*, copyright © 1998, Oxford University Press, reproduced by permission of Oxford University Press.

Figure 13.3b Adapted from the *Oxford Primary Atlas*, copyright © 2004 Oxford University Press, reproduced by permission of Oxford University Press.

Figure 13.5 From the *Oxford Primary Atlas*, copyright © 2004 Oxford University Press, reproduced by permission of Oxford University Press.

Figure 13.6 From the *Oxford Student Atlas*, copyright © 2002 Oxford University Press, reproduced by permission of Oxford University Press.

1 Introduction

Maps have never been so popular. The use of internet mapping sites for locating places and planning routes is expanding rapidly alongside growing sales of conventional paper maps and atlases. Maps are increasingly used for business, pleasure, advertising and art and the expanding availability of mapping software is democratising map making so that anyone can now make a professional-looking map with relative ease. Even books about maps have become best sellers, telling tales of geological jealousy and cartographic crime (Harvey, 2000; Winchester, 2001). Cartography and geo-information science is now a major sector in the information economy. Ordnance Survey data, for example, are estimated to underpin £100 billion of British economic activity annually (Lawrence, 2003). The number of people now using Geographic Information Systems (GIS) worldwide is more than 2 million and growing at 20 per cent per year. Locational technology has pervaded most aspects of everyday life so that few serious leisure time aviators, boaters, motorists and walkers are unaware of the benefits of Global Positioning System (GPS) receivers for satellite navigation.

In addition to their popularity, maps have never been so relevant to education. As a distinctive form of communication, 'graphicacy' has been viewed for many years as a fundamental skill: the 'fourth ace in the pack' along with articulacy, literacy and numeracy and meriting its inclusion in the curriculum from an early age (Balchin and Coleman, 1973). Free or low cost supply of hard copy maps and digital data to schools from national mapping agencies has increased the availability of teaching materials and raised student motivation. There is evidence too that map based activities are spreading to other parts of the curriculum. For example, computer mapping tools are used more in science than in geography in the United States and they increasingly feature in relation to education about eGovernment and citizenship. Much digital mapping involving young people is community focused. However, the importance of maps to education is not just driven by technological development. The irresistible romantic myth of pirates' treasure maps remains as popular as ever with children. Maps have the propensity for fantasy, taking us to faraway places with strange sounding names. They offer an escape to the imaginary geographies of children's literature: the Hundred Acre Wood; Narnia; Earthsea; Middle Earth and Oz.

We might expect, therefore, that map education for children and young people would be a vibrant enterprise. But the picture is patchy. Teaching and learning with maps takes place primarily in the context of geography at school and I know of no country in the world where geography education is increasing its curriculum share. In the UK at least, discourse in geography education has steadily, over a lengthy period, drifted away from maps as a key pedagogical issue. Whereas Boardman (1974), for example, found that the principal objectives quoted by geography teachers for undertaking fieldwork were to enhance students' map skills (such as orientating a map, following a route and relating landforms to contour patterns), replication of his research 25 years later (Smith, 1999) demonstrated that the significance of map skills in fieldwork had declined markedly. Attempts to reconfigure geography for the twenty-first century curriculum market have not positioned maps as a high profile element of the brand. Mapping in schools has not kept pace with developments in cartography, most of which have been computer based. Three quarters of the Ordnance Survey's revenue, for example, now comes from the sale of digital data and only one quarter from paper maps (Lawrence, 2003). Some years ago, Gerber noted that 'much of the mapping skills work in schools relies heavily on cartographic thinking that is at least twenty years old' (1992: 201). Progress since then has, at best, been slow. Most important of all, map related pedagogy is poorly developed. The evidence for children and young people's learning with maps is fragmented and there are few comprehensive accounts written specifically for teachers. Many teachers, even geography teachers, regard maps (and especially small scale maps) as being unproblematic for learners.

Research in cartography and children

'Maps and children' as an area of research interest represents, in one sense, a subset of the much larger enterprise of spatial cognition and cognitive mapping, which deals with how we come to understand spatial relations via direct experience of the environment as well as through external representations such as maps. Much research on children's spatial cognition has focused on their *mental* representations of spatial relationships and many investigations involving children and maps have not been driven by an interest in cartography at all (Liben and Downs, 1989). Instead, maps have more often been used as a means of accessing some other focus of interest such as children's knowledge of their local environment. There are also numerous studies of children's spatial thinking which refer not to maps in the sense in which most people would understand the term but to aerial photographs or hardware models, whilst new cartographic media such as 3D computer-generated representations of terrain and photo-maps have been almost completely neglected. What this book attempts to do is explore children's engagement with 'real' (i.e. cartographic) maps: how they read and interpret them, use them in the real world and make their own.

On the whole, research evidence in relation to young people's thinking with maps is stronger for preschool and primary age children than it is for secondary school students. Evidence is also stronger for children's thinking with large scale plans of small spaces (such as a room or playground) than it is for their thinking with small scale maps and atlases. We have almost no longitudinal studies providing evidence for the development of individual children's ability to access cartographic information or the progression in learning made by a cohort. Above all, we know very little about school students' engagement with higher order thinking in cartography and geo-information science. The contribution computer mapping can make to education is often promoted with missionary zeal but we are short of hard evidence about what students actually learn. Problem solving, making inferences and decision making (especially with interactive mapping tools) is under researched as is young people's use of maps to learn 'subject' knowledge such as geography, science or history. In most map related research the map itself (although frequently omitted from the research report) is a given. There are few examples of children having to *select* the most appropriate map for a specified purpose.

This book aims to make a contribution to the development of map and geo-information science pedagogy in school as well as to the field of educational cartography by identifying and bringing together research evidence for children's thinking with maps, much of which has hitherto only been available to readers with access to academic or professional journals. It attempts to explore the nature of map skills, to understand children's cognitive development in relation to these skills and to suggest implications for the school curriculum and strategies for classroom practice in order to promote more effective learning and teaching with maps. It also tries to identify good practice in the making of maps for children and young people.

Chapter 2 introduces a profound change that has taken place in recent years in the way we access information from maps. It clarifies some key terminology that will be used throughout the book and explains how conventional and digital maps 'work'. Chapter 3 examines several broad theoretical perspectives which have underpinned accounts of children's thinking and gives examples of how these perspectives have shaped our understanding about children's learning with maps. Chapter 4 deals with evidence for children's thinking with models, aerial photographs and large scale plans of small, familiar areas such as rooms, buildings and their immediate surroundings. How children use maps to navigate their way successfully around spaces such as these is explored in Chapter 5 and examples are provided in Chapter 6 of the strategies children use when making their own maps of the neighbourhood. Children's thinking with small scale maps (i.e. maps of countries, continents and the whole world) as well as atlases is described in Chapters 7 and 8. Chapter 9 offers broad structural guidance on planning a cartographic curriculum in school and draws attention to the nature of individual learner differences in relation to maps, particularly gender and special educational need. The following three chapters (10, 11 and 12) provide specific examples of appropriate map related activities for each of three target age ranges (i.e. the lower primary, upper primary and lower secondary years of schooling). These activities are especially designed to be readily applicable to teachers in a variety of educational contexts. A curriculum that included all these suggestions would be very full indeed and leave little room for other subjects but the listing is intended to stimulate curriculum development, not to prescribe a definitive curriculum plan. Some of the activities described are currently widely undertaken, others hardly at all. Some used to be taught but have now fallen out of favour. There are considerable resource implications for materials (e.g. of maps, hardware and software), the availability of which will influence what can be achieved and in some cases health and safety issues are raised (such as in more adventurous wayfinding with maps involving off-site visits). Chapter 13 suggests some ways in which teachers and others can make better maps for children. The final chapter summarises some key points and looks to an agenda for change.

Although the book has been written from a UK perspective, an international readership is anticipated and therefore references to specific cartographic products and curricula have been minimised. I have generally preferred the word 'legend' rather than 'key' in the text as this is the term most commonly used by cartographers.

Whether you are a parent, teacher, student, cartographer or (like so many people) just interested in maps, I hope you will take from this book an enhanced understanding of how children make meaning with them and what strategies can be used to promote map learning.

Part 1
Understanding maps

2 Cartography and geo-information science

To introduce some of the themes that run throughout this book, we start with two examples (125 years apart) of young cartographers at work.

Plate 1 shows a world map drawn by a young woman at the Leeds Ladies College, Yorkshire, in 1880. It has been painstakingly copied from an atlas into a notebook at a size of about 11cm × 16cm. Although the watercolour has faded, the pink wash of the British Empire is still just visible, its extent emphasised by use of a Mercator projection, which enlarges land areas towards the poles. The map has been fastidiously labelled: land masses and oceans are in sloping capitals; other place names are executed in a tiny, non-cursive script. We don't know how long it took her to copy this map. Ten hours? Perhaps more. The task's function as a learning activity was, presumably, straightforward: simply to show where places are in relation to each other. As the notebook is hard-backed and quarter bound in leather, we can assume it was intended to last for many years: an authoritative and unchanging inventory of the world.

By contrast, Plate 2 shows a series of screen shots from a group project carried out by school students in Yorkshire in 2005. They are investigating a proposal that the village of Hebden in the Yorkshire Dales National Park should be designated a Conservation Area. This involves them carrying out an environmental appraisal of the village and assessing the extent to which individual buildings exert a positive or negative impact on the village's character. The students' target is to make a presentation arguing a case for, or against, creating a Conservation Area and (if making a case in favour) delimiting its proposed boundary. The information they collect is stored in a database and mapped with Ordnance Survey digital data using *ArcView* (ESRI, see Appendix). They have collected and mapped data on the age of buildings (Plate 2a; oldest buildings in red; most recent in green) and linked digital images to individual properties. This helps them visualise the historic structure of the village. They notice that building materials are important in determining the character of the built environment (Plate 2b shows roof material: slate in grey; stone in yellow) and mapping the physical attributes of buildings helps the group identify those which contribute most to the character of the village and those which contribute less. To think about the proposed Conservation Area boundary they add an aerial photograph and contours to the view (Plate 2c), which helps them consider the village in its topographic context.

In both instances, the students are using maps as tools for learning but they are also learning about the *process* of mapping. In the nineteenth century example, country colour is differentiated according to attribute (e.g. membership of the British Empire) and lettering is differentiated by type of feature. Today's students, however, are empowered to use the mapping environment interactively to find answers to their questions. The maps they make are tailored to their specific needs: they are not reproducing knowledge but creating it. Their ability to select content as well as symbology (they are in control of what to show as well as how to show it) enables them to argue a case. In their hands the interactive mapping environment becomes a powerful tool for persuasion as well as analysis.

These two examples both make use of maps ('symbolised representations of a geographical reality', ICA, 2003) but they serve to illustrate profound ways in which cartography ('the art, science, and technology of making and using maps', ICA, 2003) is changing.

The 'cartographic revolution'

Until recent decades, most people experienced maps as printed on paper, objects that could be seen, handled and were (more or less) permanent. Very rapid progress in computing technology has led to increasing numbers of maps being virtual (e.g. existing in digital format and seen only on a computer screen), invisible (e.g. stored as digital data on disk) and even intangible (e.g. accessible over a network from a database) (Moellering, 1980). Traditionally, you used a map by looking at it. Increasingly, maps are interactive so that the user can select required layers of information, access spatial databases to search for and then customise data, alter the way that data is represented on the map and use tools to analyse it. Such powerful combinations of software, hardware and data are called geographic information systems (GIS or GISystems). Traditionally, maps had limited functionality. They simply displayed information. Now maps may have hyperlinks to connect to related data, images or sound. They may be dynamic so that they can show change through time. GIS represents a new generation of 'supermaps' that lie at the heart of all modern spatial decision making, whether it's locating a new superstore, planning public utilities or managing the environment. The scientific context of spatial information processing and management, including the associated technology as well as its commercial, social and environmental implications, is termed geographic information science (or GIScience) (ICA, 2003).

GIS tools enable the user to create thematic maps based on data stored in a spreadsheet or database. Data can be linked to the map in many ways – for example to an area (such as a country) or a point (such as an address) – and can also be represented as charts and graphics. GIS is dynamic – update the data and the map is automatically updated too. GIS allows the user to visualise and analyse spatial information in new ways, revealing previously hidden relationships, patterns and trends. The implication of this is that we now have to help young people understand the data on which maps depend (the so called 'deep structure' of maps, as opposed to the 'surface' form of the map itself). This brings a new responsibility for teachers.

However, despite a central role in real-world geography (probably the single biggest contribution geographers have had to make to society and economy since the age of discovery) and attempts to promote more widespread take-up, GIScience and digital cartography is a revolution which has not quite happened yet in education. Expectations are high as GIS implies a more collaborative, open pedagogy with greater emphasis on individual or small group learning and a changed relationship between learners and teachers. It offers enhanced opportunities for using 'real' data with consequent emphasis on community involvement (English and Feaster, 2003; Knapp, 2003). In the late 1990s, the most comprehensive survey to date of GIS take-up estimated an adoption rate in American high schools of only 1 per cent (Kerski, 2001, 2003) and 'only a handful' of teacher education programmes exposed beginning teachers to GIS (Bednarz and Audet, 1999).

Although these indications will certainly by now have risen, perhaps even rapidly, the prevailing 'cartographic culture' in schools in both the USA and the UK remains robustly pre-GIS. 'Many organisations, companies and individuals have gone to great length to promote the use of GIS and related classroom technologies. Yet, the number of teachers adopting GIS has remained small' (Baker and Bednarz, 2003: 231).

There are a number of reasons for this. At the time of writing (early 2005) there is a shortage of appropriate software and packaged material that is 'ready to go' in the classroom. 'Industrial strength' software takes time to learn and may be too complex for most students and teachers to work with. There is little consensus on how much GIS a teacher needs to know and whether teachers should be empowered to use complex tools in order to construct their own (particularly local) projects or simply trained to use packaged modules put together by specialists. Either way, the teacher training needs (and associated costs) are substantial. Few assumptions can be made about the capacity of hardware in schools or the technical support available to individual teachers. To date there has been a notable shortage of 'one stop shops' for software and data. For software and data providers, the most effective means of delivery (e.g. via CD or the internet) and method of recovering costs is not clear. For schools, there are well-established models for ordering and paying for books and equipment but buying data online requires new financial procedures. Internal organisation and accounting mechanisms seem slow to respond to changing needs.

None of these difficulties is insuperable but there have been enough hurdles to make most national and regional education authorities cautious about requiring compulsory teaching and learning with GIS and without that requirement the search for a solution is less pressing. Most parties (government, software providers, data providers, teachers and other support agencies) now recognise that there is an urgent need for GIS in schools that meets stated curriculum objectives, is straightforward to implement by classroom teachers under considerable time pressure and is available at a price schools can afford.

In addition to GIS, the related locational technology of the Global Positioning System (GPS) offers exciting possibilities. GPS is a network of satellites that circle the Earth transmitting signals that can be received by a device on the Earth's surface. When the receiver triangulates signals from at least three satellites it pinpoints latitude and longitude, typically to within an accuracy of about 10 metres. A GPS receiver can thus be used as a means of collecting georeferenced survey data in the field. GPS coordinates and remotely sensed data (including aerial photographs, satellite and other digital images) are increasingly combined with GIS databases. GPS is now (but very slowly) beginning to appear in schemes of work for schools. For example, a recent curriculum target in a standards-based guide to K-12 geography in the USA states that students should be able to: 'Choose and give reasons to use specific technologies to analyze selected geographic problems (e.g. aerial photographs, satellite imagery, GIS and GPS to determine the extent of water pollution in a harbour complex in South Africa or the range of deforestation in Madagascar)' (National Geographic Society, 2001: 41).

How maps work

Before addressing children's use and understanding of maps, some key cartographic terms and principles need to be introduced. All maps share some essential characteristics. They are concerned with locations (where places are) and attributes (what's there) and are reductions of reality (they are smaller than the part of the real world they represent). The relationship between the map and the real world it represents is defined by the map's *scale*. Scale is typically shown on a map by a representative fraction (a ratio such as 1:50,000 which means that 1mm on the map represents 50,000mm, or half a kilometre, on the Earth's surface). Scale can also be shown graphically in the form of a *scale bar* (a line subdivided into corresponding real world distance units such as miles or kilometres) or a *scale statement* in words (such as 'one inch to one mile'). A simple reduced scale representation of the world is a *globe*. Although globes are invaluable in enabling us to visualise spatial relationships between land masses they have a number of practical limitations: they are expensive to produce, difficult to store and carry, are only feasible at very, very small scales and even then less than half the Earth's surface can be seen from a single viewpoint. In order to overcome such limitations the spherical surface must be *transformed* to the plane surface of a flat map or computer screen. Systematic ways of making transformations are known as *map projections*. These have properties that govern their use. For example, either shape or area of the Earth's land masses can be preserved, but not both. Maps also commonly have a coordinate system for locating points. These can be *geographical* (using latitude and longitude to relate positions on the map to their position on the spherical Earth's surface) or *plane* (relating positions on the map to a rectilinear grid with a defined point of origin).

Maps cannot show everything. They show only limited aspects of the real world they represent. All maps use *signs* (made up of marks such as dots, lines and colours) to stand for elements of reality and these comprise the map's *symbology*. *Labels* are added to the symbols to identify places represented by the map or to provide additional information about what is shown. Plate 3 shows how these elements (layers of points, lines and areas, together with text) combine to produce a *topographic* or general reference map in a school atlas. *Thematic* maps concentrate on the distribution of a single attribute (or the relationship between two or more attributes) and commonly use a single type of symbol. A population distribution map, for example, may use dots to represent a defined number of people, whereas a rainfall map may use colours between isohyets (lines joining places that have the same amount of rain) to show average annual rainfall.

Point, line and area map symbols can differ in shape, size, orientation, hue (i.e. 'colour'), greytone value (i.e. 'light or dark') and texture (Plate 4). Some of these basic *visual variables* (Bertin, 1983) are better than others for showing types of geographic difference. Shape and hue, for example, are good at representing qualitative differences (such as pictograms representing different kinds of recreational activity or coloured dots to show the location of different minerals). Size and greytone value are good for showing quantitative differences (such as proportional circles to show number of employees or darker shading to represent greater population density). The combination of visual variables with points, lines and areas creates a palette of possibilities for map symbology and many of these are temptingly offered in much widely available mapping software. In the past, map making was the preserve of trained cartographers but now, anyone (including children) can make a convincing looking map. However, not all the choices offered are equally appropriate and therefore it becomes even more important that (young) users understand the cartographic choices available to them. It can be seen that the map maker has a good deal of discretion over the representation of information. Maps are not 'objective', miniature replicas of the world but are highly selective in what they show as well as in what they omit. They are powerful (Wood, 1992) and they can tell lies (Monmonier, 1996).

This chapter has illustrated some of the basic characteristics of conventional and digital cartography. Although the book as a whole espouses the 'new cartography' located within the broader field of GIScience, we have to be realistic about what is presently taking place in schools (especially those outside the highly economically developed world). It is inevitable, therefore, that much of this text will relate to traditional, hard copy maps. Much of the accumulated body of evidence in relation to children and maps is, of course, also set in the context of conventional mapping. Indeed, there is a concern that some of this evidence may be disregarded in the enthusiasm for new technology. The challenge is to reinterpret what we think we already know in the light of the new possibilities created by technological change. The next chapter examines some theoretical approaches to children's learning and illustrates each by specific reference to maps.

3 How children learn with maps

Four broad theoretical perspectives have underpinned accounts of the development of cartographic understanding through childhood. These are:

- that map learning is innate (the so-called *nativist* viewpoint);
- that map learning proceeds gradually through childhood as children progress through qualitatively different stages of intellectual development (a perspective largely based on the developmental psychology of Jean Piaget);
- that map learning is essentially a social process whereby maps come to be understood as cultural artefacts (a perspective based on the learning theories of Lev Vygotsky); and
- that map learning can best be understood using a metaphor from computer science (the *information processing* perspective).

Some commentators have found it helpful to emphasise the differences between these positions, others to emphasise the similarities. *Piagetian* approaches have been especially influential in studies on children and maps whereas, although both *Vygotskyan* and information processing perspectives are well established in relation to children's learning, relatively few studies have yet adopted these theoretical positions as explanatory frameworks for children's cartographic thinking. This chapter summarises each theory and critically reviews its contribution to the field.

Is map learning innate?

Some writers have expressed the view that children's ability to understand maps is innate, or acquired very early in life and with little or no prior map experience. Three lines of argument have been advanced for this perspective. The first is that mapping ability is claimed to be a universal survival mechanism that emerged in the Palaeolithic period (Blaut, 1991). Its function as a primitive communication system was to support behaviour such as migration and the search for food. In order to think about these necessities (so the argument runs), humans had to imagine themselves looking down on a landscape from above and then use graphic representations to communicate spatial information and propose strategies for action. The second line of argument is the number of studies that highlight children's early capacity to use maps, or surrogate maps such as aerial photographs and models. Blaut and his colleagues (Blaut *et al.*, 1970) asserted that 'children already know the skills of map reading and map using when they enter school' (Blaut and Stea, 1971: 390). They arrived at this conclusion after their studies showed that 6-year-olds in New England and Puerto Rico could 'interpret' aerial photographs of their locality by naming and pointing to known features. Some children could trace buildings and simple routes and then use these tracings without the photograph in order to solve simple navigation problems. A subsequent study (Blaut and Stea, 1974) with even younger children (aged 3 to 5) indicated that preschoolers could assemble wooden buildings, cars and cardboard 'streets' and engage through play with this model neighbourhood in a way that suggested they understood it represented a life-size environment. Further studies with children across several cultures (Blades *et al.*, 1998) have also indicated that essential mapping abilities may emerge without training by the age of about 4 years. Liben and Downs (1991), however, suggest that the skills demonstrated by these very young children may be graphic (rather than *geo-graphic*). For example, 'tracing a route' may simply reveal the ability to complete a pencil and paper maze test rather than necessarily understanding the cartographic representation of real routes. A third basis for innate mapping skill was claimed by Landau (1986), using evidence from studies with a 4-year-old girl who, although blind from birth, could use a tactile map to navigate between pairs of objects within a room. She was taught the paths between some pairs of objects but was able to use the map to infer paths between new pairings. Landau's argument is that the girl demonstrated a 'core understanding' of the correspondence between the map's reference system and that of the real space and that, as she had had no prior experience of interpreting maps, this ability must be innate. Subsequent methodological critiques, however (summarised in Newcombe and Huttenlocher, 2000), have challenged this claim.

There *is* ample evidence for children's early engagement with maps. What is at issue, however, is the nature of that engagement. A much larger body of evidence suggests that, far from being acquired early and easily, map skill is attained slowly and gradually (Downs *et al.*, 1988). Indeed, very many adults are unable to use maps effectively. There is little disagreement that very young children show *some* basic map ability but where the boundaries of that ability lie and what the implications are for education have been contentious. The nativist view (or at least findings that demonstrate early competence) has helped make the case for incorporating mapping into the curriculum of very young children. This was a positive outcome at a time when little geography was taught in primary schools, but it may also have left some educators with over-optimistic expectations of young children's mapping abilities. It may be more helpful therefore, as Liben and Downs argue (1997), to consider children's map understanding as having early *beginnings*, not that children possess early *mastery* of map skill. It is more productive to focus on which map related concepts and tasks are more difficult than others in order to establish principles of progression in learning from which to derive appropriate support strategies.

Map learning as the personal construction of knowledge

The work of Jean Piaget has been immensely influential in accounts of children's interactions with maps, especially in the field of geography education. The central theoretical idea is that cognition is a form of environmental adaptation, a process which Piaget called *equilibration*. It proceeds by 'assimilation' (whereby new information is related to pre-existing structures of knowledge and understanding) and 'accommodation' (in which the old structures are developed into new ones in the light of successive experiences). These two processes work together to enable individuals to organise knowledge into coherent systems. Understanding symbols on maps and what they refer to in the real world may, therefore, be seen as dual processes involving continual refinement. For example, through everyday experience a British child identifies a red box-like structure on the street corner as a public telephone. Subsequent encounters with public telephones in other streets reinforce this rule (*assimilation*) until a more modern style of telephone kiosk is encountered which is of similar size but a different shape and built entirely of glass. The 'red box is a telephone' rule is now adapted (*accommodation*) to embrace other instantiations of the phenomenon. Thus, when the 'public telephone' symbol is encountered on a map, the young map user has an enriched understanding of its possible range of real world referents. In Piaget's view of learning, meaning depends on the individual's cognitive structures or schemata. Learning takes place when these schemata are altered through cognitive conflict. Resolving the disequilibration requires internal mental activity and results in the replacement of a previous knowledge schema.

A feature of Piaget's theory is that cognitive development forms an unvarying sequence of coherent and qualitatively different stages: sensori-motor (extending from birth to approximately 2 years of age); pre-operational (from about 2 to 7 years); concrete operational (from about 7 to 11 years) and formal operational (from about ages 11 to 13 onwards). Children's thinking within each of these stages was said by Piaget to be relatively stable across a number of contexts.

Pre-operational thought is characterised by children beginning to use semiotic systems such as language, gestures, objects and mental images to stand for objects or events. A 4-year-old, for example, may use the word 'home', a drawing or a play house to act as a signifier for home itself. Piaget described pre-operational thought as 'egocentric', meaning that children tend to perceive, understand and interpret the world only in terms of themselves. They cannot 'see' someone else's viewpoint, either perceptually or conceptually. Pre-operational thought is also characterised by rigid thinking such as attending to a single salient feature of an object or event and disregarding others. The classic example is of comparing water poured from one container to a taller, narrower one. In pre-operational thought, children tend to centre on the greater height of the water level in the new container (disregarding the smaller surface area) and conclude (on the basis of appearance only) that there is now more water.

In the concrete operations stage, children's thinking no longer has this rigidity. An *operation* is an internalised mental process, such as being able to conserve the notion of an equal quantity of water despite a changed appearance in its level as in the container experiment described above. Other operations include being able to classify, arrange in a series, coordinate perspectives and apply reversible thinking. Once children can use operations, their use of maps takes a dramatic leap forward. They can classify map symbols into points, lines and areas and further classify the lines into those representing boundaries and those representing communications. They can use coordinate reference systems, which require the application of two or more criteria arranged in a series to locate an object. They can recognise that the distance from A to B on a map is the same as the distance from B to A, and that if you describe a route on a map as 'turn left, then right, then left' in one direction it becomes 'turn right, then left, then right' in the opposite direction. They can recognise that if Leeds is in Yorkshire and Yorkshire is in England then Leeds must be in England.

In the stage of formal operations (typically beyond the age of about 11 years) thought becomes more abstract, logical and hypothetical. Problems can be solved and theories tested using map evidence and this evidence can be systematically searched for and acquired. Contradictory sources of evidence can be evaluated. The map itself can be evaluated by reflection on its inherent biases and distortions and the effect of applying different cartographic strategies to the map (such as changing the number of data classes using a simple

GIS function) can be envisaged. Formal operational thought would be required to solve, for example, the problem of which map projection to use in order to best represent the world's major ecological zones. The task requires matching the properties of alternative map projections (e.g. retaining accurate representation of either shape or area of the land masses) with the desired visual outcome (e.g. to be able to compare the relative area of each ecosystem) and make an appropriate choice (i.e. the use of an equal area projection).

Although Piaget had little specific to say about maps, much of his work focused on children's developing understanding of space and geometry and involved the use of models or graphical representations of space (Piaget and Inhelder, 1956; Piaget *et al.*, 1960). Piaget identified three fundamental ways in which spatial relations can be understood. At first, children understand only *topological* spatial relations, based on 'primitive' qualitative properties. They can say, for example, that one item in a model landscape is 'near' another or that one mark on a piece of paper is 'inside' another. With development, children learn to coordinate this partial understanding into an integrated whole in two complementary ways. In one, items or marks can be structured relative to an observer's viewpoint so that each is seen in relation to others (e.g. 'in front of' or 'to the right of'). This relationship is referred to as *projective*. In the other, items or marks can be related to a system of independent coordinates (such as grid lines) by which objects can be related to each other irrespective of an observer's point of view. This relationship is referred to as *Euclidean* or *metric*. Children's spatial thinking does not proceed through each of these in turn (as with Piaget's general stages of intellectual development) but there is instead a development within each, and the categories themselves overlap (Hart and Moore, 1973; Moore, 1976).

One of the ways in which Piaget and Inhelder (1956) investigated the development of young children's understanding of *topological* spatial relationships was to explore their perception and mental representation of shapes. Children were handed a number of objects in turn behind a screen so that each could be felt but not seen. The objects included familiar three-dimensional solids (such as a ball, pencil and comb) and flat geometric shapes (such as a circle, ellipse and square). The task was to match the shapes that could be felt with their real or drawn counterparts in a display that could be seen. Piaget and Inhelder noted that the topological properties of shapes were the first to be recognised whereas metric properties could not be discerned until later development. For example, at about age 3 to 4 years, children could differentiate between: open and closed figures; a surface with one hole and a surface with two holes; and intertwined rings and separate rings. They could not, however, differentiate between closed figures such as a circle, triangle and square. This was partly because they seized one part of the object (e.g. a corner) rather than adequately exploring the whole and partly because they were unable to hold in their minds multiple defining morphological properties of each shape such as the number of angles *and* the number of sides. By about age 5–6, however, they were beginning to discriminate between Euclidean properties such as straight and curved lines, angles of different sizes, parallels and the relations between equal or unequal sides of a figure. A key feature of this discrimination (enabling them to distinguish between, for example, a rhombus and a trapezium) is the ability to coordinate hand movements to return to a fixed point of reference in order to conceptualise shape characteristics.

Projective spatial relations structure space from a particular perspective. This can be from the viewpoint of the observer or that of another. In projective space (unlike topological space) separate items in a model or marks on a map can be located relative to one another but only in relation to a particular 'point of view'. A number of Piaget's experiments

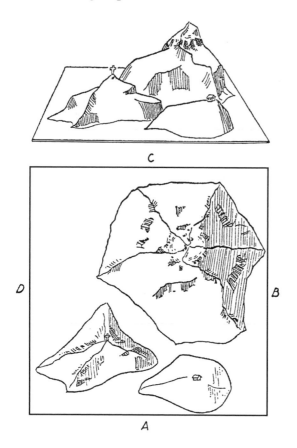

C

A

D

B

Figure 3.1 Model used in Piaget's 'Three Mountains' experiment. From Piaget, J. and Inhelder, B. (1956) *The Child's Conception of Space*, London: Routledge, reproduced by permission of Taylor and Francis.

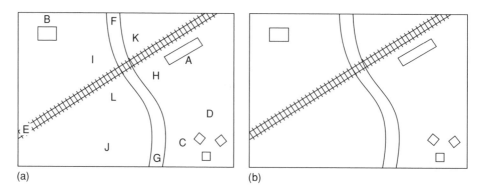

(a)   (b)

Figure 3.2 Model landscape used in Laurendeau and Pinard's 'localisation of geographical positions' test. Reprinted from *The Development of the Concept of Space in the Child* by Laurendeau, M. and Pinard, A. By permission of International Universities Press Inc. Copyright 1970 by IUP.

illustrate the development of children's thinking about projective space. In one (Piaget and Inhelder, 1956), children were invited to arrange a set of matchstick 'posts' on a table top as though they were telegraph poles running along a straight road, the first and last posts having been placed in position by the experimenter. In one form of the experiment, the first and last posts are placed equidistant from the edge of the table so that a straight line can be constructed by referring to the table's edge. In another, the posts are arranged so that a straight line will run obliquely from one edge of the table to the adjacent edge. Children up to about age 4 were unable to form a straight line even when it ran parallel to the table edge. From about age 4 to 7 years, children could construct a straight line when it ran parallel to the edge of the table but not when it ran obliquely. From about age 7 children appeared to be able to construct a straight line irrespective of where it ran in relation to the table. They were said to be able to do this because they could separate the first and last posts from the perceptual 'ground' of the table top and 'take sight' from their own viewpoint along the line in order to align the posts one behind another.

But how do children come to understand that objects look different from alternative viewpoints? One of Piaget's best known experiments (Piaget and Inhelder, 1956) was designed to explore the ways in which children discriminated between their own viewpoint and those of other observers. Children were shown a three-dimensional model of three mountains, each differing in shape, height, and colour and each having a different feature on its peak (Figure 3.1). A wooden doll was placed in various positions on the model and children were asked to demonstrate what the doll would 'see' from each viewpoint using a set of pre-prepared pictures and cardboard cut-out shapes. Up to the age of about 7, children found it difficult to distinguish between their own viewpoint and that of the doll. By about age 7 to 9 years, some spatial relationships were separated (for example, left/right and before/behind) but as the model is quite complex it is only by about age 9 to 10 years that children appeared to be able to coordinate these relations into an integrated whole.

Euclidean (or metric) spatial relations structure space as the coordination of objects rather than the coordination of a number of points of view. This is most commonly via a network of (two- or three-dimensional) axes (or Cartesian coordinates) intersecting each other at right angles. This serves as an independent frame of reference within which objects may be located in space as well as a means of identifying locations irrespective of the objects themselves. According to Piaget, children's development of projective and Euclidean spatial frameworks proceeds in parallel. Piaget explored this development through two tasks involving landscape models. Laurendeau and Pinard (1970) replicated the first of these experiments (with some methodological changes), giving a more detailed (and 'scientific') account of their procedure. It is their version of the experiment that is described here.

Two identical landscape representations were made (each 350mm × 470mm) using flat sheets of cardboard (Figure 3.2). The landscape portrayed a road and a railway line that crossed near the centre and divided the landscape into four sections of unequal shape and size. Houses of different sizes and colours were placed on the base. The tester positioned a small doll on one of the model landscapes and asked each child to place a similar doll in exactly the same place on the other model. This was repeated twelve times – the positions of the doll are shown as A to I in Figure 3.2. The tester then turned the model through 180° and the test was repeated (with the positions of the doll presented in a different sequence).

Success in the task is related to the degree to which the child is able to apply topological, projective or Euclidean spatial reasoning. The youngest children positioned their doll according to topological spatial relationships of, for example, proximity or enclosure. That is to say, they positioned their doll 'near' a reference point such as one of the houses (irrespective of its colour) or 'in' a field, but they could not relate one spatial property with another in order to obtain a locational 'fix' on the model. In the rotated condition they confused locations F and G. Both of these are topologically identical – they are both 'on' the road and 'near' the edge of the model. Similarly, positions I, K and L are also topologically the same – all being 'near' the intersection of the road and railway line. To place the figure correctly at these locations, projective relations need to be employed. For example, in the rotated condition position F becomes 'far from me' instead of 'near to me' and E becomes 'on my left' instead of 'on my right'. Euclidean concepts become necessary when positioning the figure at locations where topological and projective cues are fewer (e.g. positions J, K and L). Here, the child must estimate position by using metric relations such as 'equidistant between the road and railway' or 'twice as far from the railway as the road'.

According to Laurendeau and Pinard (1970), children at about 3 years of age seem to rely solely on topological cues when placing their doll on the model landscape. Projective relations seem to be recognised typically between about $3^{1}/_{2}$ and $5^{1}/_{2}$ years, depending on how ambiguous the associated topological cues are. Initially, the coordination of projective relations is egocentric as children cannot make the mental reversal necessary for success in the rotated model. They are more likely to be able to do so later, typically between the ages of 7 and 10 years.

The second of Piaget's 'topographical' tasks was more demanding, as it required not just the positioning of a single object on a prepared frame of reference but the construction of several objects in relation to each other (Piaget and Inhelder, 1956). A model village was displayed on a cardboard base and children were asked to replicate this arrangement in model form as well as making a drawing of the village from above on a sheet of paper smaller than the model itself. The youngest children (up to the age of about 4) were observed not to be able to make any match between the village components and their modelled or drawn representation. Children of about 4 to 6 years could clump items together but with no maintenance of left–right relations nor regard to the boundary edge of the model or drawing. Piaget also noted children's 'timorous attitude towards empty space' (Piaget and Inhelder, 1956: 435) in relation to their difficulty in spreading out the spatial representation to occupy the same range of area as the original model. From about age 7, items were placed with regard to left–right and before–behind relations but it was only at about age 10 that their representations achieved accuracy with respect to proportional reduction in scale and maintenance of correct relative distances and directions of objects one from another and from the edge of the paper.

These experiments illustrate what Piaget regarded as gradual progress through trial and error in the coordination of spatial viewpoints and the development of understanding a metric reference system. The strength of Piaget's work is that it recognises the central role of cognition in development and it has remarkably wide scope with regard to age and intellectual domains. The theory is especially useful in predicting cartographic concepts and map skills which children may find difficult and suggesting 'what comes next' in a sequence of learning. The many direct quotations in the writing from children grappling with intellectual problems also have, for many teachers, a ring of authenticity.

However, recent years have seen substantial criticism of Piaget's theory and an erosion of some of its key aspects, notably the idea that there are invariant, coherently integrated and organised stages across all domains. There appears to be as much variation within stages as between them and many adults appear not to be able to perform at tasks (including mapping tasks) requiring formal operations. Piaget (and other researchers subsequently replicating his work) paid little attention to the effect of social and emotional aspects of development. We thus know little about how children might respond to maps or models of familiar areas compared to neutral landscapes or how collaboration affects their understanding. Empirical investigations described in subsequent chapters will show that many researchers have found higher levels of performance in spatial and mapping tasks than Piaget's theory predicts. Newcombe and Huttenlocher (2000), for example, review a number of studies which show children *do* understand that observers in other positions see things differently, although they may not be sure how. Part of the reason for children's difficulties with the 'Three Mountains' task, for example, may have been the materials the children were provided with, the form of the questions they were asked and the particular choices they were required to make. Huttenlocher and Presson (1979) found that children had more success in perspective taking tasks when they were asked questions such as 'If you were over there, what toy would be closest to you?' than in tasks involving the selection of pictorial or map-like representations of another person's perspective.

Although it has been suggested that Piagetian theory has been responsible for delaying the age at which children have been introduced to maps in school and thus inhibiting educational research into very young children's engagement with maps (Spencer *et al.*, 1989), Piaget's general account remains a powerful means of organising thought and behaviour in childhood. By far the most influential neo-Piagetian research has come from the 'Penn State school' led by Lyn Liben and Roger Downs (see numerous references in the bibliography). Liben and Downs root their analysis of children's map competence in what they regard as essential truths deriving from the Piagetian tradition. Their view of the development of map understanding is one which is:

1   gradual;
2   complex and multifaceted;
3   dependent on cognitive level and experiences and thus displays major individual differences;
4   coherent in that the trends in mastery of map understanding can be predicted and interpreted from a joint developmental and cartographic perspective;
5   replete with important educational implications; and
6   linked to the larger issue of the development of symbolic representation.

(Liben and Downs, 1989: 177)

From a number of studies (see especially Chapter 4) they conclude that, although some map abilities appear early, this success only pertains under limited circumstances. Competence significantly decreases when map tasks involve greater cartographic complexity, misalignment between map and referent space and the need to apply Euclidean spatial strategies. Although quite young children appear often to recognise that a map corresponds to a real world space, detailed matching tasks requiring scale reduction and change of alignment generally prove too demanding. Liben and Downs acknowledge that the Piagetian approach is controversial but assert that the theoretical framework remains one which is particularly useful (although not unique) for explaining children's performance (Liben, 2002).

Map learning as the social construction of knowledge

In contrast to Piaget, the approach of socio-culturalists such as Lev Vygotsky is to consider human learning and cognitive development primarily as a social, rather than individual, process, whereby knowledge is shared and understandings are constructed in culturally formed settings. Much attention is paid to the role of talk as a medium for sharing knowledge and potentially transforming understanding.

In relation to schooling, Vygotsky (1962) distinguished two basic forms of experience, giving rise to two interrelated groups of concepts: scientific and spontaneous. Scientific concepts originate in the highly structured and specialised activity of classroom teaching. They do not necessarily relate to 'science' but they are characterised by hierarchical and logical organisation. Spontaneous concepts arise from the child's own reflections on every-day, primarily out-of-school, experiences. These are experientially rich but unsystematic and highly dependent on context. Vygotsky noted that scientific concepts appeared to develop more rapidly, outpacing those acquired spontaneously in everyday life and that children produced more correct answers in response to concepts learned at school. His conclusion was that education should run ahead of and support children's development, in contrast to Piaget's view that education was dependent on the level of children's prior learning.

According to Vygotsky, one of the central tasks for schooling is to bring the systematic and hierarchical structure of scientific concepts into conjunction with the concrete and unsystematic everyday concepts brought to school by the child. Vygotsky argued that progress was made in concept formation when children cooperated with more skilled learners. The key theoretical construct involved here is the *zone of proximal development* (ZPD). This rather clumsy phrase refers to 'the place at which the child's empirically rich but disorganised spontaneous concepts meet the systemacity and logic of adult reasoning' (Vygotsky, 1978: 86). The ZPD is

> the 'distance' between a child's actual development level as determined by independ-ent problem solving and the higher level of potential development as determined through problem solving under adult guidance or in collaboration with more capable peers.
>
> (1978: 87)

Children thus close the gap between their own learning and that of more skilled learners by appropriating the structures that the more skilled learners use. They are thus socialised into the cultural norms of society and also, in relation to specific domains, into the ways in which expert practitioners approach problems. Children, for example, are able to plan journeys on a map more effectively when collaborating with adults as they are guided through more successful route strategies (Radziszewska and Rogoff, 1991).

Unlike some other domains, cartography does not consist of 'natural' or 'given' prin-ciples but of constructs and procedures which are shared by a cartographic community in order to make maps and advanced in order to promote the making of better ones. Thus cartographic knowledge is both symbolically and socially negotiated. Learning to make maps is not only a matter, therefore, of individual activity in an attempt to understand the appropriate concepts, but is also a socialising process by which individuals are introduced to a culture by its more skilled members. In relation to maps, the differences between expert and novice users seems to be the procedural knowledge they bring to the task of interpreting the map and their ability to relate what they find to the conceptual models they hold (Postigo and Pozo, 1998). When children produce 'inaccurate' or 'inconsistent' maps, it may not be because they *cannot* but because they have not yet *accepted* conventional forms of cartographic representation. Younger children's maps do not look like those of older children but this may not be as a result of inability to represent or manipulate spatial information, simply that they have not yet had sufficient experience of how maps typically look in their culture. Wood (1992) provides a detailed and illustrated account of children's early exposure to hill signs in picture books, which is almost entirely of hills shown in profile. No wonder therefore, he concludes, that they take some time to draw and interpret images of hills in plan form. In order not to be misled by maps, learners have to understand the rules cartographers use to create them. Downs and Siegel (1981) propose a learning model of children's progressive *acceptance of constraint* as an alternative to the conventional wisdom, which values only their progressive (adult sanctioned) *attainment* with maps.

In emphasising the priority of social forces in learning rather than individual functioning (as Piaget had done), Vygotskyan approaches naturally focus on cooperative or collaborative classroom organisational structures. Learners in groups provide mutual encouragement and support and the burden of thinking can be shared as each group member adds ideas and strategies the others have not thought of. This is particularly appropriate in relation to cartography and geo-information science as professional practice in GIS is increasingly a collaborative activity requiring sharing of data as well as its interpretation and analysis. The significance of the social role in learning has generally been omitted from discussions of the developmental bases for map understanding (e.g. MacEachren, 1995) yet in the last few years there has been increasing interest in collaborative learning with maps. Leinhardt *et al.* (1998) set students (aged 12–13) a map enlarging task that required some understanding of scale, projections and symbology. On a post-test, students who worked in small groups had a slightly better understanding of map concepts than those who worked individually. Tshibalo (2003) grouped South African learners in secondary school in order to complete map based tasks such as locating features using grids and calculating distances, bearings and gradients. Students were arranged into teams of four persons with each individual having an assigned role. Although learning gains could not be entirely attributed to the collaborative component of the task, Tshibalo found significant improvement on test scores using this strategy.

In an attempt to unravel the relationship between the quality of student talk and the quality of map making, Wiegand (2002a, 2002b) analysed the discourse of pairs of school students engaged in a collaborative task using mapping software. A language analysis tool (Pilkington, 1999) tracked the effectiveness of dialogue in promoting learning. The dialogue 'moves' of each participant were coded according to their function. Using *inform* moves a participant makes observations and states facts about a map. *Direct* moves are instructions from one partner to the other to carry out some map making action. *Reason* moves provide explanations for mapping behaviour and *question* moves invite an explanatory response. In this study, there appeared to be an association between the quality of maps produced and the characteristics of pupil discourse during their production. Higher order maps from older students were found to be associated with *reason* and *question* discourse moves, supporting the notion that students who are able to explain their choice of decision whilst solving problems are more successful. The use of discourse analysis to explore children's collaborative cartographic problem solving appears to offer opportunities for further development (e.g. Owen, 2003).

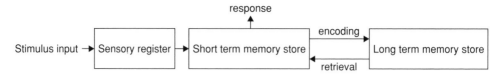

Figure 3.3 Flowchart of human information processing (after Shiffrin and Atkinson, 1969).

The strength of Vygotskyan sociocultural theory is the attention it pays to the context of learning and, in relation to maps, its emphasis on maps as cultural artefacts. Its weaknesses are the lack of a clear definition of the ZPD and a shortage of practical strategies to assist learners through it.

Perspectives from an information processing approach

Using a metaphor from computer science, the information processing approach focuses on the flow of information through the cognitive system. The flow begins with *input* (such as information via a map) and ends with *output*, such as spatial behaviour or a locational decision. Information processing psychologists are interested in the mental processes applied to incoming information such as how it is transformed, manipulated and used. The generic framework for information processing is shown in Figure 3.3 (after Shiffrin and Atkinson, 1969). A sensory register acts as a buffer to sort relevant from irrelevant information. The short term store is 'working memory' where selected information is processed further. It is where 'thinking' takes place. Information that is not further processed and transferred to long term memory is rapidly lost. Thus we have limited capacity for remembering, say, a six-figure grid reference and may have to keep saying it aloud until we've identified the feature it refers to on a map. The long term store is the repository of the learner's knowledge. Information is encoded into long term storage and retrieved when needed to assist with mental operations in working memory. Information processing research has naturally focused, therefore, on the development of memory and the limits of its capacity, the strategies used for cognitive activities such as problem solving and the way in which thinking and learning can be modelled. Some key questions in relation to information processing of maps relate to how learners remember map information and how their knowledge about maps is structured (Schwartz, 1997). Rumelhart and Norman (1985) use the term *schemata* (singular = *schema*) to refer to knowledge structures. These can be thought of as frameworks for making sense of information (such as that derived from maps) or procedures (such as how maps are made). Understanding is easier if incoming data matches the knowledge structures held by the learner.

MacEachren (1995) proposes that humans have both a general map schema and specific map schemata. A general map schema would include propositions such as:

- Features on the map are located with respect to geographic position via a coordinate system.
- Relative position of features on the map specifies their relative position in geographic space.
- Symbols are displayed by the use of visual variables.
- Symbols are specified via a legend.
- Text that is grouped with symbols provides names of geographic locations.

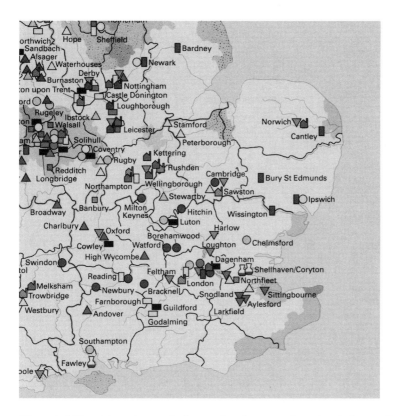

Figure 3.4 Thematic point symbol map showing manufacturing industry. From the *Oxford School Atlas*, copyright © 1997 Oxford University Press, reproduced by permission of Oxford University Press.

According to MacEachren, specific map schemata (such as those for road maps, topographic maps or weather maps) develop by modifying, expanding and filling in the details of the general schema. This happens in many ways, including formal teaching, observing and making inferences as well as applying schemata from other contexts. Application of prior experience may be successful (as in the case where knowledge from colour coding of wash basin taps is correctly applied to climate maps on which red and blue indicate hot and cold temperatures) or unsuccessful (as where green on a relief map is interpreted as land used for pasture and not land that is simply low) and so an element of trial and error is involved in the development of specific map schemata. Whilst most map users have an intuitive grasp of the main principles of the general map schema, specific map schemata generally have to be learned. The conventions of large scale topographic maps or road maps may be rapidly acquired but interpretation of, for example, aeronautical and hydrographic charts is only likely to be accomplished by persons with specialist prior knowledge.

There are few illustrations of school students' specific map schemata but one example illustrates students' understanding of how small scale economic maps work. Figure 3.4 shows an extract from a school atlas map showing manufacturing industry with the point symbols representing, for example, electronics, chemicals, motor vehicles and textiles. A cartographer might approach the task by first ascertaining some equivalence across industries (collecting data, for example, on the number of employees in each factory) then allocating symbols on some rational basis (such as making one symbol notionally equivalent to 1,000 employees). Minor isolated locations of each type of economic activity would be omitted whilst multiple instances within the same area may be grouped so that they share a symbol. In areas of high economic activity, symbols would be displaced laterally to avoid them overlapping each other and make them visible. To what extent are young atlas users aware of such conventions in the generalisation process? When school students were given a software tool which enabled them to make their own maps (Wiegand 2002a, 2002b), some students allocated symbols on the basis of how *useful* they thought the industry was, arguing for example that as clothing was more important than jewellery it should have greater prominence on the map. Others allocated symbols on the basis of *clusters* of activity, irrespective of the numbers of employees in the cluster and discarded singletons even though they were very large. Some appeared to think that symbols should *surround* the area in which each type of manufacturing took place rather than be superimposed on it. About half of the 11- to 12-year-olds who took part and about a third of the 13- to 14-year-olds appeared to have very weak understanding of how maps like these represented economic information. They would therefore be likely to have difficulty making sense of similar maps when they confronted them in their atlas.

An important strand of an information processing approach to map learning has been consideration of the different representations that map and verbal knowledge have in long term memory storage. *Dual coding theory* (Paivio, 1986) explains that knowledge is represented in two separate but interdependent memory stores. Language based information is stored in the form of sequential propositions which must be processed serially. Maps, on the other hand, appear to be stored as images which 'chunk' very large quantities of information 'at a glance'. Maps are encoded as images that contain both *structural* and *feature* information (Rittschoff *et al.*, 1994). Structural information enables map users to answer '*Where* is it?' questions and includes properties such as distance and direction as well as the visual framework provided by the map borders. Feature information enables map users to answer '*What* is it?' questions and includes properties such as detail, shape, size and colour which are used to discriminate between symbols or landmarks on the map. Map structure and map features appear to be processed in different ways (Kulhavy *et al.*, 1994). Map structure seems to be encoded in one comprehensive, overall image view whereas map feature information appears to be encoded through a combination of image and verbal processing.

Increasing attention has recently been paid to the relation between maps and written text in learning. Learners appear to be supported in their ability to make inferences about information when map and text are used in combination (Rittschof *et al.*, 1993) and appear to remember more map related facts from a text if they have reviewed a thematic map before, rather than after, reading the text (Rittschof *et al.*, 1994). This hypothesis was tested with 10- to 11-year-old children (Kulhavy *et al.*, 1985). Half the children had a map of a town and half a geographical description. Both sets heard an oral account of the history of the town. Those with a map performed better on an information recall test because, according to Kulhavy and colleagues, they had encoded the information both spatially and linguistically whereas the group with the written description were only able to encode their information linguistically. Dual encoding appears to provide a richer retrieval base from which to recall information.

Recent studies have introduced more complexity into this model. Schwartz (1997) introduces the possibility that maps are not simply encoded as copy images of what is *seen* but that encoding is related to what the learner already *knows* about the space represented by the map. Maps may not therefore particularly help memory for text where the map features are already well known by the learner. They may provide support where map features are only partially known or are unfamiliar and they may actually inhibit learning where features that appear on the map seem to be incompatible with what is already known.

The information processing approach addresses the problems of complex thinking and appears to offer particular insights into children and young people's mental processing of maps. It attempts to make explicit how children use their cognitive skills in particular situations such as problem solving or memory tasks involving maps. On the other hand, although flow charts of the type illustrated in Figure 3.3 help us understand the overall nature of information processing they generally fail to take account of children's development.

This chapter has reviewed four theoretical approaches to children's thinking with maps. However, no single approach is sufficient to explain children's learning and we await more synthesising frameworks. Elements of each perspective will be found in the next few chapters, which deal with children's understanding of specific types of map at both large and small scale.

4   Models, aerial photographs and large scale plans

The emphasis in this chapter is on children's understanding of large scale representations (such as models, aerial photographs and plans) of small referent spaces (such as a room, school playground or the immediate neighbourhood). It involves a consideration of three sets of relationships between the child, the referent space and the representation of that space. These relationships can be expressed as:

- understanding where you are in real world space;
- understanding the relationship between the real world space and its representation as model, photograph or plan;
- understanding where you are on the model, photograph or plan.

(Liben and Downs, 1993)

Models and aerial photographs can be considered as 'map-like objects' (Petchenik, 1985). They share some (but only some) important properties with maps. They all display spatial information but do so in ways that are subtly different.

Understanding that models can represent space

As models are typically three dimensional and thus 'look like' smaller versions of real world space, it may be thought that they provide an easy entry point for children's understanding of representations. DeLoache (1995), however, reported interesting results from a study of children's ability to find hidden objects. A child is asked to observe an adult hide a toy dog behind a sofa in a room. Adult and child then leave the room and, on returning, the child is asked to find the hidden toy. Most $2^{1}/_{2}$-year-old children can do this immediately. However, when asked to find, not the toy that was hidden in the room but a miniature toy hidden in the corresponding place in a scale model of the room, most children of this age fail to find it. The difficulty seems to be that children do not use the model as a tool for recalling from memory details of the hiding event they observed in the room. DeLoache's data show a remarkable increase in performance between the ages of $2^{1}/_{2}$ and 3 years as children come to appreciate the correspondence between the room and the model. This appreciation is enhanced the more the model actually resembles the real room, for example the more faithfully the details of furniture and decoration are replicated (DeLoache *et al.*, 1991). One of the potential problems with models in such experiments, however, is that they can be 'too real'. The model room is thus seen not as a representation but as a toy in its own right. In fact, children often appear to have more success with photographs and drawings as tools to locate objects in the real world than with models

(DeLoache, 1991; Dow and Pick, 1992). This is presumably because they are more familiar with the representational role of pictures. That's their purpose, compared to models which have other, more obvious uses, such as for play.

A further experiment (DeLoache *et al.*, 1997) sheds additional light on children's understanding of models as representations. Children were shown a large model of a doll in a tent-like, portable 'room' which was then exposed to a 'shrinking machine' (actually an oscilloscope with flashing green lights) whilst the child and experimenter waited in an adjoining room. On re-entering, a miniaturised version of the doll and room was discovered and, as in the previous task, the child had to use his or her knowledge of where a toy was hidden in the larger space to find it in the smaller one. In this case, all the children except one appeared to believe that the room and the model were the same thing. Performance appears to have improved because symbolic relationships did not intrude upon the children's understanding of the task.

DeLoache's results indicate that children from about the age of 3 are able to use a model to find the location of a hidden toy in a room but they appear to do so on the basis of *object* correspondence – i.e. they find the toy by correctly matching a miniature object and its real world counterpart. To what extent can young children use *relational* correspondences to identify a target location? Blades (1991a) used pairs of identical model rooms each containing a bed, a wardrobe and two chairs in experiments with children aged 3, 4 and 5 years. A toy was hidden under one of the items of furniture in the first model and, while the child's attention was distracted, an identical toy was hidden under the same item of furniture in the second model. When the toy was hidden in a topologically unique place (i.e. under the bed or the wardrobe) all the children were able to locate it. However, when the toy was hidden under one of the two chairs, only those children who were older than 4 years were able to find it and then only when the second model was correctly aligned with the first. When the second model was not aligned with the first, success was limited to children older than 5 years. Blades' study suggests that very young children's understanding of how models represent an environment is restricted to the recognition of unique items in each space rather than having a full understanding based on relational attributes.

Understanding that aerial photographs can represent space

Aerial photographs are often regarded as possessing a kind of transparency – in the sense that children are presumed to be able to see 'through' them to the real world they represent. They do, however, show aspects of the real world not always apparent from map evidence alone and may therefore provide cues that relate more strongly to children's environmental experience. An aerial photograph, for example, may reveal informal (but, to a child, very familiar) pathways worn across the grass of a public park that would be absent from a map.

The evidence for children's ability to interpret aerial photographs is somewhat contradictory. Almost all the children in one study of 5- to 7-year-olds from the USA and Puerto Rico (Blaut *et al.*, 1970) were said to perceive a test photograph as being a view of the landscape from above and were able to identify at least two unlike features (such as roads and buildings) on it. Spencer *et al.* (1980) carried out similar tests with 3- to 5-year-old British children and found that each child in their sample was able to identify a much larger number of features (up to as many as 25). Spencer and his colleagues attributed this greater performance to a less formal experimental setting and the enhanced *rapport* they were able to achieve with their sample of young participants over a longer testing period. In another cross cultural study (Sowden *et al.*, 1996) very young children across five cultures were found to be able to spontaneously identify two to six landscape features. Liben and Downs (1991), however, draw more cautious conclusions from their own studies involving similar tasks and point to a significant number of interpretation errors. Using an aerial photograph of Chicago, Liben and Downs (1989) found preschool children who identified Lake Michigan as 'the sky' (with boats on the lake as 'the stars'). A grassy area adjacent to a correctly identified road was said to be 'cheese' and the diamond of a baseball pitch was said to show 'a guitar' or 'an eye' (1989: 183ff). These findings resonate with observations in Spencer *et al.*'s (1980) study in which tennis courts were interpreted as 'doors' even though much smaller, adjacent features had been correctly identified as trees. It appears, therefore, that among young children's correct identification of features from aerial photographs there are also many fanciful suggestions, which reveal an inability to apply consistent principles of interpretation (such as relative size, or the likelihood that some features would be adjacent to others). Young children may actually view aerial photographs more as a collection of individual features than an integrated whole image.

Several studies have also reported children's limited ability to recognise known features in their own home area from aerial photographs. Preschoolers in Pennsylvania, for example, were unable to find places they knew, even when a nearby familiar place was pointed out (Liben and Downs, 1991). Only 16 out of 40 children aged 6–11, when shown an aerial photograph of their Cambridgeshire village, recognised that it was a view of where they lived (Dale, 1971). When they were told where the place in the photograph was, most children over 9 could identify most of the prominent village features, although children below the age of 9 still had difficulty. However, when the referent space is very small (such as a *model* village) even very young children appear to have little difficulty recognising features from an aerial photograph (Shevelan *et al.*, 2002) and when aerial photographs of a small and very familiar space are used in conjunction with *action* in that space, performance appears to be significantly enhanced. Children seem to be very successful in using aerial photographs as tools to find rewards and locate objects in their school playground for example, implying that such images provide a very appropriate entry point for work with maps (Plester *et al.*, 2003).

Oblique aerial photographs (looking down on the world at an angle) may present more learning difficulties than vertical ones (looking down from directly overhead). In a study involving 578 school students aged 15–16 years, many participants experienced difficulty matching features shown in an oblique aerial view with a map and only a third of students of moderate ability could identify on the map the direction from which the photograph was taken (Boardman and Towner, 1979). Coorientation of aerial photographs and maps presents a particular challenge to young learners as the scale of the map is constant whereas the scale of the photograph varies with distance from the camera. Unlike photographs, maps do not have perspective: the viewer 'looks vertically down on' all parts of the map. This means that the field of view of an aerial photograph is usually represented on a map of the same area by a triangular, trapezoidal or irregular shape, making comparison between map and photograph considerably more difficult. This difficulty increases as the land area viewed becomes larger (and the scale of the map smaller). Boardman (1983) cites evidence from examination boards that students still appear to experience significant difficulties with this relationship between photograph and map at age 16.

A number of conclusions can be drawn from the rather conflicting evidence on photographic imagery. Young children are able to identify some features from aerial photographs under some circumstances although they may not be able to relate these to their own ground level experience. The features most commonly identified are those whose properties (as seen from above) are familiar to children through play situations involving models such as road and railway layouts (Spencer *et al.*, 1980). Other commonly identified features are those having a similar appearance from above as they do from ground level (for example, the visual 'texture' of trees and vegetation). Some features may be identified by their context. Once roads have been identified, for example, it is easier to recognise the shapes on them as vehicles and the circles at their intersections as roundabouts. It would appear that preliterate, preschool children display the beginnings of interpretative skill with aerial photographs. This may form the basis, therefore, for appropriate starter activities in the nursery and early school years but much more experience may be required before interpretation is secure. There has been little consistency in the form of the photography used in these studies (e.g. scale, resolution, colour, lighting, etc.) as well as the actual content and the degree to which children are familiar with the area represented and so more controlled experiments would be welcome.

Understanding that maps can represent space

Understanding that a map represents the real world takes place at more than one level. Downs and Liben (Downs *et al.*, 1988; Liben and Downs, 1989) distinguish between the *holistic* level (i.e. the relationship between the whole map and the whole of its referent space) and the *componential* level (i.e. the relationship between individual symbols and their individual real world counterparts). At the holistic level, children must understand that the map as an artefact performs a representative function, for example that a map of France represents the whole of that country in the same way as a globe represents the Earth. At the componential level, two sets of correspondences determine the relationship between the map and the real world (Liben and Downs, 2001). *Representational correspondence* refers to the match between real world information (such as the use of a plot of land for growing fruit trees) and its depiction in symbolic form on the map (as a patterned area identified in the legend as orchard). *Geometric correspondence*, on the other hand, refers to the match between real world space and the way it is structured on the map. This includes the apparent height from which the referent space is viewed (producing map scale), the angle from which it is viewed (typically from the vertical overhead position) and its viewing azimuth (the amount of rotational turn in relation to north). DeLoache (1989) and Blades (1991a) have used the terms *object correspondence* and *relational correspondence* respectively for these two sets of correspondences between the map and the real world it represents.

Children quite quickly form views about what a map is, and what it isn't. Many 4- and 5-year-olds appear to know that maps store spatial information ('they show where things are') and can be used for wayfinding ('you can find your way home with one') (Liben and Yekel, 1996). From about 8 years, most children can consistently differentiate between a map (or plan), a sketch and an oblique drawing (Kwan, 1999). The prototypical map for many children is one that is small scale, in colour, has conventional symbols and is used to find unfamiliar places in everyday situations, such as a street or road map (Gerber, 1984; Liben and Downs, 1991; Anderson, 1996). As children become older they accept a wider variety of representations as being within the concept 'map'.

Many studies show that very young children can engage with simple maps (usually large scale plans with limited content) of an immediate small space (often a room or playground) in order to find a hidden object or to locate their own position. Even young 3-year-olds appear to understand that there is a correspondence between a map and the real world. They recognise, for example, the *principle* that 'X marks the spot' (Dalke, 1998) even if they are unsuccessful in a 'treasure finding' task. This suggests that young children understand that the map refers in a holistic way to its referent space by about the age of 4 (DeLoache, 1987). It seems likely that using a map can shape the development of children's *survey knowledge* (i.e. their knowledge of spatial relations between objects in the real world as though seen from above). Whereas most adults can mentally form survey representations of space from their direct environmental experience or even from written and verbal descriptions, children are less able to do so. Maps are an important means of supporting children's learning of multiple relations between many objects by providing a single 'at a glance' image of how space is organised (Uttal, 2000).

Using maps to find a location

The seminal experiment demonstrating that very young children could make judgements about position in a referent space from map information was by Bluestein and Acredolo (1979). They tested 3-, 4- and 5-year-olds in a small square room (Figure 4.1). The room contained identical green boxes at the midpoint of each of the four walls and distinctive, differently coloured objects in three of the corners. The door was situated in the fourth corner. A map of the room indicated in which of the green boxes a toy was hidden. The

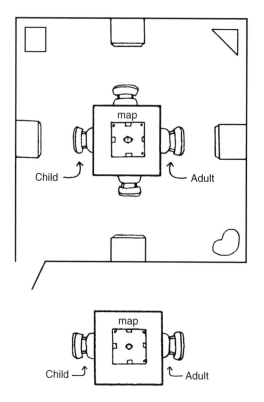

Figure 4.1 Experimental space and equipment used by Bluestein and Acredolo (1979: 693). Reprinted with permission of the Society for Research in Child Development.

children were required to find the toy in four conditions: viewing the map inside/outside the room, crossed with the map being aligned/unaligned to the room (i.e. correctly oriented to match the room's layout or not). Approximately half the 3-year-olds and nearly all the 4- and 5-year-olds were successful with the correctly aligned maps and it made little difference whether they saw the maps inside or outside the room. Inside, where the aligned map was consulted in the centre of the room, the task was perhaps easiest as the target box would be the nearest to its representation on the map. Outside the room, children appeared to code location by remembering, for example from the aligned map, that the target box was 'on the right'. Unfortunately, many also applied this strategy to the unaligned maps as evidenced by the frequent selection of a hiding place directly opposite the correct one. None of the 3-year-olds was successful with the outside-unaligned maps but 90 per cent of 5-year-olds were.

Bluestein and Acredolo's work has since been subject to a number of methodological criticisms (Liben and Downs, 1989; Blades and Spencer, 1994), which make their findings less persuasive. Nevertheless, the work remains important in that it demonstrated that very young children can apply information from a map to solve a simple 'treasure finding' task, and especially so when the map is aligned to the environment it represents. The work has been followed up by a number of studies from the highly productive 'Sheffield school' of Christopher Spencer, Mark Blades and associates, identifying the thinking behind very young children's ability to use simple maps and models to locate items in small spaces.

In one study, 3- to 6-year-old children were asked to use a map to find a hidden toy in a simple playground layout (Blades and Spencer, 1990). This consisted of a path leading to a 'crossroads' where four paths met and at the end of each of these was a box, one of which contained the toy (Figure 4.2). A 'landmark' (a large red plastic bucket) was

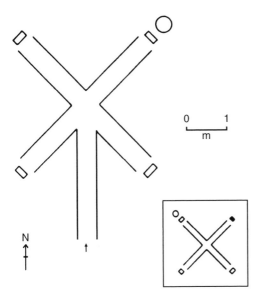

0 ____ 1
m

Figure 4.2 Layout used by Blades and Spencer for a map-using task. Inset is an example of a map showing the position of a hidden toy. From *The Journal of Genetic Psychology*, 150: 5–18, 1990. Reprinted with permission of the Helen Dwight Reid Educational Foundation. Published by Heldref Publications, 1319 Eighteenth St., NW, Washington, DC 20036-1802. Copyright ©1990.

positioned at the end of one of the paths. Children were given maps which showed the path layout, the position of the bucket and the box in which the toy was hidden. Each child was asked to find the toy 16 times (i.e. with the toy hidden in each of the four boxes and with the maps aligned with the layout as well as rotated through 90, 180 and 270 degrees). The youngest children performed better than would have been expected by chance when the maps were aligned to the layout and when the toy was hidden in the box by the bucket, indicating that they had some ability to understand that the map corresponded to the layout. Successful performance by these children was, however, limited to these two conditions and they were generally unsuccessful when maps were rotated or when the toy was hidden in another box. Although all the children performed better when the maps were aligned with the layout, the older children's performance was influenced by the location of the hiding position. They were nearly always able to find the toy when it was in the north-east box, were less successful when the toy was in the south-west box, but more likely to find it there than when it was in either of the north-west or south-east boxes. This was thought to be because both the north-east box and the south-west box each had a unique relationship to the landmark (i.e. 'next to' and 'opposite', respectively), whereas the other boxes were equidistant from the landmark and could only be differentiated by their 'right–left' relationship to it (which would have been difficult to identify in the unaligned condition). Blades and Spencer concluded that the younger children *could* use a simple map but that, as their performance was particularly dependent on being able to identify the 'landmark box', they did not yet have a full understanding of the representational correspondence between the map and the layout. This appeared to be achieved by about 6 years of age.

The difficulty younger children have in identifying location with an unaligned map was also demonstrated by Liben and Downs (1989; Downs *et al.*, 1988), who asked children from kindergarten to the second grade (Y1–Y3) to place stickers on a classroom map to indicate their own location and the location of another person who stood at various positions in the room. Most children were able to locate themselves on the map in the aligned condition but second graders were twice as successful as kindergartners when the map was unaligned. Locating another person on the map was generally more difficult, especially for the younger children. In a further study, Liben and Downs (1993) increased the task's complexity by asking children from kindergarten and grades 1–6 not only to identify their own position and the position of another person (who moved to different locations in the room) but additionally for them to indicate, using arrow stickers, the direction the other person was facing. These positions were either parallel or oblique to the nearest classroom wall. The location and orientation tasks were also given in aligned and unaligned conditions. Older children scored very highly on the location task with better performance again recorded on aligned maps. Performance on the orientation task with unaligned maps was significantly worse for all but the oldest children. Children scored significantly better when the subject was aligned parallel to an adjacent wall than obliquely to it (as Piaget's theory predicts on the basis of the table top alignment tests described in Chapter 3).

Most 4- to 5-years-olds appear able to locate the position of at least some objects correctly in their own classroom by placing stickers on a plan (Liben and Yekel, 1996), suggesting they have some understanding of the relation between map and referent space. However, performance is poorer when they are asked to identify on their plan the location of markers placed on open areas of the floor than when required to match stickers to markers placed on individual items of furniture. Liben and Yekel concluded that the status of floor area on the map as undifferentiated, but nevertheless representational, is not apparent to young children (it is interesting to note in this connection that most of the simple plans and maps used in experiments with young children rarely appear to have used area symbols). Pre-school children appear to be better at locating 'bounded' items, e.g. those near classroom walls, presumably because the walls offer topological 'near to' clues (Siegel and Schadler, 1977; Liben *et al.*, 1982).

Understanding the map's alignment and viewing angle

As we have seen, directional information on a map may be interpreted much more readily when the map is aligned to the real world. If it is not, alignment must be carried out by the user, either physically or mentally. Physical alignment (i.e. turning the map around until it is aligned with the real world) allows the user to match perceptually the relationship between the representation and referent space and appears to enhance children's performance on orientation tasks (Rosser, 1983; Newcombe, 1989). Mental alignment, however, requires a conceptual strategy. This may consist of mentally switching 'left–right' and right–left' relationships where the map is rotated 180 degrees relative to the referent space. An alternative strategy is to identify the spatial relationships of the target location relative to other features in ways that are not affected by the rotation. Imagine, for example, a misaligned map being compared with a model village layout. Searching for a unique target (say, a church with a spire) is a relatively easy task as no spatial relationships with other features are involved. All that is required is for a match to be made between the representation of the church on the map (e.g. by symbol or pictogram) and the church in the model (the only building with a spire). If, however, the target is one of two telephone boxes then the search strategy needs to be different. The target telephone box might be the one nearest the crossroads, in which case its location is readily encoded and the location can be found irrespective of the map's rotation. If both telephone boxes are equidistant from the crossroads then a more complex strategy is required, for example encoding the target telephone box as being between the church and the public house. Mental rotation is difficult. Many children (and adults) have problems doing it.

Up to about the age of 5, children's spatial thinking may be limited by the degree to which they have to use their own position as a reference point for solving orientation problems (Pufall and Shaw, 1973; Pufall, 1975). So, what strategies do older children employ that younger children don't? According to Blades (1991a), one reason for older children's greater success is that they are able to combine more items of information in order to identify a location correctly. Four- to 6-year-old children were given pairs of circular boards around which were painted black and coloured circles. The first pair of boards had black and uniquely coloured circles clearly grouped in *pairs*. A token was placed on one of the black circles on one board and the children were asked to place another token on the matching circle on the other (rotated) board. To pass this test children had to adopt a 'next to' strategy – i.e. recognise that the correct black circle was always paired with a unique colour. They were then given a pair of boards on which black and coloured circles were *evenly distributed* around the rim. In this case the 'next to' strategy would only lead to a 50 per cent success rate, as they would have to guess which of the two possible black circles was adjacent to a coloured circle. For complete success, children had to adopt a 'between' strategy, identifying that the target black circle was located between two unique colours. Only the older children were able to use a spatial strategy that took into account more information from the representation.

Success in a perspective-taking task is partly determined by the child's ability to match a map to a layout by making reference to the layout's own internal features. However, problems can also stem from a conflict between two or more frames of reference (Newcombe and Huttenlocher, 1992). Consider, for example, a common perspective-taking experiment, where a child sits at a table on which an object is located and is asked to select, from a number of alternatives, the correct 'map' of the object in relation to the table top. The object could be coded according to the child's own position in relation to the table (e.g. 'the side furthest from me') or to the position of the object relative to the table top ('opposite the side with the drawer'). However, it could also be coded according to an external frame of reference such as the walls or items of furniture within the room in which the task is set ('the side nearest the door'). Newcombe and Huttenlocher suggest, therefore, that perspective taking represents a challenge in which 'two or more frames of reference must be maintained at once, yet distinguished from each other and interrelated' (2000: 125).

Most research on children's map use has employed plans where the viewing angle is from vertically overhead and yet this perspective appears not to be easily recognised by very young children (Liben and Downs, 1991) and 4- to 5-year-olds appear to perform better on object location tasks using oblique views of their classroom than with plans (Liben and Yekel, 1996). It seems likely that the more 'pictorial' representation inherent in an oblique view provides important clues to what is being represented as, for example, key features of familiar items of furniture (such as the legs of tables and chairs) can be seen. Children who use an oblique view first appear to perform better when using a plan later, suggesting that learning is more effectively supported if iconic symbols are experienced before abstract ones.

In relation to children's development of concepts associated with plan view, there appears to be little or no research evidence about understanding of cardinal directions although some confusion may exist between cardinal directions and body direction reference (i.e. left and right). In a computer simulation of navigating through a park, for example, students equated the 'turn right' button (regardless of which way they were actually pointing) with moving east (Liben *et al.*, 2002). North–south discrimination appears to be secured earlier in childhood than that between east and west and the false notion that north is *always* 'at the top of the map' appears to be a persistent one (Boardman and Towner, 1979).

Understanding scale

Perception of size and distance develops early in childhood and is used to guide spatial behaviour. Children have early experience of scale through play with models and with increasing age they reject toys that are 'too big' or 'too small' for others (Boardman, 1983).

Understanding the correspondence of spatial relations between a map and the real world requires *scaling ability*. One aspect of this appears to emerge at about the age of 3 years. In one study (Huttenlocher *et al.*, 1999), a small disc was hidden in a five foot long sand box and children had to find the disc by using a 'map', which showed the location of the disc as a dot on a small rectangle. Four-year-olds and many 3-year-olds could do this, suggesting they were able to recognise the correspondence between map and sandbox and could encode, and correctly scale, linear distance. Note, however, that this is only a one-dimensional task. Scaling is much more difficult when multiple spatial relations have

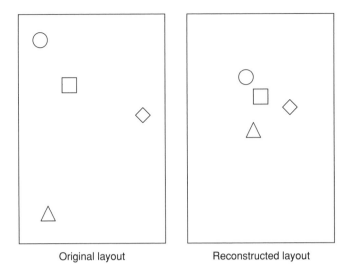

Original layout   Reconstructed layout

Figure 4.3 Scale error in reconstructing a layout. Angular relations are maintained but not scale relations. From Uttal, D. (1994), reproduced from the *British Journal of Developmental Psychology*, © The British Psychological Society.

to be encoded and children are much more likely than adults to make scale errors of 'shrinkage' or 'expansion' when invited to make a reconstruction of a spatial arrangement (Uttal, 1994, 1996). Figure 4.3 shows (on the left) the original arrangement of a set of features and (on the right) a child's typical reconstruction of them. The nature of these errors suggests that knowledge and use of *scale* relations may develop later than the *angular* relations between individual elements. Teachers setting a task therefore involving redrawing a map at a different scale may need to ensure that children have detected not only the correspondence between individual elements but also the correspondence in their overall configuration.

The scale at which the reconstruction of a referent space is made also appears to have an effect on performance. Siegel *et al.* (1979) familiarised children with a model town at two scales (a larger scale at which the model town could be walked through and a smaller scale at which a small model vehicle could be 'driven' through) and asked them to reconstruct the town layout in either a large or small scale version. Children's reconstructions were more accurate when they were tested in the same scale environment at which they had acquired the spatial information or when they were required to reconstruct at a smaller scale information which had been acquired at a larger scale.

Many children continue to find scaling difficult at the age of 10–11. In an early study, children's scaling ability was assessed using a model of a toy farm on a board (Towler and Nelson, 1968). They were also given a smaller board at a scale of 1:4 and asked to select from an array of symbols at different scales a matching set representing the buildings on the farm. Only the oldest children could do this and Towler and Nelson concluded that children do not develop the ability to make scaled reconstructions before the age of about 10 or 11 years and that school tasks requiring them to (for example) compare maps of the same area at two different scales are generally too demanding. However, it has been noted (Spencer *et al.*, 1989) that performance on Towler and Nelson's test was partly affected by the materials used as some symbol shapes were selected with greater accuracy than others.

More advanced work on scale is dependent on the ability to measure (a skill made considerably more complex by the coexistence in many educational contexts of metric and imperial units). About half of a sample of 6- to 8-year-olds were able to make a reasonable estimate of the dimensions of their classroom in metres but their judgement of longer distances (tens or hundreds of metres) was often very inaccurate (Gerber, 1981). We know little about the development of children's estimation of these sorts of distances in relation to their real world experience but being able to estimate distance on the ground is an obvious precondition for understanding map scale.

Using coordinates

The ability to use a coordinate system is a key map reading skill. Early studies emphasised children's difficulties in using coordinates. For example, Piaget and his associates (1960) explored children's ability to locate a point in two dimensions. Given a rectangular piece of paper with a dot marked on it, they were invited to copy the position of the dot onto a second piece of paper. The task required measurement and construction of coordinates and then transfer of the information to the second piece of paper. Not surprisingly, this task was seldom completed successfully before the age of about 8. In a variant of this experiment, Towler (1970) gave children rectangular cue cards, each with a pattern of eight dots. They were asked to replicate the pattern on a blank card. The cue cards varied in the degree of support they gave (such as the presence or absence of an overprinted grid). Towler noted that only children older than about 9 were able to use a coordinate system when transposing the pattern of dots onto another card. Other commentators at about this time also concluded that the use of grid references is more appropriately limited to the later years of primary school (e.g. Catling, 1979).

With the intervention of more ingenious materials, however, children do appear to show the ability to deal with coordinate tasks. Somerville and Bryant (1985) provided children with an opaque square board under which were two rods. The rods protruded from the board to give a vertical and a horizontal coordinate and the children were asked to indicate where they thought the rods would cross under the board (extrapolating from the visible ends of the rods) by selecting from four locations marked on its surface. Most 6-year-olds and some 4-year-olds were able to perform this task successfully. Blades and Spencer (1989a) devised a coordinate game whereby a wooden board was constructed with 16 sunken squares, each containing a photograph hidden by a cardboard cover. 'Grid references' were provided so that children could locate the photographs using, in one condition, an alphanumeric grid code and, in another condition, pairs of coloured circles (see Plate 5). Once they had located the square they could take off the cover to reveal the photograph and self-check by turning over the grid reference card which had a duplicate of the photograph on the reverse. Younger children experienced some difficulty when they were required to use letters and numbers but were successful when they were provided with more appropriate support (i.e. the coloured circles). Blades and Spencer reported that the use of the grid was reversible: children could work from the grid reference to the grid and also from the grid to the grid reference.

Experience of a coordinate system is likely to support children's learning with maps. The presence of a grid may help children encode spatial information more efficiently as well as retrieve it, for example when drawing a sketch map (Uttal, 2000).

Understanding symbols and text on large scale maps

Ability to make use of map symbols is dependent on the achievement of *representational insight* (DeLoache, 1995), which involves having a mental representation of the referent, of the symbol and the relationship between the two. Liben and Downs (1992) postulate a tentative model of progression in understanding symbology. In *syncretic representation* the individual understands that a symbol 'stands for' the referent but incorrectly syncretises (or 'combines') aspects of the symbol and the referent. This may operate in two directions. An arbitrary aspect of the symbol (e.g. its colour) may be assigned to the referent. Thus a house painted yellow is thought, necessarily, to be shown as yellow on the map – and vice versa. In *naïve conventional representation* the individual understands that the relationship between the referent and the symbol is arbitrary but there is a naïve belief that some aspects of the representational system are necessary or at least preferred. Thus the symbology adopted by a national mapping organisation is necessarily thought to be better than that devised specifically for another purpose. In *meta-representation* the individual understands that there are a variety of symbolic systems, that each has relative merits and demerits and that some may be better used under some circumstances than others. With this level of understanding, the user is empowered to make, for example, an appropriate selection of symbols for the needs of a particular map readership.

Children have much experience of symbolic media in everyday life including road signs, pictograms on toilet doors and logos for fast food outlets. It is not surprising therefore that, at one level, young children appear to understand that marks on the map stand for things in the real world. Very young children's interpretation of both pictorial maps and maps using conventional symbols is aided by the properties of the pictograms and symbols as shape, size and colour provide clues to meaning (Anderson, 1996). However, they often make mistakes. According to DeLoache (1989), one of the problems is that they attempt to apply the rules they know for interpreting pictures and photographs to maps, expecting much greater agreement between the representation and its referent than really exists. In Liben and Downs' (1992) terminology they over-interpret or 'reify' symbols. There is some evidence that children find pictorial symbols easier to interpret than abstract ones (Liben and Yekel, 1996).

Map symbology is closely associated with text and text on maps can present challenges for young users. English language place names are often difficult to pronounce and spell and there are many inconsistencies. For example, Scarborough has two 'o's whilst Middlesbrough has only one and the letter string 'ough' is pronounced differently according to whether you're at Brough, Houghton-le-Spring, Lough Neagh or Broughton. Loughborough has two 'ough' pronunciation traps in a single name. Many British streets carry names that evoke Britain's history and commemorate landed estates, imperial battles and colonial expeditions. Thus few residential areas in the United Kingdom are without numerous challenging place names such as Beaulieu, Montague, Blenheim, Marlborough, Grosvenor and Belle Vue.

Figure 4.4 represents a fictitious British suburban area drawn in a common 'street finder' style. Space on street maps is tight and so abbreviations are frequent. Short streets may have long names and long streets may have short names, creating unpredictable spaces between letters. Notice the challenge to an insecure reader presented by the spacing between letters of Low Lane and the spacing between words in Waterside Park. Even where letter spacing is predictable and the type face is distinctive, the names of residential areas (Waterside and Victoria Park) are difficult to pick out from the underlying street

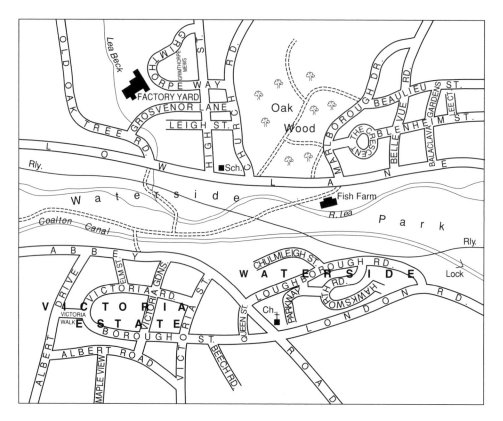

Figure 4.4 Street maps pose particular challenges for young map readers.

pattern. Street names necessarily cannot always be read from left to right and are frequently intercut by the names of streets that cross them. River, canal, railway, road and path in the middle portion of the map in Figure 4.4 cannot easily be distinguished although most adults would be able to interpret the line symbols using knowledge not derived from the map (e.g. footpaths bend more than railway lines; rivers vary in width more than canals). The pocket book format of many street maps, although convenient for use in the field, also presents its own difficulties for young users. Turning the pages usually provides continuity of coverage west to east but tracking a route north to south involves skipping of pages (generally aided by marginal page indicators or by reference to a smaller scale sheet line map, but requiring another meta-level map use skill not generally taught at school).

In this chapter we have examined several aspects of children's understanding of large scale representations of the real world, including models, aerial photographs and plans. We have also examined children's understanding of the *properties* of large scale maps. In the next chapter we turn to children's *use* of such maps and especially their use for wayfinding.

5 Using maps to find the way

Wayfinding refers to the ability to navigate effectively. In a familiar environment remembering the route and recognising landmarks on the way are enough to get you to where you want to go but in an unfamiliar environment additional support is needed, such as information from road signs, asking for directions and reading a map. The literature on wayfinding is large (Golledge, 1999) and, in relation to children, it is growing (see Blades, 1997 for a methodological review) but empirical evidence on children and young people's wayfinding *with maps* in age-appropriate environments is more limited.

A life skill we don't teach

Finding the way with a map isn't easy – many adults cannot do it. In one study, one quarter of a sample of adolescents were found to be unable to use a street map to navigate through a town (Gerber and Kwan, 1994). The general low level of skill in using maps to find the way must call into question the almost entirely classroom based nature of map instruction in schools and the almost complete lack of navigational practice with maps in real world settings (Blades and Spencer, 1987b). Most children and young people's practical experience of wayfinding with maps appears to take place within the voluntary sector (in organisations such as scouts and orienteering clubs) but this often involves a restricted range of map styles and may not include ancillary skills such as giving and receiving oral directions. There are, of course, important health and safety implications for off-site visits from school as well as the need for greater staffing levels but not getting lost is a significant life skill and it is unfortunate that first hand navigational practice with a map does not generally form part of all children's educational entitlement. However, despite the obvious 'common sense' view that teaching students to navigate in authentic circumstances should be more effective than classroom based instruction, the evidence (such as there is) for learning gains in one context compared with another is inconclusive. Students who are taught wayfinding with maps in a real world context *can* do better in another similar environment but may not be able to generalise what they have learned to a contrasting environment (Griffin, 1995).

Children's use of large scale maps for wayfinding is underpinned by their developing adaptation to the physical environment. This begins early. Even toddlers are able to make shortcuts and detours (Huttenlocher *et al.*, 1994). With increasing age, children's adaptation becomes more refined. For example, the ability to make left–right discriminations is first mastered in relation to themselves and then later in relation to other people and objects. Piaget noted that children's early descriptions of journeys made little or no reference to the environment but were instead essentially self referenced (for example, a 4-year-old

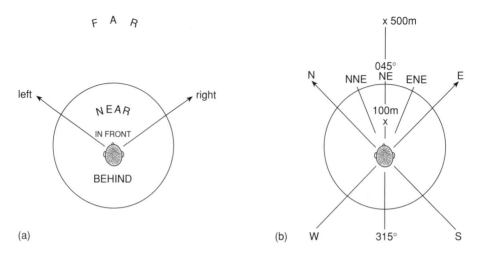

Figure 5.1 Subjective and objective frameworks of spatial relations.

described his route home as: 'I turn, I turn, I turn, I turn' (Piaget *et al.*, 1960: 11). Gradually, children develop the ability to encode spatial information in relation to the environment. Landmarks are the first building blocks of environmental awareness. At first, children often use personal or ephemeral landmarks in their route descriptions, such as a favourite colour or a curious architectural detail or something immediately diverting such as an ice cream van. Later, they come to understand that more serviceable landmarks are those which are permanent, memorable and shared by others such as statues, public monuments or prominent buildings (Spencer *et al.*, 1989). Landmarks are first encoded with reference to self (e.g. 'the toy shop is on *my right*') or topologically (e.g. 'the toy shop is *in* the shopping mall') and then joined together sequentially to form routes. These are learned first ordinally (e.g. 'the coffee shop is *after* the book shop and *before* the hairdressers') and then by reference to distance and direction from known points (e.g. 'the cake shop is *50m*, or *5 minutes* from the Town Hall, going towards the market') (Newcombe *et al.*, 1998). Figure 5.1 illustrates some dimensions of an individual's progression from a qualitative, self referenced, subjective framework of spatial relations to a quantitative, externally referenced, objective frame of reference.

Eventually, knowledge acquired from multiple routes is mentally 'joined up' to achieve an understanding of the overall spatial relations of landmarks in an area. This is known as *configurational* knowledge (Kitchin and Blades, 2002). Small local frameworks of configurational knowledge are then progressively grouped into larger frameworks.

Using maps to identify a route

Two sets of studies shed light on children's ability to identify a route using a map. In the first, children are asked to describe a route from map information. In the second, children are asked to follow a real world route indicated on a map.

Children's ability to describe routes increases significantly in the middle years of primary school. On the whole, children of age 7 or below appear to find giving directions from map information difficult. More success is achieved after this age, but how do children's route descriptions with a map compare with those of adults? Brewster and Blades (1989) asked 6- to 8-year-olds and adults to give a verbal description of a route using a map which showed roads and landmarks (such as a church, post office, fire station, etc.). Cardinal directions were marked on each edge of the map. The route included eight choice points and was identified with a pecked line. None of the children gave completely accurate directions. Turns associated with a landmark proved easier to describe than those without and directions were more accurate when they involved choices made when moving 'up' the map than 'across' or 'down' the map. Adults provided nearly twice as much information as the children but the sequence and type of information was significantly different. Adults often referred to the *order* in which roads were encountered, offering instructions such as 'first right, third left'. None of the children did this. Adults also nearly always referred to the specific type of road junction encountered (e.g. a crossroads, T junction, fork), a distinction which children never made. By having a road junction vocabulary, therefore, adults were able to use the junctions themselves as landmarks whereas children were unable to do so. The maps included cardinal direction and scale information but this was little used by either children or adults. A subsequent larger scale study (Blades and Medlicott, 1992) including children up to the age of 10 and 12 showed markedly greater ability in direction giving among 12-year-olds.

Successful wayfinding with a map in the real world includes the skills of being able to locate your own position on the map, identify the location of the destination, orient the map to the environment, plan an appropriate route using map symbols and then follow the route, matching landmarks to map symbols as you travel. On the way, continual monitoring of progress is required and, where necessary, errors must be rectified (Sandberg and Huttenlocher, 2001). For obvious reasons, studies with very young children have been limited to the scale of room-sized spaces and smallish areas such as playgrounds. Nevertheless, even with adolescents there have been few studies of extended wayfinding in action in larger scale, age-appropriate environments.

Navigating small spaces

To what extent are young children able to describe where they are on a map? A study by Blades (1991a) sheds light on how 4- to 8-year-old children use landmarks to locate themselves. A rectangular grid was marked on a playground. Two landmarks (a red and a green bucket) were placed on the grid and the children had to locate themselves on a map which showed the grid and the landmarks. Ingeniously, the map itself was oval, preventing the children from locating themselves by reference to the edges or corners of the grid. They could thus only relate the map and the playground area by referring to the landmarks. Some 4-year-olds and most of the older children could locate their position on the map in the correct, or an adjacent, grid square when the map was aligned to the playground. In general, the nearer the children were to the landmarks, the easier they found it to locate themselves. When maps were rotated through 180° the most common error was that they positioned themselves in a mirror image location on the map, suggesting that they had related their own position to only one of the landmarks, not both.

Several studies suggest that preliterate children can use a map for navigational tasks in small spaces. Older 4-year-olds, for example, were found to be able to follow a route marked out by coloured buckets in a school playground using a simple map (Blades and Spencer, 1986b) when they had an unobstructed view of the whole route. In another experiment (Blades and Spencer, 1987a) a 25m maze was constructed with screens set up so that children taking part could not see the route ahead. Three- to 6-year-olds were asked to find their way through the maze using a map. To follow the maze successfully they had to make correct route choices at several T junctions. Blades and Spencer reported that all except the youngest children performed better than would have been expected by chance and that older children did significantly better. Subsequently Freundschuh (1990) reported that 4-year-olds following a route through an obstacle course were able to update their location on a map, identifying both their current location and the next waypoint.

In these studies, children referred to the map whilst navigating the referent space but young children also appear capable of using a map in advance in order to learn a route. Uttal and Wellman (1989) constructed a large playhouse with six rooms, each of which contained a different toy animal. Children were asked to travel through the playhouse and identify which animal lived where by pointing 'through the wall' to the appropriate adjoining room. Many 4- and 5-year olds and all 6- and 7-year-olds who had learned the map in advance learned the playhouse more quickly than those who had not seen the map. Uttal and Wellman concluded that these children's map acquired information took the form of an *integrated representation* of space, i.e. one that captures the relational correspondence between map and objects in the environment rather than one which, say, only retained a linear 'what comes next' relationship.

Within small defined spaces, children seem able to take account of the relations between self, map and environment with some fluency by about 6 years of age. They are able to construct and follow quite complex routes involving reorientation *en route*. Navigating in a series of corridors (two long hallways with four short interconnecting hallways in a local high school) for example, kindergartners appear to have some understanding of route efficiency, generally selecting (without being asked to do so) the shortest possible linear path from start point to end point (Sandberg and Huttenlocher, 2001).

Navigating in the real world

It is clear that very young children are able to demonstrate some, albeit limited, aspects of navigation skill in carefully controlled settings but how do children navigate with maps in a large, real world environment? In one of the few studies of its type, Ottosson (1987) tested the ability of 36 children aged 5–12 to find their way to a marked point on a map of the area around their school. The children adopted a great variety of strategies. Some were able to find their way spontaneously. They did not appear to spend time studying the map but immediately 'saw' the solution. Most of the successful wayfinders aligned the map correctly at the outset. For some this seems to have been a painstaking, gradual matching of map and surroundings. For others, it was done speedily and with ease. Some children misaligned their maps and set off in the opposite direction. Of these, some recommenced their route once they realised their error but did not take into account the fact that they had already moved to a new starting position. From detailed transcripts of the children's thinking aloud during the task, Ottosson distinguished between those children who appeared to understand that their position on the map changed as they progressed through the environment (they could read their position anew as they travelled) and those who seemed to read the map as a set of linear instructions ('turn right, follow street, take second left', etc.) to be decoded at the outset but which could not be reconfigured during the trip or after error.

It is possible that two different strategies are used in map wayfinding and that these vary according to age. Younger children may use the map to learn very small sequential

Figure 5.2 A portion of the Leeds Picture Map. © James Brown Designs 2004. email: james@bbbrown15.freeserve.co.uk Updated from 1932 OS map by local survey. No part of this map may be copied without a licence from the publisher.

portions of a route. This means they must consult the map again to obtain more information as each part of the route is completed. Older children may store in memory a more extensive and organised pattern such as a sequence of left and right turns. Each strategy makes different demands on the user. The first involves easy coding but frequent updating and the possibility of losing track of one's position *en route*. The second involves a larger capacity for initial data storage but requires less attention to updating (Scholnick *et al.*, 1990).

Ottoson used a conventional map but in recent years more pictorial representations of urban environments have become popular, providing enhanced environmental information and creating a powerful 'sense of place' (see Figure 5.2). These picture maps appear to offer greater support for wayfinding as the identity of individual buildings can be discerned from the architectural detail of the visible elevation. This provides significant clues for navigating in one direction (i.e. 'up' the map in Figure 5.2). It would be interesting to know to what extent wayfinding may be hindered travelling in the opposite direction where building elevation detail is hidden on the map.

Map alignment is a key factor in navigational success. In orienteering (a navigational sport whereby participants use a large scale map and a compass to compete in locating and navigating between a series of control points) younger children (aged about 7) appear to use a trial and error route finding strategy when navigating whereas older children (9 years) appear to turn the map to assist in their orientation (Walsh and Martland, 1993). When children have extensive experience with orienteering maps, however, they appear able to achieve success at least as well as unpractised adults (Blades and Spencer, 1989b).

Another key feature of real world navigation is continual monitoring over time. If you are given directions they must be matched to the environment as you follow the route. Mismatch indicates that either the individual is following the wrong route (for example a turning was missed) or that the directions are incorrect (for example a key turn was omitted from the instructions). Adults and older children are able to hold in mind possible ambiguity in directions when making a judgement about whether they have reached a target destination. In a case where the first part of a set of directions received is ambiguous in relation to the route experienced but the second part is unambiguous, older wayfinders remain sceptical about whether or not they have arrived at the correct place. Younger children, however, forget the early ambiguity and tend to have unfounded confidence in having arrived at the correct destination solely on the basis of an unambiguous match between directions and environment on the last part of the route (Flavell *et al.*, 1985).

Map alignment and monitoring over time are functions that are provided automatically by satellite navigation technology. We have little or no evidence as yet for the ways in which handheld GPS receivers could support young people's wayfinding or their ability to interact with such 'mobile mapping' technology but this would appear to be a promising area for future research.

This chapter has considered the (rather limited) evidence for children's attempts at using maps to find the way. In the next chapter, we examine children's ability to make their own maps, especially those of small familiar spaces and their own home environment.

6 Children's neighbourhood maps

Making a map is more demanding than simply using one (Newcombe and Huttenlocher, 2000). This chapter considers evidence for the nature of children's maps of the familiar area around their home and identifies some factors that determine what is included and how these features are represented.

Recreating the view from above

Three dimensional models provide a useful medium for children to make representations of their neighbourhood and they seem to create more accurate 'maps' with these than when they draw in two dimensions (Hart, 1979). However, in the early years this is a skill that needs to be taught. Very few preschool children are able *spontaneously* to assemble a town layout with model materials (Blades *et al.*, 2003). At about the age of school entry, children often have difficulty recreating the spatial relations between items in a familiar space such as the classroom by, for example, arranging furniture in a small scale model (Siegel and Schadler, 1977) or even (with the experimenters' help) replacing real furniture after it has been moved to one side (Liben *et al.*, 1982). Their representations improve if they are able to refer frequently to the referent space instead of relying on memory (Golbeck *et al.*, 1986), although actually being present in the environment you are mapping does not necessarily guarantee that you will use it to monitor the progress of your map (Liben, 1997). Younger children frequently have difficulty drawing the view from above. Most 6-year-olds, for example, have difficulty drawing relatively small everyday objects, such as a bucket, in plan view whereas most 8-year-olds don't (Gerber, 1981). Younger children also find it hard to relinquish what they may consider to be the defining features of some objects (such as the legs on a table) even if they are invisible in plan view. This difficulty can persist into later childhood when attempting, for example, to draw the plan of a tall chimney or steeple. The plan view alone just doesn't seem 'enough' to capture the essential characteristic of the building, i.e. its height.

Children's maps of their home area

Studies of children's map making typically ask participants to draw a map of a familiar area or route but more use has been made of sketch maps as a technique for collecting data on children's *cognitive* maps than on their ability to draw cartographic maps. Although freehand sketch maps have been considered a reliable method of retrieving environmental knowledge (Blades, 1990) we need to be cautious about what such representations tell us as this knowledge is not necessarily stored mentally in a map-like form (Downs, 1985).

Neither does skill in map drawing necessarily have much relationship to skill in environmental behaviour. Children's maps may appear partial, inaccurate or incomplete yet 'children do not walk into things; they do not get lost with any noticeable frequency' (Downs and Siegel, 1981: 239).

An individual's ability to represent a referent space such as the locality or neighbourhood in map form is dependent to a large degree on knowledge of that space. Children's expanding horizons are reflected in the maps they draw. Their *home range* (i.e. the area around home that is travelled during play and recreational activity) expands with increasing age. For most children, the extent of this area is negotiated with parents and may differ for boys and girls, social class and ethnicity. Hart (1979) identified three conditions sanctioned by parents: 'free range' (places children could go without asking permission), 'range with permission' (places where children could go alone but only after receiving permission) and 'range with permission and with other children' (places where they were allowed to go but only accompanied by another, often older, child). Each of these conditions showed an increase with age. Using the same categories as Hart, Matthews (1992) reported from field work in Coventry that the typical free range of a 6-year-old might be about 100m but this doubled with permission and trebled when accompanied by other children. Matthews found that a significant shift in the range occurred at the age of about 8 or 9 years and that by the age of about 11 all three categories of range were approaching a kilometre. Moore (1986) proposes a socio-spatial model of the development of children's territorial range. He distinguishes the *habitual range* (highly accessible contiguous space based on the child's home, mostly available to children between arrival home from school and the evening meal); the *frequented range* (less accessible extensions of the habitual range reached with the help of a bicycle and/or with older children, available mostly at weekends) and *occasional range* (variable extensions of the frequented range made as special trips and representing the frontier of children's environmental experience). The increase in real and perceived threats to children's security (from traffic and stranger danger) and the attractions of indoor play (such as personal computers and electronic games) may have reduced earlier estimations of the size of home range in recent years. On the other hand, more widespread ownership of mobile phones by children and young people and the element of security they provide may be slowing this reduction.

Assessing children's maps

It is difficult to make generalisations about, or comparisons between, the maps children draw of their locality or their journey to school not only because there are great variations in their ability to represent space but also because the environments and routes they have each actually directly experienced may be very different. The map making media used (type of drawing instrument or characteristics of the software, availability of colour, size of paper, etc.) will also influence the cartographic product. Map making involves depicting many spatial relationships simultaneously yet, as the task is sequential, the first marks on the page will influence subsequent ones. Thus early minor errors are likely to be compounded as the map proceeds. Left and right handedness and the bias implicit in drawing lines of different orientations due to ease of wrist and hand control may also influence the finished form of the sketch map and account for differences between one child's map and that of another. The resulting maps are not easy to assess or classify, not least because they are 'usually distorted, fragmented and incomplete' (Matthews, 1992: 101). Some researchers have graded maps according to a broad, overall, composite assessment of the level of mapping (e.g. Catling, 1978; Matthews, 1984b) whereas others have identified elements of progression within each of a number of separate attributes such as scale or perspective (e.g. Klett and Alpaugh, 1976). Harwood and Usher (1999) graded maps according to five criteria: accuracy of spatial arrangements, representation of scale and proportion, perspective, degree of abstraction, type of symbolisation and (on a route map) the amount of linear content.

A further issue is the yardstick against which children's maps should be judged. The implication of Piaget's work is that children progress towards some 'higher' stage of cognition yet we know that adults often have difficulty drawing maps. If a child's map is to be assessed for accuracy, what external standard should be used? Although what is included in, or omitted from, professionally produced maps is usually done in a consistent, explicit and controlled way, maps are themselves selective so a child's map that shows elements missing is not necessarily 'wrong' (Downs and Siegel, 1981). Harwood and Usher (1999) point, for example, to pictorial maps as being a highly appropriate form of representation for town trails rather than being 'childish'. Figure 5.2 presents a vivid and accessible view of a city centre, not at all an inferior alternative to a conventional map.

We shall consider three aspects of children's maps of their home area: first, the *content* of their maps, second, the way the information is *structured* and third, the *symbology* used in the representation. These criteria have frequently been used to classify children's maps.

There have been several approaches to analysing the *content* of children's neighbourhood maps. Matthews (1980, 1984a) coded children's maps according to an influential classification of physical elements of the cityscape by Lynch (1960). These elements were defined as:

Paths   linear elements such as roads and pedestrian walkways along which the observer moves;

Edges   linear elements not used as paths but which form boundaries between distinct parts of the environment and include rivers, walls and railway cuttings;

Districts   medium to large scale homogeneous zones that the observer is conscious of being within, including shopping areas and housing estates;

Nodes   strategic points (often the core of districts or the junction of paths) such as city squares that can be entered and from which new directions can be taken;

Landmarks   well defined physical phenomena that serve as points of reference. They may be large and distant like a mountain or small and local such as a statue or distinctive item of architectural detail.

Matthews found that the number of mapped elements increased throughout the primary school age range. Unsurprisingly, paths were the dominant element in journey to school maps, whereas landmarks were more dominant in maps of the home area. Districts and nodes were the weakest elements in both types of map. An increase in map detail has also been noted at the older end of the age range. Maps of 16- to 17-year-olds in Barbados, for example, were found to be more complex than those of 11- to 13-year-olds (Potter, 1985).

Children's socio-environmental experience may influence the content of their maps. In one study (Dupre and O'Neil-Gilbert, 1985) village and city children were asked to make a representation of their home range using construction blocks. Village children made representations of the whole village, building coherent and comprehensive models that provided an overview of the community, irrespective of where precisely they lived. City children, on the other hand, were more likely to anchor their models on their own home and then expand outwards in successive concentric circles of urban features. Dupre and O'Neil-Gilbert concluded that the simpler and more clearly delimited village environment was easier to organise mentally and represent in model form than a complex city neighbourhood. Children who are accompanied to school by adults, either on foot or by car, have been found to record more landmarks on their maps of the route than unaccompanied children (Joshi *et al.*, 1999). This greater awareness of detail by accompanied children seems to attest to the power of adult–child conversations *in situ* to promote environmental awareness. Some observations have also been made of the affective content of home area maps with younger children appearing to include more personal and idiosyncratic content (Spencer and Lloyd, 1974; Moore, 1986).

Early research into children's mapping produced classifications based on the *structure* of the maps using schemes derived from Piaget. Moore (Hart and Moore, 1973; Moore, 1976), for example, proposed three distinct stages of cognitive reference system that could be applied to maps of larger environments. These are:

Egocentric	Map content is limited to features of personal significance. Landmarks are organised in relation to the individual's own position in the environment.
Fixed, or Clustered	Map content is structured as clusters of content around certain landmarks or along particular routes. These clusters or routes are not, however, related to each other and cannot be 'joined up' in any systematic way because they are each dependent on a single viewpoint.
Coordinated	Map content is constructed with a systematic and abstract system of coordinates. Map elements are hierarchically integrated.

Later work has shown that this classification still broadly appears to hold true, with older children making maps that are less egocentric and more coordinated but that they may use different frames of reference when making maps of different areas (Matthews, 1985b). In complex and lesser known environments, for example, children seem to employ simpler frames of reference (Acredolo, 1976).

Children frequently fail to apply scale and viewing perspective consistently. Some parts of their maps are 'stretched' whilst others are 'shrunk'. This may be due partly to scaling errors, as seen in Figure 4.3 (Uttal, 1994, 1996) and partly to the sequential way in which many maps appear to be drawn. Biel and Torell (1979) noted from verbal accounts whilst the children were on task that most children drew their maps as though they were walking around the area, mentally following routes they knew. In a case study (Golledge *et al.*, 1985) of a single 11-year-old drawing free recall sketch maps as part of the process of learning a new route, the route was remembered in segments and, with increasing experience, these were gradually linked together. However, even though children can often draw separate maps of overlapping routes, combining them into a single composite map often proves difficult (Golledge *et al.*, 1991).

In relation to children's use of *symbology*, more attention has generally been paid to children's use of pictorial images than to their conscious use of points, lines and areas and there seems to be general agreement that most children under 8 years tend to draw pictorial maps with elevation views of buildings, most children over 10 draw maps using plan forms and most children in between draw hybrids that use both forms of representation within the same map (Matthews, 1984a; Liben and Downs, 1994; Catling, 1998). Typical maps in each category are shown in Figure 6.1.

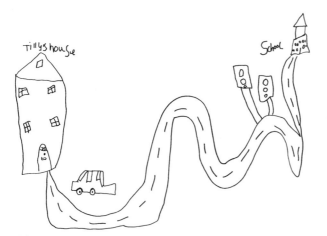

(a)

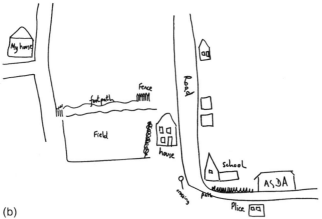

(b)

(c)

Figure 6.1 Journey from home to school maps: (a) Pictorial; (b) Pictorial-plan; (c) Plan.

In a study of the free recall sketch maps of school students aged 8–15, Gerber (1984) found that the youngest children used a mixture of pictorial and abstract symbols, whereas older students relied almost wholly on abstract ones. These were also drawn smaller, which enabled adolescents to include more information on their maps. Some studies have suggested that differences in expressive style may exist between the map making behaviour of children from different cultures. Matthews (1995), for example, reported greater use of pictorial representation in young Kenyans' maps compared to those of British children, as well as lower geometric accuracy. Potter (1985) found that maps of young people in Barbados consisted almost entirely of point symbols.

Using mapping software

The availability of appropriate electronic tools has now shifted research attention towards young children's map making using new technology. In Plate 6 the village previously illustrated in Plate 2 has been represented using *Local Studies*, a simple interactive mapping software tool. Linework can be drawn with the computer pointing device and pictograms can be dragged from a palette to the right of the screen in order to make a map. Alternative (e.g. standardised) symbols are available as well as simple measurement functions using a 'trundle wheel' that is clicked and dragged from one point to another. Areas can be coloured or shaded and text added. Digital maps (e.g. from the Ordnance Survey) and aerial photographs can be included in the view. Hot spots on the map (only one is shown here) are linked to spatial data – in this case a digital image of the location marked by the hotspot (No. 1, by the bridge) and some lines of text. Owen (2003) has explored primary school children's map making using *Local Studies* as well as another electronic tool: *Textease* (see Appendix). The *Textease* examples in Plate 7 are some children's responses to a task inviting them to create a trail around their school for different categories of map user (e.g. younger children and adults new to the area). The software enables them to use realistic photographic images as well as pictograms and conventional symbols in differentiating their map design. It seems likely that empowering children to readily alter their map symbology and move map elements on screen will support learning of how visual variables operate and help them overcome scaling errors.

This chapter, and the previous two, has explored children's understanding of large scale mapping of relatively small areas. The next three chapters consider aspects of children's thinking with smaller scale maps.

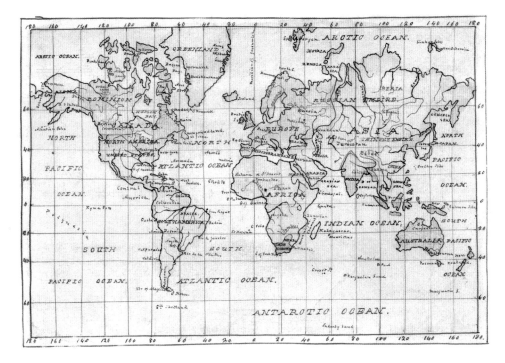

Plate 1 A map of the world by Miss Vevers, Leeds Ladies College, 1880 (from the author's collection).

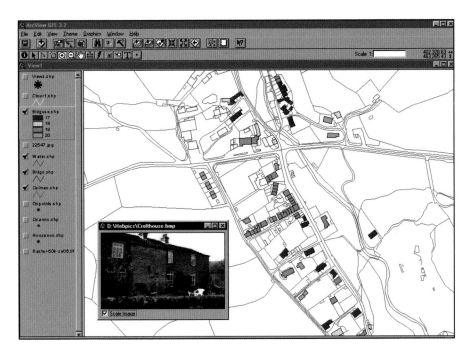

Plate 2a Character appraisal of the village of Hebden using ArcView GIS, 2005: age of building survey.

Source: ESRI. © Crown copyright Ordnance Survey. All rights reserved.

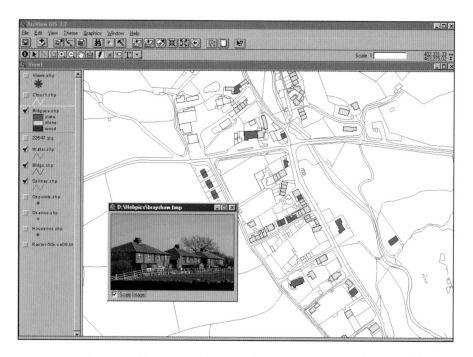

Plate 2b Character appraisal of the village of Hebden using ArcView GIS, 2005: building materials
survey.
Source: ESRI. © Crown copyright Ordnance Survey. All rights reserved.

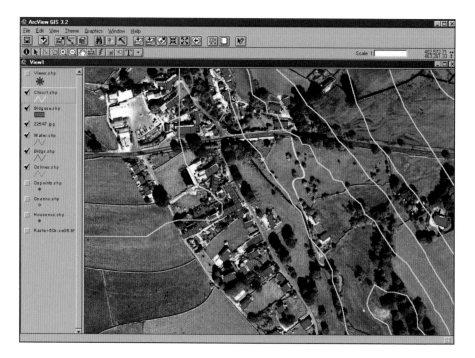

Plate 2c Character appraisal of the village of Hebden using ArcView GIS, 2005: topographic
context.
Source: ESRI. © Crown copyright Ordnance Survey. All rights reserved. Aerial image © Getmapping plc.

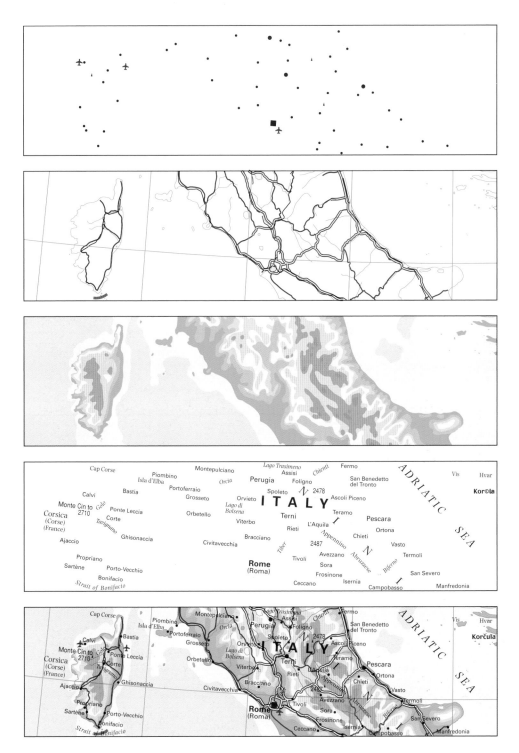

Plate 3 Point, line and area symbols combine with text to make a topographic map. From the *Oxford Student Atlas*, copyright © 2002 Oxford University Press, reproduced by permission of Oxford University Press.

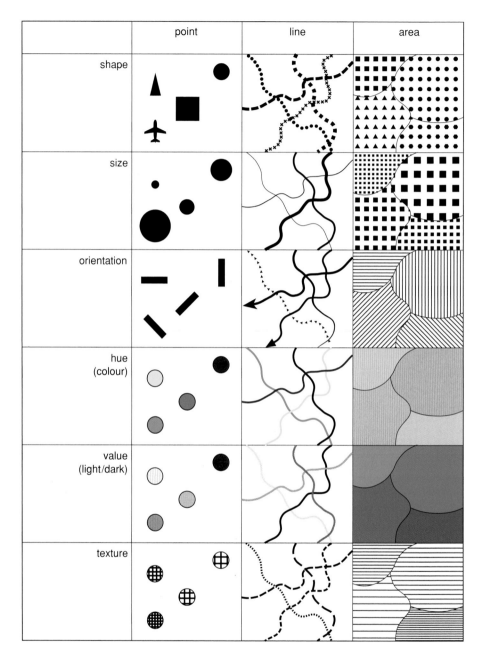

Plate 4 Visual variables used in map symbology (after Bertin, 1983).

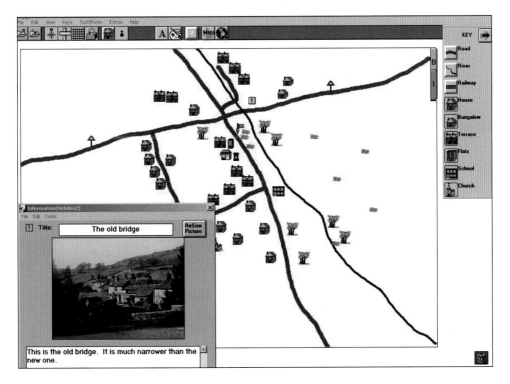

Plate 5 Coordinate game devised by Blades and Spencer (1989a, 1994).

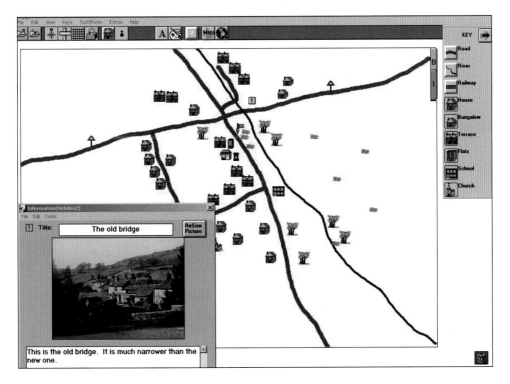

Plate 6 A village study using *Local Studies* (Soft Teach Educational).

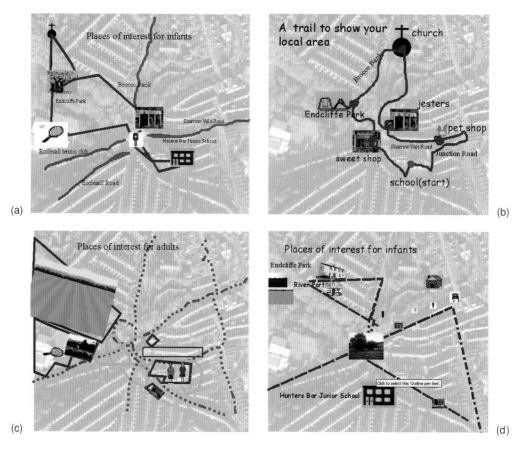

Plate 7 Children's electronic map making using *Textease* (see Appendix). Reproduced by kind permission of David Owen from his research in progress on children's electronic mapping. Map b also by permission of the Register of Research in Primary Geography (Catling and Martin, 2004). Background aerial image © Getmapping plc.

Plate 8 Picture maps provide a 'sense of place'. Map by Digital Wisdom Publishing; illustrations by Ray Grinaway, James McKinnon, Claudia Saraceni, Michael Saunders, Rode Westblade and Ann Winterbotham from *The Reader's Digest Children's Atlas of the World* © Weldon Owen Pty Ltd.

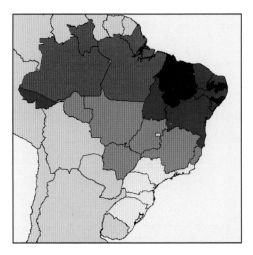

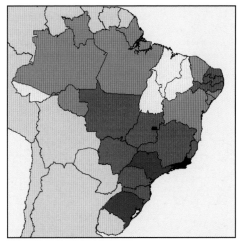

Plate 9a Arcview GIS project on the quality of life in Brazil: illiteracy.
Source: ESRI.

Plate 9b Arcview GIS project on the quality of life in Brazil: participation in higher education.
Source: ESRI.

Plate 10 Atlas map legend from *Atlas Rodinoznanie*, edited by Dr Temenoujka Bandrova, copyright © Data Map Europe, reproduced by permission of Data Map Europe, Sofia, Bulgaria.

How is the Italian economy changing?   1 - GDP Index

The interactive maps below are linked to economic and social data for the regions of Italy in 1988 and 2000. Use these maps to discover similarities and changes in the Italian economy since the late 1980s.

1988

2000

GDP Index 2000
Less than 70.9
From 70.9 to 82.8
From 82.9 to 94.8
From 94.9 to 106.8
106.9 or more

GDP Index
Less than 81
From 81 to 95
From 96 to 109
From 110 to 124
125 or more

	Mapref	Region	Area	Pop Den
1	1	Nord-Ovest	34081	18
2	2	Lombardia	23872	3?
3	3	Nord-Est	39816	18

	Mapref	Region	Area	Pop
5	5	Centro	41142	
6	6	Lazio	17227	
7	7	Abruzzo-Molise	15232	

GDP is the usual measure of a country's wealth. The 1988 map above shows the GDP Index of the Italian regions. Create a similar map for 2000. Use the maps and data tables to find out whether the distribution of rich and poor regions in Italy changed between 1988 and 2000.

1. 1988	2. 2000
Name the 3 richest regions in rank order, with their GDP Index 1 2 3 Highlight and label these regions List the 3 poorest regions in reverse order of wealth, with their GDP Index 9 10 11 Highlight and label these regions.	Name the 3 richest regions in rank order, with their GDP Index 1 2 3 Highlight and label these regions. List the 3 poorest regions in reverse order of wealth, with their GDP Index 9 10 11 Highlight and label these regions.

3. Describe the distribution of the richest and poorest regions in Italy in 1988. Did the pattern of distribution change in 2000? 4. What has happened to the GDP Index of all the Italian regions since 1988? Give examples of the greatest changes. 5. Use the maps to find the number of regions wealthier than the EU average and replace the ? to complete the sentences. 6. Does this mean that the regions of Italy were poorer in 2000 than they were in 1988? Explain your answer.	3. 5. In 1988 there were ? regions above the EU average. In 2000 there were ? regions above the EU average. ? went from above the EU average in 1988 to below the average in 2000

Plate 11 Project on regional variations in Italy using *AEGIS 3*. The Italy worksheet is part of the *AEGIS 3* interactive mapping (GIS) package for schools. © AU Enterprises Ltd. For information about *AEGIS 3* refer to www.advisory-unit.org.uk

7 Understanding topographic and thematic maps

This chapter considers children's understanding of maps as made by national mapping agencies (such as the Ordnance Survey and the United States Geological Survey), typically produced in separate sheets at scales of, say, 1:25,000 and 1:50,000 and used by walkers or motorists, as well as atlas maps of much larger areas of the world such as countries and continents. The former are commonly referred to as large scale maps and the latter as small scale maps. These terms are relative, however, and there is no clear definition of what constitutes large or small. Children frequently have difficulty remembering the difference. Although the terms appear counterintuitive (a large scale map shows a small area and vice versa) they actually refer to the size at which places are represented (a large scale map shows the place large, or close up).

As maps within this range of scales generally deal with areas too extensive to be seen or looked down upon from above, it seems likely that a different schema from that applied to large scale plans must be employed in their interpretation. The larger linear units involved, such as 10, 100 or 1,000 kilometres, are more difficult to relate to everyday experience and very large areas (such as continents) are distorted on a flat map because of the sphericity of the Earth. Making sense of maps that show large areas of the Earth's surface therefore typically requires the user to go beyond the cartographic representation and apply additional knowledge to what is seen. This chapter deals with children and young people's understanding of *topographic* maps (i.e. general reference maps that show a variety of landscape features such as the height of the land, coastlines, communications and settlements) and *thematic* maps (i.e. maps that show the distribution of a single phenomenon or the relationship between several). Typical thematic maps introduced to children at school include maps showing the distribution of temperature, rainfall, population and wealth.

Some learning difficulties with scale

Figure 7.1 illustrates some contrasting representations of scale, each providing different levels of learning support. The solid fill of the graphic scale (or 'scale bar') in Figure 7.1a creates a bold visual impression of 100km but probably makes visual separation of the scale bar into smaller units of 25km more difficult. Estimation of smaller subdivisions is probably easier with the graphic scale in Figure 7.1b but readers who want to put a paper edge below this scale bar in order to mark off and transfer distances to the map will find themselves obscuring the numbers as they are positioned below, rather than above, the bar. Figure 7.1c further subdivides a portion of the scale bar to the left of zero. This is probably unhelpful, as most children invariably assume that the left edge starts at 0 (Bartz,

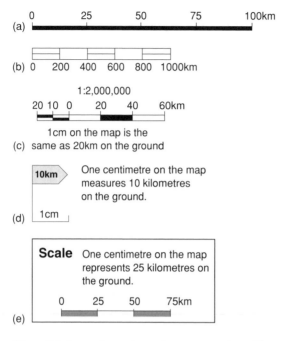

Figure 7.1 Some alternative scale representations. Figure 7.1d from the *Oxford Junior Atlas*, copyright © 1996 Oxford University Press, and Figure 7.1e from the *Oxford Primary Atlas*, copyright © 2004 Oxford University Press, reproduced by permission of Oxford University Press.

1965). Figure 7.1d uses a 'signpost' device in an attempt to show the equivalence between a distance of 10km in the real world and the unit (1cm) used to represent it on the map. Figure 7.1e attempts to combine some of the best features of each of the preceding examples and perhaps provides the best support for learning.

Bartz (1971) describes some (roughly hierarchical) misconceptions children hold about the use of a graphic scale. These include children:

- not understanding that distances can be measured on the map and that these measurements relate to distances in the real world;
- understanding that the graphic scale has something to do with the relationship between the map and the real world but not being sure what the nature of that relationship is;
- understanding that the total length of the graphic scale relates to the stated distance in the real world but that it can only be used to measure that stated distance, not fractions or multiples of it;
- using a previously learned scale (e.g. 1:50,000) without realising that scales vary from one map to another.

A number of practical problems can also be identified when children use map scale information. Accuracy of measurement tends to decrease as distance measured increases. If the graphic scale treatment is different to that previously encountered, children may have difficulty understanding the new form (Bartz, 1970a). Scale statements (such as '1cm to 10km') are often impenetrable, especially when children's experience of 'real world' distance units is of miles and the units taught at school are in kilometres. In relation to world maps, it is also not generally recognised that the scale is usually only true for the equator and therefore inappropriate measurements are often made for other parts of the map. Many school students also appear to have difficulty relating the scale of an inset map to the main map on a page (Towler and Nelson, 1968).

Comparing maps at two scales presents particular challenges. Boardman (1988) notes in his evaluation of the Schools Council *Geography for the Young School Leaver* project that 14- to 16-year-olds found particular difficulty making comparisons between pairs of maps when they were provided with incompatible scale information. For example, the scale of a map of Yellowstone National Park in the project materials was given in miles whereas that of a map of the Peak District National Park was given in kilometres and an historical map of Margate at a scale of 3cm to 400 feet was to be compared with a modern map at 3cm to 500m. Unsurprisingly, such comparisons proved a challenge.

Generalisation

The smaller the map scale, the more generalised the map. Generalisation involves processes such as: the *selection* of the most significant (and omission of less significant) features; *simplification* of level of detail; *smoothing* of linework such as coastlines and contours; *aggregation* of symbols whereby one symbol replaces many; and the *conversion* of areas to points (Buttenfield and McMaster, 1991). The resultant map will probably also show some exaggeration of symbol size (the width of roads, for example, will no longer be 'to scale') and displacement of symbol position (the symbols may need to be separated one from another in order to make each one legible). Generalisation brings both difficulties and opportunities in map interpretation. Less can be ascertained about particular points (entire cities may be represented by small dots) but more can be appreciated about the spatial relationships between them (as a larger area is represented).

The generalisation involved in small scale mapping may underpin learning difficulties in relation both to what is shown on the map and what is not shown. Nearly half of 1,600 students in the first four years of secondary school thought that because only three towns were marked on a small scale map of New Zealand there were only three towns in the country (Sandford, 1972). Sandford (1981) also found urban areas to be underrepresented on school atlases. Children describing an imaginary journey from London to the south coast of England therefore substantially underestimated the degree of urban sprawl as the individual point symbols used for towns created an erroneous view of compact settlements surrounded by fields, farms and forests. Misunderstanding of generalisation also led students to conclude that there were lakes in China and Russia – because they were shown on the map, but none in India – because they were not (Sandford, 1980a). Despite these errors, 'most teachers assume that little or no help need be given to children in atlas mapwork' (Sandford, 1972: 86). The very low level of classroom attention currently paid to *how* atlas maps represent spatial data (Wiegand, 1998b) suggests this assumption is still current.

Understanding conventional symbols on topographic maps

Before being able to *interpret* a map using conventional symbols, the map user must *detect* the individual symbols, *discriminate* between them and then correctly *identify* them (Keates, 1989). Detecting the symbols seems straightforward enough yet being able to pick out the relevant marks on the map from the irrelevant background 'noise' can be problematic for young map users. Some linework, for example, is commonly superimposed on other linear features (political boundaries may follow rivers or parallels of latitude) and may be hard to follow. Practical classroom circumstances can also cause difficulties. Low light levels, wall maps placed too far away and students sharing atlases may all result in significant map detail being overlooked. Discriminating between point, line and area symbols can be problematic if too many symbols share the same shape, size or colour. Discrimination is also made more difficult if children do not have an adequate vocabulary to describe symbol characteristics (for example, to distinguish between navy blue and royal blue or between a pecked line and a dotted line). Identification involves matching the symbol to its counterpart in the legend and correctly interpreting the legend text entry. Many children are unable to match more subtle map colours to their equivalent among the legend swatches as the relative areas of each are generally different (which may influence perception of hue) and in the legend, colour blocks are generally set against white rather than against other colours as on the map. Matching symbols between map and legend also involves holding the symbol characteristics in memory whilst the eye moves from one to the other and this may pose a challenge if symbols are not adequately differentiated. Reading the legend entry is, of course, not the same as understanding it. Most school students will be able to read the words 'national park' next to the appropriate symbol in the legend but if (in a British context) they understand this to mean, say, land in national ownership and having some (park like) attributes such as swings and roundabouts, they will have misinterpreted the symbol.

Many symbols are 'identified' by children without reference to the legend at all. This is partly because many marks on the map do not appear in the legend (some symbology, such as the use of blue for water, is commonly assumed to be intuitive). In many cases this is unproblematic. Bartz (1965), for example, reported near 100 per cent intuitive comprehension of a black dot for settlement, a star for capital city, blue line for rivers and blue fill for sea (the latter also noted by Ottoson, 1987). On political maps most children appear to understand that the non-target land area (often grey or a neutral colour) represents something other than the main focus of the map (Bartz, 1967a). However, in other cases children can make significant errors. Colour is particularly problematic: a 'cartographic quagmire' according to Monmonier (1996). Layer tints (the colours applied to areas between contours) showing land height are especially vulnerable to misinterpretation. On small scale topographic maps such as that illustrated in Plate 3 for example, green (a colour more or less arbitrarily selected to represent low elevation) is often interpreted by children to mean lush grassland, whereas brown is frequently interpreted as representing areas of sparse vegetation (Bartz, 1965; Patton and Crawford, 1978; Sandford, 1980b). Even absence of colour can cause difficulties. In a test, 12- to 15-year-olds were asked to identify land cover using an Ordnance Survey 1:25,000 map. These maps show detail of the built and human environment but leave much of the map white. The white areas could potentially represent cultivated fields, limestone pavement, peat cuttings or rough pasture but nearly half the candidates interpreted the white areas as 'empty', 'barren' or 'where nothing grows' (Sandford, 1979: 300). A control group, using unfamiliar land use maps without a legend, correctly interpreted the same areas as farmland, responding to the brown and green colours used on these maps.

Context is important in symbol identification. A railway line and a river are not simply differentiated by, say, a black line and a blue line but also by the map user's expectations of their form and association with other symbols. Rivers and railways each have subtly different relationships with relief, settlement and coastlines and these are absorbed by the map reader in addition to the description in the legend. Text is also a contributory factor in symbol interpretation. Bartz (1965) gives the example of children's interpretation of a white area symbol superimposed with blue dots. This symbol was associated on a map with the text: *Arctic*. When children correctly associated the text with 'cold' they interpreted the symbol as ice. When the word *Arctic* held no meaning for them they were as likely to interpret the symbol as salt or non-target land area. However, even among fluent readers there are pitfalls. Where settlement names, for example, incorporate topographic elements (such as Lake or Beach) children can assume that reference is being made to these topographic features, not to settlements (Ottoson, 1987). Maps contain many linguistic 'false friends' such as, in Derbyshire, The Peak (actually a plateau) and Peak Forest (actually a village) (Boardman, 1983). Fairbairn (1993) distinguishes between narrative text (which names places) and descriptive text (which labels features according to some other property such as function) and draws attention to the potential for muddling one with the other. FISH FARM, for example, could name a specific farm or describe an economic activity. The potential for confusion is enhanced where descriptive text is unhelpfully printed with the initial letter(s) capitalised (as in Weir and Stepping Stones).

Visualising relief

Visualising relief from a map is a considerable challenge for many young map users. Early maps showed relief by small drawings of hills (a method still employed in maps and atlases for young children) until these were superseded by hachures (lines drawn in the direction of slope with thicker lines representing steeper slopes). Contours were generally adopted from about the beginning of the nineteenth century, with the later addition of hypsometric tints and shaded relief.

The cartographic problem of representing a three-dimensional surface in two dimensions has now been at least partially solved by the ability to readily create a near replica of the landscape through computer generated surfaces using digital elevation models (DEMs). These are collections of elevation points for an area and can be displayed to show the terrain surface in three dimensions and from a choice of viewpoints. Figure 7.2a shows a DEM of Reno, Nevada, from the north. Peavine Peak is the highest point to the west, at an elevation of 8,266 feet. A digital orthophoto quadrangle (DOQ) has been draped over the south-east quadrant of the DEM. DOQs look similar to aerial photographs but have uniform scale and do not contain the image distortions of photographs caused by tilting of the camera and terrain relief. DOQ data can therefore be superimposed directly on a map or DEM to provide additional information such as, in this case, city detail. Figure 7.2b shows the view rotated so that it is seen from the south.

This technology has pushed the boundaries of what counts as a 'map' and would appear to provide considerable opportunities for enhancing children's understanding of landscape although there are very few studies which detail the learning gains. As the surface of the Earth is three dimensional it seems obvious that children's understanding would be supported by 3D landscape displays. For younger children, hardware models providing tactile experience of landscape surfaces remain popular. They will continue to be an essential prerequisite for the use of computer generated perspective views, which only *look* three-dimensional and in which some features may be shielded from view behind others. We know little, as yet, about the degree to which computer generated 3D views promote learning about relief nor about how children's learning may be supported by enabling young map users to pan, zoom, rotate, or 'flyby' using 3D displays.

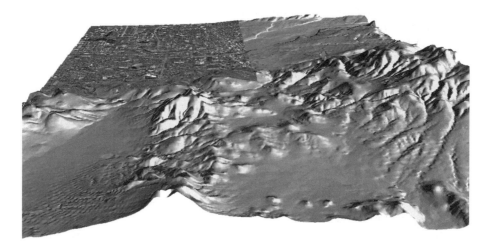

Figure 7.2a Digital Elevation Model (DEM) of Reno, Nevada, from the north. Peavine Peak is the highest point to the west, at an elevation of 8266 feet. A digital orthophoto quadrangle (DOQ) has been draped over the south-east quadrant of the DEM.

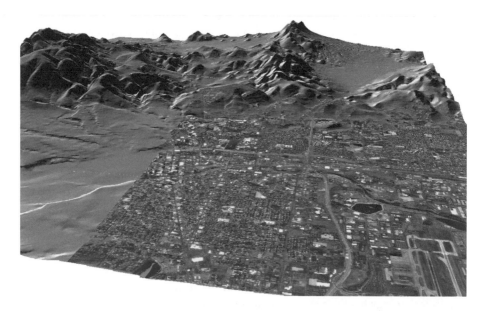

Figure 7.2b The same view rotated so that it is seen from the south.
Courtesy United States Geological Survey.

A significant barrier to children's understanding of relief on maps is the limitation on their language development. The language of landscapes is imprecise. 'Steep' is a label and concept far more readily grasped and unambiguously applied to slopes, for example, than 'not steep' (often described as 'gentle', 'moderate' or 'gradual'). There may be significant regional variations in topographic vocabulary (e.g. in Great Britain: valley, dale, strath, glen, cwm) and many local topographic terms are difficult to say and/or spell, such as: clough, knoll and tor (Boardman, 1983). Children's use of language is also limited by their experience. A 'hill' is more likely for city children to mean a street with a steep gradient than a landscape feature with three dimensional form; 'the coast' may be interpreted as 'seaside'; and 'river' can have associations with leisure activity entirely unrelated to the core concept of water flowing in a channel. In the primary phase, children's understanding of apparently simple physical landscape concepts such as mountain, hill and valley is frequently not secure (Harwood and Jackson, 1993; Dove *et al.*, 1999). Differentiating a hill and a mountain, for example, relies on the application of multiple criteria, such as relative (not absolute) elevation as well as steepness of slope, form and surface character-istics such as land cover or land use. In the real world, few landforms resemble their idealised prototypes as illustrated in text books. Even for secondary school students, many landforms remain difficult to visualise without a 3D representation (for example, hanging valleys and truncated spurs).

Other aspects of children's cognitive development are involved in their attempts to grasp landscape concepts. At first, children's drawings of hills show houses and trees drawn perpendicular to the hill slope. Later, they are drawn perpendicular to the gravitational vertical axis. In between there is a transitional stage when the houses and trees are no longer drawn perpendicular to the slope but neither are they yet coordinated with a fixed, external frame of reference and so they bend, appearing to 'grow towards the light' (Liben, 1981). In a remarkably prescient book, Lucy Sprague Mitchell (1934) described a similar phenomenon in relation to a 12-year-old drawing a map of Russia. Although he 'knew' that water flowed downhill he could not connect this first hand experiential knowledge with drawing the small scale map, commenting that the River Ob (which flows northwards) flowed from the Arctic Ocean 'down' to Siberia. Sandford (1980b) cites evidence for secondary school students' misunderstanding of precisely the same geographical example.

How do children themselves solve the problem of mapping a three dimensional surface? Wiegand and Stiell (1997b) explored the attempts of 5- to 11-year-olds to represent the relief of model landscapes. These were formed from damp sand in boxes with transparent tops. The children were asked to look down into the box and draw the relief from above on plexiglass laid directly on the box lid (Figure 7.3). When they had finished their

Figure 7.3 Mapping relief in 2D using a sandbox.

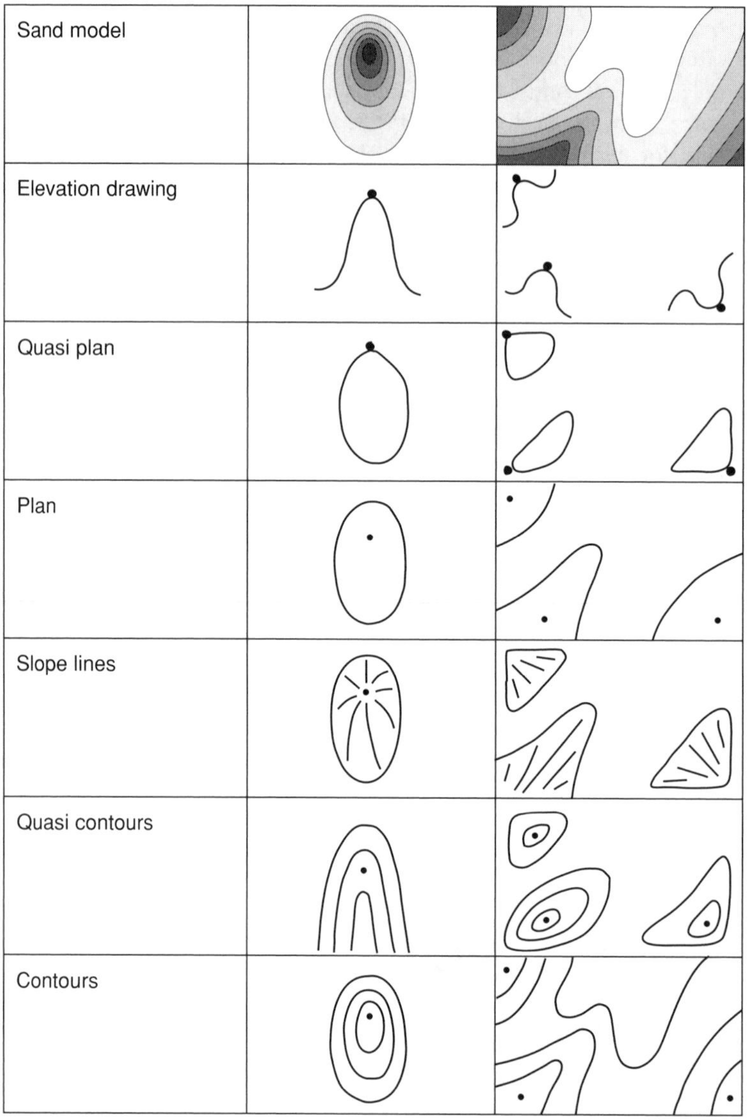

Figure 7.4 Hierarchy of children's 2D representations of relief (after Wiegand, P. and Stiell, B. (1997b) 'Children's relief maps of model landscapes', *British Educational Research Journal*, 23: 179–92. Reproduced by permission of Taylor and Francis. www.tandf.co.uk/journals

drawing they were asked to indicate the highest point with a dot. Figure 7.4 shows typical attempts to draw an oval hill and the confluence of two valleys.

The youngest children drew hills in elevation whilst those in the middle primary years drew simple plans or plans embellished with slope lines. In Figure 7.4 note the distinction between the hills shown entirely in elevation and the quasi plan view where the 'footprint' of the hill is shown in plan but highest point (shown by the dot) shown 'at the top'. Many children devised imaginative systems of slope lines to show distinctions between slope facets they were unable to describe adequately in words. Older children attempted contours with varying degrees of success. Children were frequently unsure how to terminate contour lines on the more gentle slopes or failed to appreciate the relationship between the contour pattern and the position of the highest point. The more complex landforms were often 'chunked' into several discrete elements, rather than a single, continuous form (as the quasi contour map of the valley confluence in Figure 7.4).

Contours

Interpreting contour lines has long formed the basis of much topographic map work in school and the challenge presented to learners has long been recognised: 'The teaching of contour-map reading is generally regarded as one of the most difficult problems the geography teacher has to face' (IAAM, 1954: 195). Liben and Downs (1989) reported striking variations in the degree to which individual children were able to match a 3D model landscape of their local area with a contour map. Children in grades 1 and 2 (Y2 and Y3) were asked to match flags positioned at a number of points on the model with small stickers on a map which showed the same area but at a smaller scale. Performance was generally poor but was highest in the case of a distinctively shaped mountain peak set away from other mountain ridges and also for a corner location where the edge of the frame presumably provided a strong locational cue.

The main difficulty with interpretation of contours is interpolation of slope. Map readers need to recognise two-dimensional patterns from their perception of the contour lines (such as closely or widely spaced parallel lines, nesting of 'V's and circles) and then 'interpolate mentally the infinity of intervening contours' (Sandford, 1979: 298). In tests where they are required to add rivers to contour maps children may often draw them along spurs or ridges rather than in valleys because they haven't yet identified the direction of slopes. Later, children must learn to chunk together slope fragments (such as concave and convex slopes, spurs and valleys) and mentally resolve them into larger landscape patterns such as undulating terrain, dissected plateaux or cuestas. Although children at about age 11 begin to interpret simple, discrete landforms, the difficulties increase when the contours are open and unresolved at the map edge or where the landscape does not match a known ideal. Strategies suggested in teachers' handbooks are often limited to helping children understand discrete, distinctive landforms (such as isolated hills, which they generally don't find problematic) rather than continuous, understated landscapes (which they generally do).

A number of common misconceptions appear to persist in relation to contours among 11- to 14-year-olds. Boardman (1989) gave school students a test based on part of an Ordnance Survey 1:50,000 map. This map (dating from the transition between imperial and metric units) had contours drawn at 50 feet intervals but with the heights converted to metres. On a worksheet showing only contours (Figure 7.5), students were asked to shade all the land over 91m. Some failed to shade the land inside the unnumbered contours at the northern edge of the map, suggesting their understanding was impeded by the absence of numerical cues. Others shaded only the land between 91m and 107m, suggesting they may not have understood that the land continued to rise beyond 107m. When asked to identify the higher end of each of lines A to C, more were successful for line B (which may have been as a result of the proximal cue from the contour numbered 122m). Fewer than half of the 14-year-olds identified line C as the steepest and the majority who chose line B may have confused height of the land with steepness of slope. Asked to

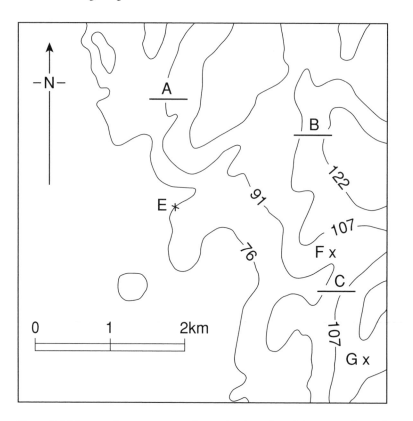

Figure 7.5 Map used to test secondary school students' interpretation of contours (from Boardman, 1989: 324 and reproduced with permission of The Geographical Association).

estimate the height of the land at points E–G, most gave the height of E correctly as it lay on a contour. Few were able to estimate the heights of F and G and many stated that F was at 91m and G at 107m. This may suggest that they visualised the land as rising in a series of steps. Contour interpretation errors such as these seem to persist into the later years of secondary schooling (Boardman and Towner, 1979).

Given the difficulty of interpretation, it is surprising that more use appears not to be made by teachers and learners of a significant cue in the way contours are numbered: numbers are most commonly (for example, on Ordnance Survey maps) read 'uphill' so that the top of the number is on higher ground (Phillips, 1979). Other important support is provided by relief shading. Map readers are generally faster and more accurate when interpreting relief from layer tinted maps than from contours alone (Phillips, *et al.*, 1975; Potash *et al.*, 1978; Castner and Wheate, 1979), not least because the colours resolve the ambiguity of which side of a line is higher, especially when the lines are sparse. Legend information may also have a significant effect on interpretation of relief. Children do not always correctly interpret colour *ranges* in the legend. A colour may be interpreted, for example, as representing land at 1,000 *or* 2,000 feet but not the intended *range* of 1,000–2,000 feet. The phrase 'below sea level' may also be too cryptic for many young readers who often interpret this as meaning 'land beneath the sea' (Bartz, 1965).

To identify symbols efficiently, point, line and area information has to be held in memory between viewing the map and the legend and children's ability to do this can be supported by a high degree of 'match' between legend and map. De Lucia and Hiller (1982) make a distinction between 'natural' and 'standard' land height legends. A standard legend consists of a linear sequence of boxes containing colour tints used on the map. A natural legend recreates a portion of the mapped landscape and identifies elements of it by means of labels. De Lucia and Hiller tested each style and found that overall map reading accuracy was improved when subjects used the natural legend. This was especially marked on tasks involving visualisation of the topographic surface of the landscape (for example identification of valleys). The standard legend, however, performed slightly better for some tasks such as those requiring relative height judgements (for example, identifying the highest town in an area). If standard legends are to be used for land height it is preferable that they are arranged vertically rather than horizontally and, if land height steps are uneven, that this is reflected in the relative thickness of the colour swatches.

Reading and understanding text on small scale maps

Almost everything about text on small scale maps is potentially difficult for young map users. Spelling and pronunciation problems are compounded with foreign place names, even where diacritical marks are not used and place names are shown in the form most familiar to readers. Bartz (1967a) reported children muddling Niger and Nigeria, apparently thinking that they were the same or that the former was an abbreviation for the latter. Some features change their name from one country (and language) to another. The River Danube, for example, is called the Donau in Germany, the Duna in Hungary, the Dunav in Bulgaria and the Dunarea in Romania. Many small scale maps carry abbreviations. Some are common (such as: R., Mt., Is., Pen. for physical features), whilst others are unique (such as FYRO Macedonia, i.e. the Former Yugoslav Republic of Macedonia). Conventions on the use of brackets after place names may also need to be decoded. These can be used inconsistently. For example:

Corsica (France)	gives name of country;
Cabo de Hornos (Cape Horn)	gives translation;
Beijing (Peking)	gives alternative transliteration (i.e. from Chinese to the Roman alphabet);
Chennai (Madras)	gives former name.

Insecure readers need the support of clear text that runs from left to right with predictable spaces between words and letters. That's exactly what doesn't pertain with text on small scale maps. In addition, place names can be long in relation to small areas and thus condensed into a small space (Liechtenstein), or short for large areas and thus spread out over a large area of the map (USA). It is not surprising, therefore, that children often cannot relate a label to its referent area, particularly if an irregular coastline and many islands are involved, such as in the case of Indonesia (Bartz, 1967a). Insensitivity to typography also causes errors, with students unable to distinguish between those labels that are capitalised or bold or italic or in different point sizes. Sandford noted that the question 'Name the two largest islands in the West Indies' was commonly answered by 'Cuba and the Dominican Republic' (the latter for Hispaniola), 'an error resulting from the usual combination of unobtrusive physical names and an ineffectual and unstated typographical code' (1980a: 87).

Understanding picture maps

In an attempt to make cartography accessible for young children, much use has been made of pictorial maps. These come in many forms (Holmes, 1992) but a common application is of small map located items of artwork that create a 'sense of place' by illustrating animals, buildings, activities, landscapes, etc. characteristic of the area in which they are placed (see, for example, Plate 8). Black (1997) draws attention to the ways in which these images can be a source of bias, citing the example of a map of south east Asia bearing bucolic illustrations of rural life with no evidence of industrialisation, modern buildings or motor vehicles. The maps reviewed by Black tended to be dominated by animals (apparently living in perfect harmony with no predation by other animals or human poachers). The suggestion is not that negative images should be employed but that sanitisation of content for young readers is misleading.

Although pictorial maps appear to enhance motivation in browsing and provide particular support for children who struggle to learn, the messages embedded in the located pictures are not always received. In one study (Wiegand and Stiell, 1996c), children were asked to identify the pictures on a selection of atlas maps. Several images (almost certainly unproblematic for adults) proved difficult, especially those of industrial features outside the children's experience (such as an offshore oil rig, pit head winding gear and several representations of factories). It is possible that at least some of these identification errors could be reduced with multimedia atlases that use animated images and sound to give young readers better clues to what the pictures show. Even when children could readily *identify* the image they frequently were not able to *interpret* it. Artwork of a car, for example (positioned at a city well known for motor vehicle assembly), was interpreted variously as 'a car park', 'a car sales showroom', 'a traffic jam', 'a place where they like red cars' or 'a breakdown'. Children are, of course, more likely to have direct experience of all these things than they are of motor vehicle manufacture and so their misinterpretation is entirely understandable but it does point to the need for some support in clarifying for children what may be self-evident to adults. In Plate 8, the map maker has anticipated this difficulty by labelling the car artwork appropriately (it's the addition of the word *manufacturing* that makes the difference). In another example, children correctly identified a picture of a woollen garment as clothing but had difficulty interpreting its meaning. A (loosely hierarchical) set of notions appeared to be held:

1   Correct identification but no understanding of meaning ('I know it's a coat but I don't know why it's there').
2   Literal misinterpretation ('Someone lost a coat there').
3   Misapplication of metaphor (the garment is a metaphor for scarecrow: 'They grow crops there'; the garment is a metaphor for temperature: 'It's a cold place because you need to wear a coat there'; or, interpreting the metaphor differently: 'If you wore a coat like that you'd be hot so it's a hot place').
4   Partial application of correct metaphor (the garment represents wool: 'Wool comes from there').
5   Correct application of metaphor (the garment represents woollen garment manufacture: 'They make and sell woollen clothes there').

(Wiegand and Stiell, 1996c: 22)

Children were also challenged with two maps from different picture atlases, each of which showed an image of an elephant on a map of India. In one atlas the image was located in southern India; in the other it was located to the north west. Although earlier questions indicated that the children understood each single elephant picture to represent many elephants on the ground, further probing elicited ambiguous understanding. The difference between the location of the images on the two maps was explained, for example, by '*the* elephant moved' or '*he* went to live somewhere else'.

Understanding thematic maps

Thematic maps can be *qualitative* (such as a map showing the location of factories through the use of point symbols) or *quantitative* (showing the number of employees at each through the use of proportional circles). Children's understanding of quantitative symbols generally comes later than understanding of qualitative symbols (Gerber, 1984). Thematic maps emphasise patterns of phenomena and spatial aspects of numerical data. They are extremely common in school atlases and geography textbooks, with the implicit assumption that this type of cartographic representation is readily understood by school students. However, although children in the early years of school can access some thematic information from maps (Trifonoff, 1995), for many school students interpretation may be more problematic than has hitherto been recognised. Students often do not have appropriate strategies for analysing thematic maps, probably because the school geography curriculum places greater emphasis on declarative knowledge (knowing *that*) rather than procedural knowledge (knowing *how*) (van der Schee *et al.*, 1992; van Dijk *et al.*, 1994).

Point symbols are commonly used in educational cartography to show the location of economic activity (Figure 7.6). For nominal data such as types of economic activity the graphic variable of shape is generally used to differentiate between symbols. These are usually *mimetic* (i.e. they resemble the feature being represented), especially where the feature being represented has unambiguous distinguishing characteristics, such as cattle, sheep, pigs and camels. Where features can be less easily distinguished, such as between minerals, or types of related industry, such as cotton textiles and woollen textiles, then abstract, geometric symbols, often differentiated by colour or orientation, may be more appropriate. These are sometimes grouped into 'families' so that, for example, triangles might represent sources of energy, whereas squares might represent types of manufacturing industry. This is good cartographic practice. Good educational practice would be to make such distinctions explicit to learners so that they could decode the map more easily. Mimetic symbols provide support for learners as their shape gives a clue to meaning but readers who surmise meaning incorrectly have little incentive to check their understanding with the legend. Abstract symbols, on the other hand, cannot be so readily guessed so the reader is compelled to go to the legend to discover what they mean. However, even when the reader refers to the legend there may be pitfalls. School students often interpret legend entries such as 'furniture', 'motor vehicles', 'food and drink' (notwithstanding that the legend may be clearly titled *Manufacturing industry*) to mean a location where these goods are *sold* rather than where they are *made* (Wiegand, 2002a).

Some common errors with economic point symbol maps are illustrated below in relation to the map in Figure 7.6.

- The map shows agricultural activity. The student may conclude that there is no industry in Africa (incorrect).

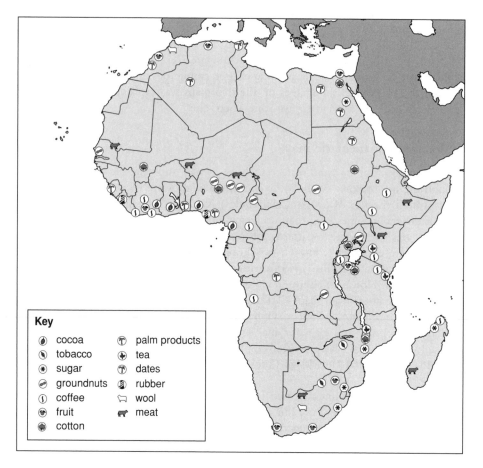

Figure 7.6 Crop and livestock production in Africa: a thematic point symbol map. Adapted from *The Oxford Practical Atlas*, 2003, copyright © 2004 Oxford University Press, reproduced by permission of Oxford University Press.

- Libya has no economic point symbols. The student concludes that Libya is relatively unproductive economically and may assume this is because much of Libya is desert (correct) or that much of Libya is mountainous (incorrect).
- Symbols representing wool and meat are shown in South Africa. The student concludes that livestock are raised in South Africa (correct). There are, however, no symbols for wool and meat in Namibia. The student concludes that there is no livestock in Namibia (incorrect: there *is* livestock but it is below the threshold for inclusion on a map at this scale).
- Two fruit symbols are placed along the coast in South Africa. The student concludes that much fruit is grown in South Africa (correct) but that it is only grown at the coast (incorrect, as the scale of the map means that the symbol covers a very large area. Fruit is also grown elsewhere in the country but at levels below the threshold for inclusion on the map).
- Without referring to the legend, the student identifies a palm tree symbol in Nigeria and interprets it as meaning the production of dates (incorrect, as the legend

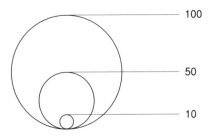

Figure 7.7 Children's interpretation of proportional circle legends (after Elg, 2003).

shows that this (reversed) palm tree symbol stands for the production of palm oil).

(Based on examples provided by Elg, 2003 and Sandford, 1972; 1980b)

Point symbol maps can also be used for quantitative data with symbol size varying in accordance to the quantity represented. Compact forms that are easily scaled (such as circles and squares) are usually used, rather than figurative shapes. Nevertheless, most studies indicate that individuals exhibit weak ability to compare the size of symbols whose area is proportional to a quantity, for example proportional circles representing the tonnage handled at ports. This is especially difficult where symbols are not located near each other. Errors are greater for circles than for squares and even greater for volume symbols than area symbols as volumes are scaled to the cube root of the data, hence the range of symbol sizes is reduced. When three dimensional volume symbols are presented on two dimensional paper maps it is the surface area, not the apparent volume, that is perceived by readers. Legends for proportional circles are easily misinterpreted. In Figure 7.7, for example, students may interpret the diagram to mean that there are three discrete categories only, not three indicative points on a continuous scale (Elg, 2003).

It seems reasonable to assume that most children find a one-to-one relationship between symbol and referent relatively easy to understand but thematic maps (such as dot maps) frequently have a many-to-one relationship. Each dot stands for a quantity in geographical space. Dot maps have an intuitive appeal in education because of their apparent simplicity (more dots equal more of the phenomenon) and, for example in different colours, they allow several distributions (e.g. sheep *and* pigs) to be shown on the same map. Most map readers, however, appear to underestimate the number of dots and therefore also the densities represented (Provin, 1977). Support for young learners can be provided in the legend through *visual anchors* in the form of samples of dot densities with appropriate descriptive labels (e.g. 'crowded' or 'empty' for population distribution). Legend entries that refer only to statistical relationships can be too cryptic for children. Passini (2003) cites an example of a child, confronted with a legend entry for a population density map of 'less than 1 person per square kilometre', asking 'Are they dwarves?'.

Choropleth (or 'graduated colour') maps are a very common way of representing statistical data gathered for areas such as countries or counties and are popular in school atlases and geography texts. Anecdotal evidence from teachers suggests that a frequent student misunderstanding is that there is a sudden intensity change at the edge of the enumeration area. Although student construction of choropleth maps by hand has been a traditional part of geography education for many years, the educational use of GIS tools massively increases the possibilities for student exploration of the effects of changing the number of data classes and the basis for classification which can radically alter the appearance (and therefore interpretation) of the map. The most common form of classification (and the default on many software mapping programs) is where data are grouped into classes based on similarity so that numerical differences within groups are less than the differences between groups. This method of classification was traditionally achieved only after laborious graphical representation of the data so that the class boundaries could be determined visually. Although the computer now performs such calculations instantly, the rationale for classification can appear opaque to school students. One of the possible alternatives to this basis for classification is where each class interval encloses equal amounts of the total range of mapped quantities. In this form of classification, legends have an intuitive, orderly appeal but although the classification is easier for school students to understand, it may not be best suited to the data.

Choropleth map data for educational use are almost always 'normalised' so that values are related to area or some other variable such as total population. Thus choropleth maps generally show ratios or proportions, not absolutes (e.g. population density, not total population). The usual rule in symbol selection is that the darker the area, the greater intensity of the phenomenon being mapped.

Some aspects of student thinking with choropleths can be illustrated by their use of GIS tools (Wiegand, 2003). Following a brief training session in which they were introduced to the functionality of *ArcView*, pairs of students aged 14–15 and 16–17 were invited to make a set of maps that showed how the quality of life varies in Brazil. Analysis of their talk during the task reveals some common 'bugs' in learning. As Plate 9 shows, there is 'directionality' in the datasets. North East Brazil is high on illiteracy (a 'negative' variable) and low on participation in higher education (a 'positive' variable). This directionality of data has an obvious impact on student visualisation of the map. Darker area shading can mean 'better' or 'worse' depending on the variable being mapped. Data directionality in Plate 9 caused interpretation difficulties (albeit in the short term only for many) for about half the students. Students also showed a tendency to exaggerate when they described the datasets. For example, areas with only relatively high illiteracy rates were described as 'where they can't read or write' and areas with relatively lower percentages of homes with running water were described as 'where they have no bathrooms'. This may be a way of dealing with a high information load (simplifying saves processing space) but the descriptions are misleading. The scale of the map used for this task was also generally not recognised as students referred to 'there, near the coast' for places that were perhaps 500km from the sea (a phenomenon also reported by Bartz, 1967b). Students struggled to explain the concept of normalising to themselves and to each other and some found the distinction between '0' (i.e. a value of zero) and 'no data' (i.e. no information available) difficult to grasp. Concepts of ratio and proportionality are not well established, even in the middle years of secondary schooling, and these concepts may need rehearsing at the point at which students create their maps. Having worked through the decisions necessary to make their maps, however, students are much better equipped to make an effective selection of appropriate symbology and to evaluate maps in atlases and texts, achieving what Liben and Downs (1992) call *meta-representation*.

This chapter has examined some characteristics of children's learning with topographic and thematic maps at medium and small scale. The next chapter identifies some particular learning issues in relation to maps at the smallest scale of all: maps of the world.

8 World maps, globes and atlases

Maps can exert a significant influence on children's thinking about the world as a whole. They offer a powerful picture of spatial relationships between countries and land masses. The properties of some map projections (i.e. systems for transforming the spherical surface of the Earth into a flat map) may suggest misleading distortions so that children come to believe, for example, that Greenland is the same size as Africa or that 'we' are in the middle of the world whilst others are on the periphery. This chapter examines some common misconceptions about the Earth, how children's world knowledge typically develops and how maps, globes and atlases (both conventional and digital) may shape their understanding of how parts of the world beyond their immediate experience 'fit together'.

Understanding the Earth

Even older students in secondary school often fail to understand spatial relationships at the scale of the whole world. When asked, for example, to indicate the direction of Australia and the South Pole, British students generally (eventually) point 'down' towards the antipodes but the notion of, say, Paris being far enough south to be below the horizon is generally poorly understood (Sandford, 1980b). In the UK, at least, children (and many adults) frequently have little idea of the approximate dimensions of the Earth (the equatorial circumference is about 25,000 miles or 40,000 kilometres) and often greatly exaggerate its size and the time it would take to travel round it.

Children's thinking about the Earth as a planetary body exhibits some common misunderstandings. Consider, for example, the problem of locating a small model human figure on a large globe. Many children find it difficult to resolve the cognitive conflict inherent in positioning the figure in the southern hemisphere. They know it has to be attached to the Earth by the feet but that people cannot be 'upside down', yet for the figure to be the 'right way up' it has to be attached by its head – also an impossibility. Now suppose that such a figure on the Earth's surface is holding a rock. If the rock is dropped, which way does it fall? If the figure is standing on the northern hemisphere of the globe it may be said to fall 'down', towards the Earth, but what if the figure is standing on the southern hemisphere? Does the rock fall 'up' towards the Earth or 'down' away from the Earth? And if there was an imaginary hole right through the Earth would the rock fall out of the other side or would it stop in the middle? Children's thinking about problems such as these has led to the development of a number of alternative notions about the Earth as a cosmic body (see Figure 8.1) (Nussbaum, 1985).

Notion 1 was ascribed to children who, although they *stated* that the Earth was round, answered questions as though they *believed* it was flat. Pictures they have seen of the Earth

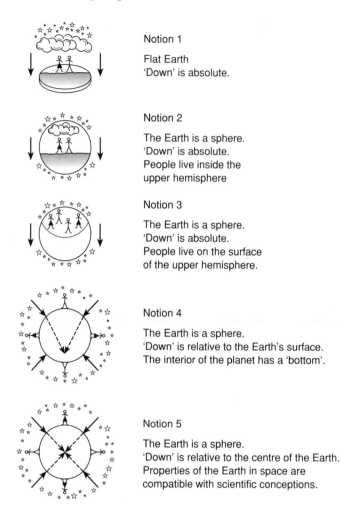

Notion 1

Flat Earth
'Down' is absolute.

Notion 2

The Earth is a sphere.
'Down' is absolute.
People live inside the
upper hemisphere

Notion 3

The Earth is a sphere.
'Down' is absolute.
People live on the surface
of the upper hemisphere.

Notion 4

The Earth is a sphere.
'Down' is relative to the Earth's surface.
The interior of the planet has a 'bottom'.

Notion 5

The Earth is a sphere.
'Down' is relative to the centre of the Earth.
Properties of the Earth in space are
compatible with scientific conceptions.

Figure 8.1 Children's conceptions of the Earth as a cosmic body (after Nussbaum, 1985). Arrows point to the direction believed by the child to be 'downward'.

from space contrast with their own direct experience of its flatness. When challenged with the inconsistency some refer to the roundness of mountains or the curvature of roads. Others appear to believe there are two Earths – the one photographed by astronauts and the one they themselves live on. Yet others believe that the Earth is 'round' (that is, like a disc) but not spherical. Children holding notion 2 believe that the Earth is a huge ball made up of two hemispheres. People live inside this sphere on the flat planar surface of the lower hemisphere. The sky is the inside surface of the upper hemisphere. Outside the sphere is 'space'. Children holding notion 3 have some idea of unlimited space surrounding the Earth but they lack the idea of gravity – it is possible to 'fall off'. Objects thrown from the northern hemisphere will fall to Earth; those thrown from the southern hemisphere will continue falling downwards. 'Up' and 'down' are not defined by reference to the Earth itself but by a more universal sense of 'right way up' of which the Earth itself is a part. People can therefore only live on the surface of the upper hemisphere. In notion 4 children appear to believe that the Earth is spherical and that objects will fall to Earth because of gravity. Yet when questioned about the internal structure of the Earth they are confused. The interior of the planet is thought to have a 'bottom', even though 'down' on the surface is always towards the ground. In notion 5 the properties and nature of the Earth are consistently construed as compatible with scientific conceptions. The Earth is spherical, surrounded by space, and 'down' is towards the centre of the Earth.

Nussbaum's findings were validated by Sneider and Pulos (1983), who showed that most children below the age of 10 held notions 1, 2 or 3 and most children aged 13 and over held notions 4 or 5. The widest spread of notions was held by children in the 11- to 12-year range. Similar findings have also been reported by Vosniadou and Brewer (1992).

Development of world place knowledge

Very young children have generally heard of a number of distant places even if they have little experience of them directly (e.g. through travel) or indirectly (e.g. through pictures). Several attempts have been made to chart the development of the 'known world' of childhood by mapping the places children spontaneously name in play or tests (Lambert and Wiegand, 1990; Wiegand, 1991). For children in the UK a typical pattern of developing world awareness might be as shown in Figure 8.2.

The first distant places preschool children appear most consistently to have heard of include France, Spain, America, Australia and Africa. Seven-year-olds can generally name seven or eight countries but these frequently include fantasy lands, both real (Disneyland, Legoland) and imagined (paradise, never-never land). Although, on average, 11-year-olds appear to be able to name about 15 countries and some can name up to 30, some very significant gaps in British children's world view commonly persist by the time they enter secondary school. These typically include much of central and South America (with the exception of the well-known footballing nations of Brazil and Argentina) and most of the countries of Africa, eastern Europe and south-east Asia. This fairly stable, but distorted, pattern of developing awareness of the rest of the world is likely to be different for children from other countries (and therefore exposed to different media sources) and modified in response to topical events (or at least events that have significance for children). Overjørdet (1984), for example, found that Norwegian children's world maps (drawn after the seventh week of the Atlantic War between Britain and Argentina) portrayed the Falkland Islands (Islas Malvinas) as being more prominent than both the USA and Argentina itself.

Children's maps of the world

Several studies have used free recall sketch maps as a means of accessing children's understanding of the configuration of the Earth's land masses. As a research instrument, free recall sketch maps have the methodological shortcoming of relying heavily on the subject's drawing ability but they are flexible in their application, the task is easy to administer and much information can be collected rapidly. Free recall world maps drawn by school students appear to exhibit systematic biases (Saarinen, 1973). A common perception, for example, is that Africa and Europe are thought to be much further south than their true latitudinal position, whilst South America is often envisaged as being further west than its

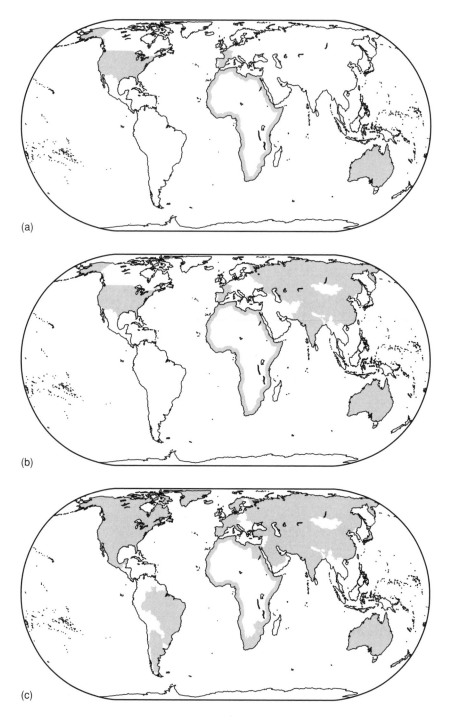

Figure 8.2 Typical development of the 'known world' of childhood from a UK perspective (after Lambert and Wiegand, 1990; Wiegand, 1991).

true longitudinal position (Nelson *et al.*, 1992). Evidence of these and other errors in the alignment and rotation of the landmasses were also noted by Tversky (1981) and Muller (1985). Wiegand (1995) reported the results of 268 primary school children's attempts to draw a free recall sketch map of the world. The resultant maps were analysed and classified into five types, which showed a strong association with age (see Figure 8.3). The youngest children drew maps (Figure 8.3a) characterised by a number of enclosed, roughly circular shapes, each identified as a discrete place. Most were countries but there were also many instances of towns (especially seaside and holiday resorts both in Britain and overseas), districts, suburbs and even streets. With increasing age, children attempted to draw (Figure 8.3b) the shapes of places as irregular outlines rather than circles but with few instances of 'correct' maintenance of shape and none of correct spatial relationships between the shapes. Spaces between these 'lands' were often identified by name or by colouring as sea or ocean areas. Some maps (Figure 8.3c) revealed embryonic elements of contiguous spatial relations, even though the elements themselves were generally inaccurately located. Great Britain and Ireland were commonly shown in an appropriate relative relationship (i.e. Ireland to the west of Great Britain). Other typical maintained contiguities included France/Spain, America/ Mexico, China/Japan and USA/Canada. Older children's maps (Figure 8.3d) were characterised by multiple instances of correct contiguity and inclusion. Up to four continental land masses were usually depicted, the most common being North and South America, Europe and Australia. By the end of the primary phase, children were often able to depict all seven continents and some maps in this category exhibited a striking degree of country detail (as can be seen in Figure 8.3e, drawn by an exceptionally able younger child).

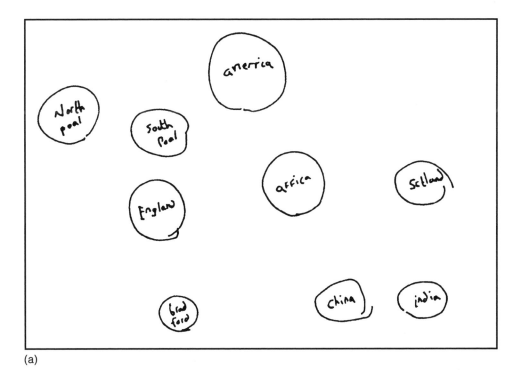

(a)

Figure 8.3 Children's free recall sketch maps of the world (Wiegand, 1995).
8.3a World map type 1 (girl, age 6)

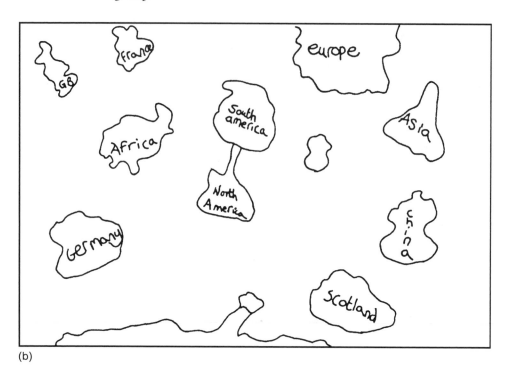

(b)

Figure 8.3b World map type 2 (boy, age 9)

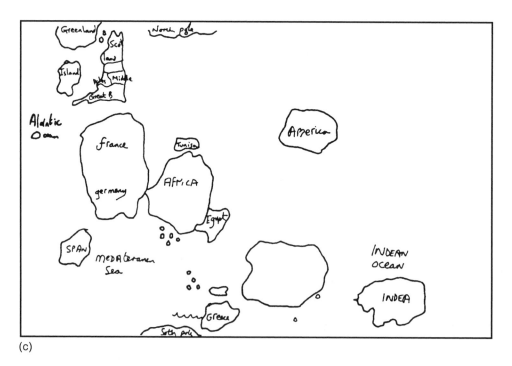

(c)

Figure 8.3c World map type 3 (boy, age 8)

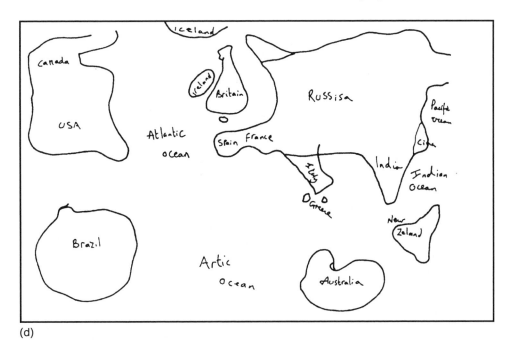

(d)

Figure 8.3d World map type 4 (girl, age 10)

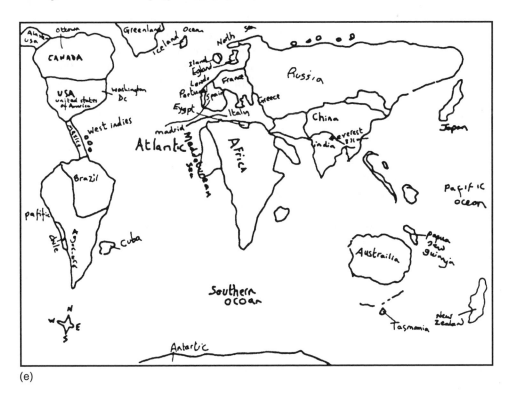

(e)

Figure 8.3e World map type 5 (boy, age 9)

School students' sketch maps of the world are influenced by their experience of the prevailing representations of the world available to them. European students tend to produce Atlantic centred maps and Australian students tend to produce Pacific centred maps. The dominant bias, however, from students all over the world is to exaggerate the size of Europe (Saarinen, 1999), whereas the size of Asia is generally underestimated. This may be because children assume that the rationale for grouping land masses into continents is that they cover approximately the same area. Students' maps are also generally ethnocentric. In one European study (of 300 children from five countries) all participants showed their own country with greater accuracy and represented it as being at the heart of Europe (Axia *et al.*, 1998). When making comparisons between the size of continents, students often significantly overestimate the size of Antarctica (Wiegand and Stiell, 1996a). Its appearance on many projections as a long strip at the foot of the map may contribute to this error but the application of other information may also intervene. One girl, for example, knew that 'Antarctica gets bigger in the winter'. In a more controlled comparison of children's representations of the location, size and shape of continental land masses, using separate schedules to assess each attribute, Harwood and Rawlings (2001) noted that children were significantly better able to depict location and size than they were shape.

Map projections

Map projections systematically transform the curved, three dimensional surface of the Earth into a flat two-dimensional plane. In so doing, some distortion is inevitable. This affects shape, distances and directions. Figure 8.4 illustrates the contrasting characteristics of a selection of map projections. Figure 8.4a and b show two, differently 'centred' versions of the Eckert IV projection (i.e. the fourth projection devised by the German cartographer Max Eckert, 1868–1938): one as it might appear on the wall of a classroom in Europe; the other as on a classroom wall in Oceania. It is an *equal area* projection, i.e. the area of the land masses (for example Greenland and Africa) are shown in their correct relative size. Shape, however, is distorted and increasingly so west and east of the map centre as the meridians of longitude become more curved. Nevertheless, the shortening of the parallels of latitude towards the poles, giving the map outline an elliptical appearance, does echo the sphericity of the Earth and the Eckert IV projection is considered by many to be a good compromise for educational use. Its use in the documentation for the National Curriculum has led to its widespread adoption in school atlases in the United Kingdom.

Figure 8.4c is the projection devised in the sixteenth century by Gerard Mercator (1512–94) and was in common use in school atlases and wall maps in the nineteenth century and for much of the twentieth. Comparison with the Eckert IV shows how badly relative area is distorted. Greenland looks about the same size as Africa yet is actually about 14 times smaller. To use this projection to show, for example, ecosystems would be entirely misleading (as it would appear as though a third of the world was tundra and coniferous forest). However, although areas are distorted on the Mercator projection it has an invaluable navigational property: a straight line on the map is a line of constant compass bearing. This key property has been somewhat overlooked in education (being not much concerned with practical navigational matters) and the Mercator projection has fallen out of favour. The dominance of the northern hemisphere (and thus in particular the misleading relative proportions of rich and poor nations) has been thought to reinforce Eurocentric bias in children's graphical world view. Particularly influential in this debate was Arno Peters (1916–2002) whose 'new' projection (actually a replica of one devised by

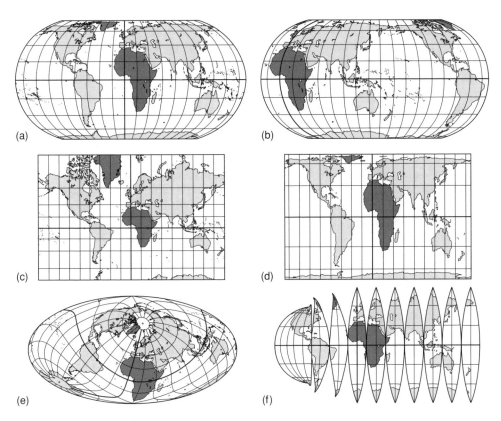

Figure 8.4 Some contrasting map projections: (a) Eckert IV (Atlantic centred); (b) Eckert IV (Pacific centred); (c) Mercator; (d) Peters; (e) Oblique Aitoff; (f) Globe with gores.

the Rev. James Gall in 1871) was vigorously promoted as a fairer view of the world (Figure 8.4d) and boosted by its widespread use in international development publications and its adoption by the global education movement. Although the map itself was roundly criticised by cartographers, the Peters projection controversy is now more commonly viewed as an episode with positive outcomes in that it attracted immense social, political and educational interest in alternative ways of representing the world (Vujacovic, 2003).

Figure 8.4e illustrates the oblique Aitoff projection, one of the many alternatives to more traditional representations of the world and one which helps counter some common misconceptions held by school students as a result of over-reliance on use of world maps rather than the globe. This particular map would be useful in an educational context for illustrating themes such as the history of the Cold War (because the spatial relations between North America and the former Soviet Union can be more readily appreciated) or the distribution of major world air routes (which primarily traverse the northern hemisphere). Figure 8.4f shows the globe 'unpeeled' into strips or 'gores' and this is a common illustration in school atlases to explain the impossibility of representing the three dimensional surface of the Earth as a rectangle without stretching, squeezing or snipping parts of the map. 'Snipping' the meridians is a principle employed in 'interrupted' projections (which typically cut the meridians in mid ocean and thus leave less distortion in the largest land areas). Bartz (1965) reported that 10- to 14-year-old children had little difficulty understanding interrupted projections and could readily explain (on a projection which cut Greenland longitudinally) why there were two parts labelled 'Greenland' on the map. However, the same students appeared to have considerable difficulty with the similar-sounding terms latitude and longitude, and had very sketchy notions of how they were numbered. When asked to find the equator on a world map, many searched for the *word* rather than relating the concept to 0° latitude. Few were able to relate insets to the main map using latitude and longitude coordinates, neither could they draw conclusions about relative location using coordinates alone.

The need to familiarise children with the size and shapes of the world's land masses creates a paradox for teaching. We want children to understand that each world map is only one of many possible representations. This suggests providing a variety of projections, each centred on different parts of the world, in order to counter conventional views and stereotypes. On the other hand, children require a stable frame of reference to which they can anchor their developing place knowledge and this suggests the complementary strategy: regular presentation of the same projection. Teachers need to find their own way through this paradox but it is generally agreed that the projection presented most commonly to school students should be equal area. This is because the most common applications for the world map in education are those for which an equal area map are best suited.

The significance of understanding map projections has risen dramatically in recent years. What was once a rather obscure topic with practical exercises requiring hours of calculation has now moved centre stage as even young users can reproject their data using cartographic and GIS software with just a few mouse clicks. Figure 8.5 illustrates this with a classroom example. A group of 13-year-olds are studying earthquakes and volcanoes and their relationship to the boundaries of the Earth's plates using *ArcVoyager* (an adaptation of *ArcView* for educational use: see reference to ESRI in the Appendix). They build up a map of plate boundaries and earthquakes using the Robinson projection, familiar to them from their school atlas (Figure 8.5a). They then raise the question of how the plate boundaries look around Antarctica, poorly served by most world maps, and so alter their projection

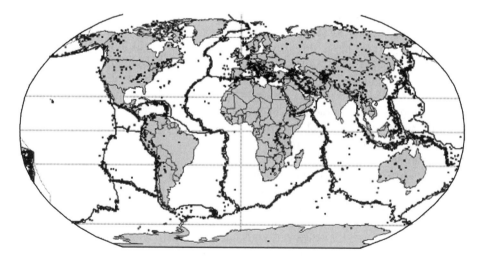

Figure 8.5a Earthquake and volcano project using *ArcVoyager*. Robinson projection.
Source: ESRI.

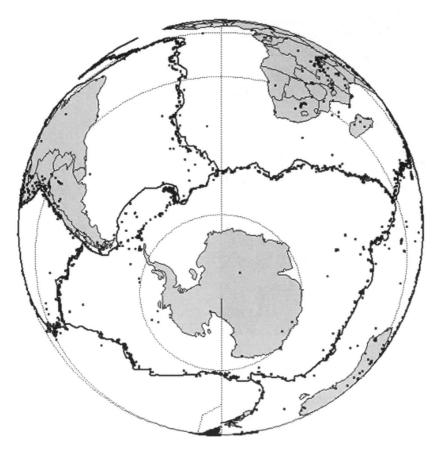

Figure 8.5b Earthquake and volcano project using *ArcVoyager*. View of the Earth from space.
Source: ESRI.

to one of the Earth from space (Figure 8.5b). To do this, they must specify latitude and longitude coordinates for the centre of their view (Figure 8.5b is centred on the Prime Meridian and latitude 70°S). After some trial and error they produce a view of the Antarctic plate. Later, they add volcanoes to the map and make further adjustments to the coordinates in order to display the Pacific Ring of Fire at a single view. The enormous potential of the software therefore can only be harnessed with some understanding of latitude and longitude.

Understanding the spherical Earth

Children's exposure to particular map projections is likely to have some influence on their thinking about the configuration of the Earth's land masses. But what if, instead of drawing free recall world maps on paper, they were invited to draw on a spherical surface? Children were provided with 'blank' globes, made by spraying a regular globe with blue paint (Wiegand, 1998a). It was explained that there had been a fault in manufacture, the land masses were missing and had to be drawn back on the globe (Figure 8.6). In order to facilitate comparison between drawings, a 'projection' was devised for transferring the

Figure 8.6 Drawing land masses on a spherical surface.

spherical drawing to a flat sheet of paper by using a small nylon net bag stretched tightly across the ball. A diamond-shaped 'graticule' was derived from this net so that each child's drawing could then be copied, diamond by diamond, from the spherical surface to the flat map. The resultant maps were categorised according to the classification devised for world maps drawn on a plane surface (Wiegand, 1995) and a similar age related sequence was observed.

Videotape replay enabled some assessment to be made of the strategies children employed in making their spherical representations of the world. Antarctica and the Arctic Ocean (or, more commonly, the 'South Pole' and 'North Pole') were generally drawn first. This may have been an attempt to impose some initial order on the sphere before the remaining land masses were sketched in, a function performed by the edges of the paper or the map frame when drawing a flat map. Both north and south polar areas were generally drawn as land masses and in their comments during the task it was clear that most children regarded the North Pole as dry land rather than frozen ocean. Drawing on a spherical surface is an unfamiliar task (although one which motivated and intrigued the participants) and so, in a further study (Wiegand and Stiell, 1996b), self adhesive vinyl shapes of the continents were used. Videotape evidence indicated that the 'equator' (i.e. the seam where the two hemispheres had been joined during manufacture) formed a significant reference line for positioning the vinyl shapes. All the children knew that the equator was 'hot' and this knowledge informed their placement of the land masses. Many children knew (from direct experience) that southern Europe was also hot and therefore positioned Europe so that at least part of it touched the equator. This left insufficient space for Africa and the African template was therefore often tilted so that as much of the continent as possible was aligned with the equator. Africa appears consistently to be the continent most likely to be omitted from children's sketch maps and was the least well located and most inaccurately orientated continent on their world maps and reconstructed globes.

Children's maps of their own country

There have been relatively few studies of children's representations of individual countries. Wiegand and Stiell (1997a) invited a sample of over 1,000 children from a secondary school and four of its feeder primary schools to draw a free recall map of the British Isles. The relative spatial relationship of Scotland and England appeared to be well established early in childhood, although Scotland was almost always shown significantly smaller than its area relative to England. Similarly, the Orkney and Shetland Islands (often shown in school atlases as insets and therefore perhaps not often perceived in their correct relative location), as well as the islands to the west of the Scottish mainland, were rarely drawn and representation of Wales was generally extremely inaccurate. Approximately one fifth of all school students participating in this study drew maps of the British Isles similar to that in Figure 8.7. A parallel study involving the very complex configuration of the Greek mainland and islands has been described by Filippakopoulou, (2002).

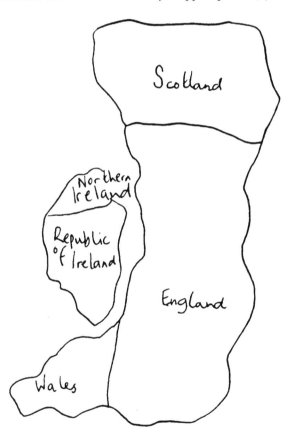

Figure 8.7 Free recall map of the British Isles drawn by a girl, aged 10 years (Wiegand and Stiell, 1997a). From *The Cartographic Journal*, 34(1): 13–21, published by Maney Publishing on behalf of the British Cartographic Society (BCS) and reproduced by permission of the BCS.

The national boundaries in Figure 8.7 have been drawn nearly vertically and horizontally. There is other evidence for this systematic distortion in memory for elements of small scale maps. Asked to estimate the positions of continents and the location of cities, many respondents align them more in relation to vertical and horizontal lines than is really the case. It seems likely that irregular shaped figures are difficult to anchor in the mind and there is thus a bias in perceptual organisation to 'straighten up' the mental representation according to a vertical and horizontal frame. North America and Europe are generally therefore remembered as more horizontally aligned and North America/South America more vertically aligned. San Francisco Bay, for example, which actually runs northwest–southeast, is most commonly remembered as being aligned north–south (Tversky, 1981). This phenomenon has a knock-on effect on memory for the location of points embedded within these shapes such as the locations of cities. German primary and secondary school children, asked to mark the position of Paris on a map of France, placed it further south of its true location, suggesting a tendency to 'centre' remembered locations within areas (Nebel, 1984).

Understanding nested spatial hierarchies

Piaget carried out several studies (Piaget and Weil, 1951) into Swiss children's understanding of their homeland and their nationality. A frequent answer to the question 'Are you Swiss?' was 'No, I'm Genevese' (i.e. from Geneva). Three quarters of the children up to the age of nine denied the possibility of being both Swiss *and* Genevese. Other children knew that Geneva was in Switzerland but denied that they themselves were Swiss. Only from about 11 years did children appear to understand that all people from the Swiss cantons were Swiss and that one can be Genevese and Swiss at the same time.

Piagetian theory interprets the development of this understanding in terms of the logical operations of class *inclusion* and *transitivity*. Class inclusion is asymmetric. If Geneva is in Switzerland then Switzerland cannot be in Geneva. Class transitivity means that if Geneva is in Switzerland and Switzerland is in Europe, then Geneva must be in Europe. Although many children appear to 'know' their home address at an early age, Piaget suggests that these logical operations are essential prerequisites for an understanding of how the components (e.g., street, town, county, country) fit together. Gustav Jahoda (1963) made use of cut out shapes to explore further children's thinking about this 'nested spatial hierarchy'. Children (aged 6–11 years) were first shown the materials illustrated in Figure 8.8a and asked to assemble them to represent 'me, in the classroom, in the school'. They were then given similar materials that represented, respectively, Britain, Scotland, England and Glasgow and asked to arrange them to demonstrate their understanding of the relationship between these places. A correct response is shown in Figure 8.8b. Nearly three quarters of the children who had been able to make a correct *verbal* statement that Glasgow was part of Scotland could not reflect that understanding with the practical materials.

Later studies in London by Piché (1981) employed extended clinical interviews, drawing and mapping tasks and puzzles with children aged 5–8 years. Piché found that their understanding of places was principally formed by concrete experiences of the locality through play and everyday activity. Their construal of 'extended places' was weak. Only five children appeared to understand they could live in London and England simultaneously. Similar findings were reported by Daggs (1986, cited in Downs *et al.*, 1988) with children in grades 1 to 3 (Y2–Y4) at a public elementary school in the United States. Daggs used a verbal test in conjunction with a model of a small park (e.g. 'If you were in the sandbox

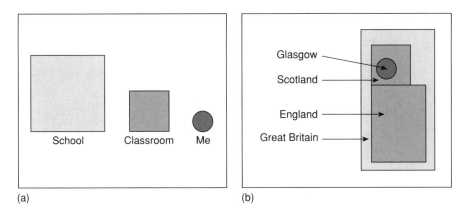

Figure 8.8 Materials used by Jahoda (1962) for exploring children's thinking about nested spatial hierarchy: (a) Materials used to test relations between 'me, my classroom, my school'; (b) Materials arranged to show relations between Glasgow, Scotland, England, Great Britain.

could you be in the playground?') as well as asking about larger areas (e.g. 'Are the people in (town X) in Pennsylvania?'). A graphic test was also used (e.g. 'This circle shows Pennsylvania. Draw a circle to show (town X). Colour Pennsylvania.'). Performance improved with grade level but there were differences in performance according to the type of task used. In the case of the model (in which the geographic relationships were concretised) performance across all grades was close to perfect. Compared to the concrete familiar context of the playground, many children did not understand the nature of Pennsylvania as a state (labelling it instead as a town or a 'place where people live') and therefore could not relate it to a hierarchy

Harwood and McShane (1996), however, suggest that young children's understanding may have improved since this earlier work, possibly as a result of curriculum change, increased opportunities for travel and vicarious experience of places through the media. They replicated Jahoda's (1963) experiment with children aged 5–6, 7–8 and 9–10 years from Nuneaton, England. These children had experienced the (then new) National Curriculum which explicitly required children aged 5–7 years to be taught that the places they study exist within a broader geographical context (e.g. within a town, a region or a country), and that they should be taught to locate and name on a map the constituent countries of the United Kingdom, marking on the map approximately where they live. Harwood and McShane tested whether children's performance was enhanced when maps were used instead of geometric shapes. Templates were used to assess children's understanding of the 'Home–Nuneaton–England–British Isles' hierarchy. The pieces were arranged in random order and orientation and each child was asked to sort the pieces and suggest what the shape represented. If the child was unable to do this, the tester arranged the pieces in their correct orientation. If the child still could not complete the puzzle the tester arranged the pieces in the correct positions and asked the child to name the shape formed and its constituent parts. Finally, the child was asked to place a 1cm × 1cm yellow square on the map to represent Nuneaton and then show his/her home with a small black circle. Only four children out of the sample of 36 failed to recognise the British Isles at any stage during the test and 50 per cent of the youngest children could arrange the

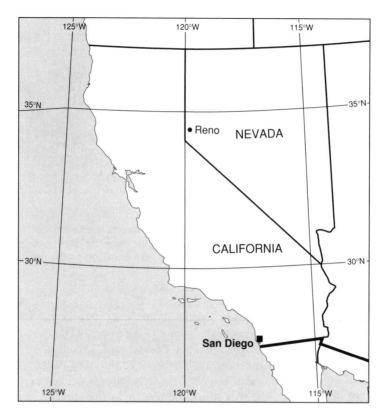

Figure 8.9 Relative locations of Reno and San Diego.

pieces correctly and name the British Isles without prompting. Only one child out of the sample failed to represent the 'Home–Nuneaton–England' hierarchy correctly. Children performed better using the map pieces than they did on an oral test and they appear to have significantly outperformed Jahoda's sample, although direct comparisons proved difficult to establish. Harwood and McShane suggest that changes in children's typical experiences in the intervening 30 years may account for the discrepancies between their findings and those of Jahoda. Availability of learning materials is also likely to have had an effect. Harwood and McShane point out that the children in their study had had, for example, access to jigsaw puzzles as a means of developing place concepts.

Another example of how map memory is structured comes from McNamara (1986) who, in an analysis of the errors people make when judging spatial relations, cites the example that most Americans are likely to say that Reno, Nevada is east of San Diego, California. Indeed, as Reno is in northern Nevada and San Diego in southern California many people might say that Reno is north-east of San Diego. In fact Reno is north-west of San Diego (Figure 8.9). According to Stevens and Coupe (1978) the error is a result of the hierarchical way spatial information is stored. Larger 'regions' (such as states) are encoded before smaller ones (such as cities). This is shown diagrammatically in Figure 8.10. In this example, the relations between California and Nevada are preferentially encoded before the relations between the cities and their respective states, whereas relations between the cities themselves are not encoded. Hierarchical storage may be responsible

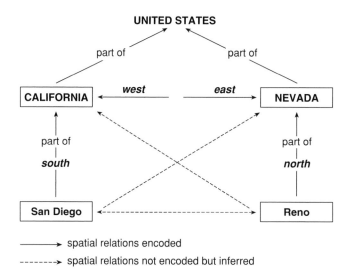

Figure 8.10 Hierarchical coding of spatial relations. Adapted from McNamara, T.P. (1986) 'Mental representations of spatial relations', *Cognitive Psychology*, 18: 87–121, Copyright 1986, with permission from Elsevier.

for many common errors in judging spatial relations (for example, it is not often recognised that the most northerly part of the Republic of Ireland lies north of Northern Ireland, witness Figure 8.7) but it is also likely that there are perceptual errors associated with map projections. This effect is particularly strong where meridians converge within the area of the map. Figure 8.11 shows the relative locations of Edinburgh and Madrid. Reference to the Prime Meridian shows clearly that Edinburgh is north of Madrid yet many observers would code it as being north-east. In another example, Sandford (1980a) reports that the majority of candidates in a national school examination at age 16 years thought that the USA lay north-west of Mexico according to their interpretation of a Mercator projection.

School atlases

We have seen that small scale maps have the power to shape children's perception of the world. This influence extends to collections of maps in the form of atlases. School atlases in particular are not objective accounts of the world. The selection of maps often emphasises the home country and the locations of selected case studies. These case studies are generally approved by examination and curriculum authorities, reinforced by school textbooks and, once established, may be perpetuated for many years. School atlases therefore help to carry long lasting messages about relations between the home country and the rest of the world as well as about 'what's worth knowing'. They can therefore be said to represent a category of 'establishment' mapping (Monmonier, 1981), resistant to innovation. Atlases for school often contain images legitimated by school (front matter explaining scale, compass directions and symbols is usually illustrated with pictures of school buildings or equipment) and they rarely start from children's interests (such as football teams, pop stars and soap operas). Of course, children's interests are often ephemeral and don't sit easily

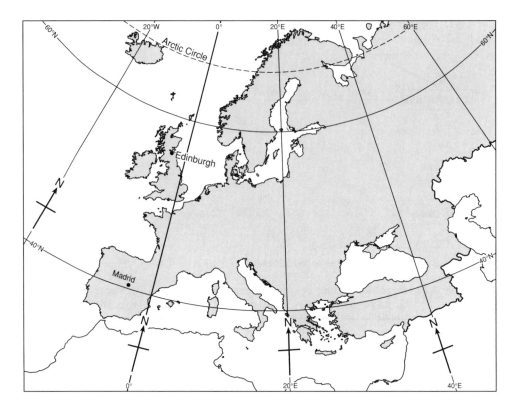

Figure 8.11 Relative locations of Edinburgh and Madrid.

with the economics of book production, but that is another feature of the social message delivered by most conventional school atlases: that they come in bound volumes (often 'badged' by examination boards and learned societies) and are made to last.

The format of conventional atlases can influence children's perception of the world. There is, for example, a finite number of pages available, requiring careful decisions to be made about contents and map scales. An example illustrates some alternative choices. Figure 8.12a shows the sheet lines for topographic coverage of Europe in a popular school atlas, for which ten pages were available. France, Spain, middle Europe, Italy and the Balkans are shown at a scale of 1:5 million; Eastern Europe/Turkey and Scandinavia (with an inset for Iceland) are shown at 1:10 million; Benelux is shown at 1:2.5 million and the British Isles (in addition to larger scale mapping of the UK elsewhere) is shown at 1:4.5 million. An alternative strategy (Figure 8.12b) would have been to represent Europe at a constant scale (much as a road atlas might do) of, say, 1:7 million and there is a strong case for doing this in order to avoid perceptual bias. However, on the whole, school students in the UK study individual countries or coherent groupings of countries and north-western mainland Europe is particularly rich in curriculum exemplars. There is also merit (particularly in a continent consisting largely of peninsulas and islands) in students being able to see coherent geographical units (e.g. the Iberian peninsula, the 'boot' of Italy, the Scandinavian peninsula, etc.). The pragmatic solution adopted is one that is generally preferred by teachers but it may come at a cost. British students' sketch

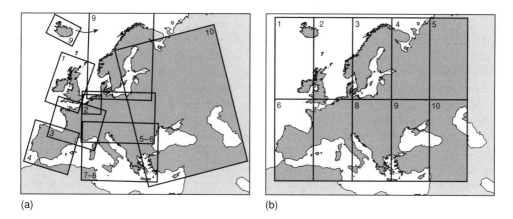

Figure 8.12 Contrasting approaches to sheet lines for Europe: (a) Groups of countries at variable scale. From the *Oxford Student Atlas*, copyright © 2002 Oxford University Press, reproduced by permission of Oxford University Press; (b) Sheet lines mapping Europe at a constant scale (areas of overlap not shown).

maps of Europe frequently under-represent the area of Scandinavia (Axia *et al.*, 1998) and a possible reason for this is that they have so frequently seen it at a much reduced scale, compared to the rest of Europe. It is important therefore for teachers to be alert to possible side effects of editorial decisions and adopt appropriate complementary teaching strategies (in this case for example, by making frequent reference to locator maps and the map of Europe as a whole).

Atlases are essential reference tools in school but concern has often been expressed about the extent to which they are up to date and age-appropriate. Schools appear to 'buy for growth', often using atlases intended for older students throughout the school rather than buying editions specifically designed for the needs of younger students (Wiegand, 1998b). Much commentary on the way atlases are used in classrooms has been pessimistic. Sandford attributed the generally low standard of atlas map work by examination candidates to 'a long period of self-deluding complacency among teachers, apparently assuming an innate or intuitive ability with atlases' (1985: 3) among school students. An atlas has too frequently been seen simply as a tool for looking up the location of places (Sandford calls this 'lexical' usage) rather than, for example, visualising complexity and deriving generalisations from it (Castner, 1987).

Electronic atlases

Electronic atlases are advanced mapping environments that offer some advantages over conventional hard copy formats (Kraak and Ormeling, 1996; Kraak, 2001). They vary from non-interactive electronic versions of paper atlases to those with GIS-type functionality. Electronic atlases intended for educational use can provide learning support by, for example, displaying additional information on rollover of the cursor. In simple cases this may involve naming a feature, providing explanations of terms, giving the population of a town or providing continual update on latitude and longitude coordinates. More complex instances include showing the relationship between two variables. For example, wind chill is a measure of the cooling effect of wind on exposed skin. It increases as wind speed rises and temperature falls. A wind chill of −45°C can be achieved with a temperature of −30°C and a wind speed of 20km/hour as well as with a temperature of −20°C and a wind speed of 50km/hour. Lines on a map joining places of equal wind chill can therefore be linked on rollover of the cursor to a two dimensional table showing all the possible combinations of temperature and wind speed that make up the wind chill value. Point to the area on the map that gives a wind chill of −45°C and all the cells in the table that equal this value are highlighted (this example can be seen on the *Oxford Student Atlas* website – see Appendix). Other examples of learning support to assist understanding of complex concepts include linking hotspots on the map to images, text, sound or multimedia (including animation, flybys and virtual reality). Sound, for instance, can clarify the pronunciation of place names (a valuable element of learning support for insecure readers) or promote a sense of place through music and video clips. Other learning support may be provided by additional explanatory text linked to the map face itself.

Electronic atlases generally provide a set of navigational tools that enable users to record the route they have followed through the atlas, compare two or more maps or themes at a single view, scroll the map by using a compass indicator, and follow the location of the screen view on an interactive locator map. Map manipulation tools enable the user to change scale (by zooming or determining the scale ratio), measure distances and areas, change projections, add to or subtract from the map layers, annotate or add symbols to the map face and query all the map objects. Sometimes these and other functions are accomplished through the agency of an electronic assistant (often a motivating character who helps steer the user through the required tasks).

The overwhelming advantages of ease of distribution and updating make it likely that electronic mapping will be increasingly delivered to schools via the internet yet most internet maps have not been designed specifically for young people. Web cartography therefore offers both opportunities and challenges for schools. The opportunities include access to vast quantities of maps and data as well as being able to use 'real world' tools, for example location-finding sites such as *Multimap* and *Mapquest* as well as itinerary planning tools like *Mappy* (see Appendix) which help to bridge the gap (noted in Chapter 1) between the school curriculum and practical life skills. Immediacy is highly valued by most young people and web maps can be updated rapidly giving access to 'happening now' information. Maps can be hotlinked to webcams and other reality aids such as 360° photographs. Weather and current events can be mapped as they take place and the enormous reserves of information available increase the likelihood of making connections with children's immediate (often ephemeral) interests, increasing motivation for learning. Challenges include the ongoing requirement to adapt the curriculum to a real world rate of change. This involves frequent reconsideration of concepts and skills as they become more, or less, relevant to contemporary needs. Grid references, for example, remain significant in relation to paper maps as devices for locating places but electronic maps make greater use of postcodes. Children need therefore to be taught how postcodes 'work' alongside more traditional teaching about the operation of grid references and coordinates. Young users also need support in a complex online learning environment which offers the distraction of advertising and material irrelevant to the task in hand. As with GIS, the boundaries of what constitutes genuinely independent learning within web cartography and the way it could be achieved remain difficult issues to resolve. Practical challenges include the availability of internet access during scheduled class time as well as the resource implications of maintaining computing capacity in the public sector that keeps pace with cartographic innovation. Although electronic atlases are increasingly popular, in most educational settings (including schools in more economically developed countries) conventional hard copy atlases still dominate in classrooms.

This chapter has examined children's thinking about the Earth as a whole and how its representation in maps and atlases influence their understanding of it. The next chapter considers the implications for children's thinking about maps at all scales and explores some principles that underpin the construction of a balanced curriculum in cartography and GIScience.

Part 2

Better teaching with maps

9   Planning a map and GIScience curriculum

Although there is significant map teaching in the voluntary sector (through various youth organisations such as the scouting movement), most systematic instruction in maps is at school and most of this is delivered through the geography curriculum. What gets taught in schools in relation to maps, however, is distinctly slanted with the overwhelming emphasis on map *reading* rather than map *using* (Blades and Spencer, 1986b). Important life skills such as giving directions and navigating with a map are rarely taught. By contrast, skills which are emphasised in school (such as the use of cardinal directions and scale) appear to be little used in everyday life (Blades and Medlicott, 1992). In a South African study (Innes, 2003), the most common maps used by cartographic professionals were found to be cadastral (property ownership) maps (very rarely met at school) and the most common professional map task (but one seldom encountered in school texts or examinations) was identification of property boundaries. By contrast, calculation of gradient was given high priority by teachers but rarely used by professionals. The most obvious example of mismatch between map education in school and the workplace is in the use of digital mapping and GIS.

This chapter considers the implications for curriculum planning of the evidence for children's thinking with maps described in previous chapters. The nature of map skill is reviewed, some principles of progression in learning are identified and some key elements of a map and GIScience curriculum are suggested. The chapter concludes with a brief discussion of planning for individual student differences – especially gender and special educational need.

Map skills

Map using is a complex activity and a distinction is commonly made between *map reading*, *map analysis* and *map interpretation*. In this view, map *reading* is characterised as simply extracting information from the map. Map features are identified and named and their attributes noted. Map *analysis* involves processing that information in order, for example, to describe patterns and relationships or to measure distances between places. Map *interpretation* goes beyond what is shown on the map and involves the application of previously acquired information in order to solve problems or make decisions.

A number of sub-skills in map use can also be identified. Winston (1984) separates these into:

- using symbols;
- finding location;

- orienting and using directions;
- using scale and finding distance;
- selecting media;

whereas Sandford (1986) suggests:

- map confidence (e.g. finding the map you want and finding places on the map);
- sense of scale (e.g. comparing the representation of towns and countries on maps at different scales);
- verbal mapwork (e.g. recognising and understanding symbols and displaying a working vocabulary of geographical terms for features shown on the map);
- numerical mapwork (e.g. using scales, contours, gradients, compass directions, coordinates, time zones, projections);
- map comparison (e.g. between pairs of political and physical maps and between maps at different scales and with varying themes);
- presentation of data (e.g. converting information from one map form to another, making selective tracings from maps, drawing cross sections);
- related work (e.g. understanding day and night, seasons, phases of the moon and tides).

This general approach to map skill has, for many years, underpinned the content of secondary school map textbooks, most of which have started with basic principles of map reading and analysis (understanding scale, measurement, grid references, representation of relief, etc.) followed by map interpretation (recognition of land forms, identification of rock types, types of settlement, communications and land use) and concluded with application of these skills to selected maps chosen to illustrate distinctive physical regions (glaciated highlands, limestone uplands, etc.) or geographical themes (e.g. inner city redevelopment, intensive farming or coastal defences). Traditionally such texts have made use of a restricted range of map types (typically 1:25,000 or 1:50,000 topographic maps).

A contrasting approach to curriculum design is adopted by Castner (1997), who proposes a taxonomy of *map use function* as a basis for planning. These map use functions are: inventory (answering 'what is where' questions); navigation; and measurement and analysis tasks. Each map use suggests a particular family of maps. For example, map use as inventory suggests a set of maps differentiated by scale, such as a globe, atlas map, topographic map, city plan and architectural plan, whereas map use as analysis suggests a set of maps differentiated by how the data are depicted, such as dot, flowline, isoline and choropleth maps. This approach helpfully emphasises curriculum breadth and balance in respect of *cartographic representation* and associated skills rather than solely *geographical* knowledge and understanding.

Progression

Progression is a key feature of curriculum structure which refers to the advance in students' attainment as they move through the school system. It is closely related to differentiation, which refers to the match between curriculum provision and the interests, experience and capabilities of pupils of roughly the same age. The challenge for curriculum developers is to match the increasing complexity of map learning activities with the maturation of students.

Progression from concrete experiences to abstract representation was characterised by Bruner (1966) as a three tier process in which intellectual growth depends on the individual's ability to internalise events. In Bruner's first, 'enactive', system of representation, children engage in physical action, directly experiencing the environment and manipulating objects in it. In the second, 'iconic', system, children use objects to stand for others in the real world. In the third, 'symbolic', system, abstract symbols such as language and mathematical notation are used as forms of representation which enable individuals to hypothesise, speculate, predict and extrapolate. This progression can be illustrated by a simple teaching and learning sequence with very young children. The teacher takes the children out on a visit to the fire station. On the way, they talk about the houses and shops they pass. Back at school they create a town scene using blocks. The red block stands for the fire station. The children 'drive' a model fire engine through the 'streets' made by the spaces between the blocks. Their teacher then shows that by drawing around the blocks on a large sheet of paper the model town can be easily reconstructed the next time they want to play. A convenient way of making the link to two-dimensional representations is to have the children draw round the blocks ('so that we know where to put them next time'). Later the blocks can be dispensed with and the plan itself used as a substitute for the model. This 'map' can be used in place of the model as a tool to think with, for example to solve problems such as finding the shortest way from the fire station to a particular house. The progression in this teaching sequence clearly leads the children from direct experience of the local environment, through modelling it with concrete materials to its symbolic representation in map form.

We now consider two aspects of progression in relation to maps: increasing complexity of the cartographic resource, and increasing complexity of the mapping task. There is a general consensus that large scale maps should be taught before small scale ones. Educationists have generally taken the view that large scale maps of small and familiar areas are easier to understand than small scale maps of larger, unfamiliar ones. The symbology is usually simpler, the features represented more concrete and there is less generalisation involved in the mapping (one symbol usually representing one item in the real world). Large scale maps also avoid the additional complication of shape and/or area distortion as a result of the Earth's curvature. However, whilst these characteristics do make large scale maps more accessible to young users it must also be borne in mind that children are exposed to small scale maps as part of their everyday experience from an early age (in the form of, for example, TV weather maps and advertising), suggesting that attention should be paid early in childhood to at least maps of the world and the home country. This argument runs counter to the approach of a traditional 'concentric' geography curriculum, which treats the world as a series of expanding environments from the home locality to the home region, then to country, continent and finally the whole world. Whilst this sequence has an appealing logic for the curriculum developer, children's experience is not so predictable.

Maps become more difficult to make sense of the more the user is required to bring additional information and understanding to the map. Simple plans, for example, only require the user to make a match with a viewed or recalled environment, whereas complex representations such as geological maps and aeronautical charts require extra understanding of specialist abstract concepts such as dip and flight levels. Greater precision in data description also adds complexity to map interpretation. Younger map users may readily understand the description of countries as 'rich' or 'poor' but complex notions involving relations between sets of abstract concepts such as Purchasing Power Parity (i.e. the Gross Domestic Product per person, adjusted for the local cost of living) or the Human Development Index (a measure combining life expectancy, adult literacy, average number of years of schooling and purchasing power) make far higher demands of the reader.

Perhaps the most influential account of progression in cognitive abilities has been that proposed by Bloom (1956) as a 'taxonomy of educational objectives'. In this scheme, the cognitive domain is arranged hierarchically so that higher level categories of intellectual skill encompass more complex abilities than the lower ones. Bloom's lowest category, *knowledge*, comprises the recall of specific facts (such as the button functions on a particular GIS software package or the meaning of a conventional symbol). *Comprehension* includes: the translation of information from one mode of representation to another (such as converting information from a map to text or diagrammatic form); interpretation of map evidence (such as explaining the geomorphological history of an area); and extrapolation (such as predicting weather outcomes from a weather map). *Application* involves the use of abstractions in particular situations (having established, for example, a relationship between earthquake magnitude and certain types of plate boundary (see Figure 8.5a and b), students might then apply the same concepts to an enquiry into the relationship between plate boundaries and earthquake depth). *Analysis* requires the breakdown of previously unseen information into its essential or key elements. Using the maps, field data and aerial photograph shown in the Yorkshire village project (Plate 2), for example, students might identify the key environmental characteristics of the village. Putting these elements together in the form of a report in order to make a persuasive case for or against designation as a Conservation Area would constitute *synthesis*. Bloom's highest order category, *evaluation*, involves making informed judgements. An example might be the selection of a particular world map projection to represent given data, such as the choice of an equal area projection to compare the global distribution of deserts and ice caps.

Another important kind of relationship in subject matter – that of 'learning prerequisites' – was identified by Gagné (1965). In this view, educational content is best sequenced in such a way that prerequisite sub-skills are always taught before the skills for which they are a prerequisite. Thus, using Gagné's terminology, *Higher order rules* require as prerequisites *Rules*, which require as prerequisites *Concepts*, which require as prerequisites *Discriminations*, which require as prerequisites *Basic forms* of learning. Prerequisites for understanding map scale, for example, would include being able to measure with a ruler, use standard units of measurement, relate these to the real world, understand ratio, compare measurements on the map with those made using the scale bar, etc.

Schemes such as those by Bloom and Gagné have been used to identify progression in map learning; for example progressive levels of complexity in thinking with GIS tools have been matched to Bloom's taxonomy by West (2003). However, the categories in these schemes can be rather difficult to apply in practice. Curriculum reform in many countries in recent years has led to specification in increasing detail of what should be taught to students at each stage of their schooling but identification of curriculum targets for children is often made in the absence, or in advance, of empirical evidence for performance. Downs *et al.* (1988) and Harwood and McShane (1996) refer to the complexity that underlies apparently simple curriculum objectives such as 'use simple classroom maps to locate objects' (what constitutes evidence for 'use'?) and 'give your home address' (what constitutes evidence for understanding how the component elements nest together?). As a further example, Castner (1990) draws attention to the objective in many curriculum statements of 'knows and uses cardinal directions'. An appropriate classroom activity might consist of assigning labels to classroom walls and 'using' them, 'but it is quite a different matter to understand that these labels transcend the classroom and bear abstract and complex relationships to the sun, Polaris and the axis of the Earth' (1990: 36). Even where progression appears obvious it is not always clear how the rate of advance might be most appropriately timed. For example, in many curriculum statements the use of four compass points is specified at a lower 'level of attainment' than the use of eight (another example is the use of four figure grid references compared to six), yet in practice these intellectual gains are often made within a lesson or two rather than over a year or more.

Another misleading notion that is sometimes found in curriculum documentation is that children should necessarily proceed from imaginary maps to those of real places, as though increasing accuracy of representation is the only desirable educational goal. Stimulating counterbalances to this view are provided by van Swaaij and Klare's *Atlas of Experience* (2000) in which familiar-looking, but imaginary, topographic maps are labelled with text cleverly juxtaposed to create playful associations, or Simon Patterson's artwork *The Great Bear*, modelled on the London Underground map, in which stations are renamed as figures from history and popular culture in order to suggest unexpected connections between them. These are sophisticated examples of imagination and creativity, not childish make-believe.

A number of practical frameworks for a map-based curriculum have been proposed. These have taken the form of normative statements about expectations of student learning (e.g. Catling, 1981, 1996; Winston, 1984) as well as exemplification of the sequence and structure of this learning through teacher advice and classroom materials (e.g. Catling, 1992). This has resulted in at least partial agreement about what types of activities are appropriate at each phase of education (see Chapters 10–12).

Less consensus exists about how learning with GIS might be structured, partly because software use is highly dependent on the particular demands made by specific programs. Some innovative American examples of GIS learning activities provide helpful models of curriculum development and assessment. In the first comprehensive series of GIS lesson outlines for teachers in book form, Malone *et al.* (2002) base their model lessons on five sets of skills identified as key steps in *geographic enquiry* by the National Geography Standards (1994):

- ask geographic questions;
- acquire geographic resources;
- explore geographic data;
- analyse geographic information;
- act upon geographic knowledge;

and identify a set of basic technological skills as a starting point for learning. Other suggestions are to be found on the ESRI and ESRI Canada websites (see Appendix). English and Feaster (2003) and Knapp (2003) showcase community projects by students and teachers using GIS and the former has a teacher's companion guide (Malone *et al.*, 2003) providing practical and pedagogical recommendations with implicit suggestions for curriculum structure for teachers who wish to implement their own projects. The projects described by Knapp are undertaken as part of the Orton Family Foundation Community Mapping Program (see Appendix).

An important issue in relation to GIS use is the extent to which students are ultimately empowered to use the technology independently. At present (2005) there are ample examples of supported, structured teaching and learning modules in GIS applications (see the examples cited above) but few accounts of how teachers and students can 'make the break' into more genuinely independent enquiry. Anecdotal evidence suggests that despite the powerful potential, without extraordinary levels of teacher and other support, relatively few achieve this.

Evaluating map teaching strategies

Suggestions for teaching with maps are not often supported by evidence for the effectiveness of particular strategies (Blades and Spencer, 1994). However, instruction on how to *make* maps does appear to make significant improvements in children's mapping skill. In a study by Harwood and Usher (1999), primary school children were asked to draw the journey from school to a local church (a frequent walk undertaken by all the children, thus providing a common basis for comparison, unlike the usual 'journey to school' studies where each child follows a different route). Teaching was found to improve (albeit for a limited period) the quality of their route maps, especially the representation of perspective, use of symbols and the amount of geographical content depicted. Similar improvements were found in children's recall of continent location, size and shape following a teaching unit involving world mapping (Harwood and Rawlings, 2001).

In the secondary years, there have been very few attempts to investigate the effectiveness of teaching children to *interpret* maps, investigate spatial relationships or solve problems (Liben and Downs, 1989). Many students appear to have difficulty applying procedural knowledge to maps (e.g. by identifying the spatial relationships between two or more variables). In one study (van der Schee *et al.*, 1992) students were asked why one country on a map of Europe was unusual (Finland was the only one which was both wealthy, as shown by a located point symbol, *and* from which a large number of workers left in order to work abroad, as shown by area shading). Many students failed to identify the association between these two mapped variables citing other (irrelevant) knowledge in their answers. Van der Schee and his colleagues suggest specific teaching interventions are needed in which students are systematically trained to analyse cartographic data.

Perhaps the most developed recent evaluation of a map teaching programme is that of *Where Are We?*, a multimedia map skills software application and associated curriculum (Kastens *et al.*, 2001; Liben *et al.*, 2002). The software links a map of a park with live action video and users can 'move' through the park using directional buttons. Evaluation of the programme with second to fourth grade (Y3–Y5) students suggested that students' map using strategies improved on both a reality-to-map test (marking the position of flags in the field with stickers on the map) and a map-to-reality test (marking the position of stickers on the map with flags in the field), indicating that real world map use can be enhanced by prior training with a computer simulation.

Although there are rich descriptive accounts of teaching with GIS in both classroom and community contexts, there is little empirical evidence for its impact on learning. Most studies to date in authentic classroom settings have reported a positive effect on student motivation (Linn, 1997; Keiper, 1999). It is claimed that GIS supports students in higher order thinking as it exposes them to more efficient strategies for problem solving (West, 2003) and there is some evidence that there have been positive pedagogical outcomes compared to conventional map use (Kerski, 2003). Collaborative work with GIS appears to have improved attitudes towards technology, individual learners' own assessment of their ability to complete a task and their capacity for data analysis (Baker and White, 2003).

So far, this chapter has reviewed some principles that determine how a cartographic and GIScience curriculum might be structured on the basis of cartographic complexity and map skill. But a curriculum also has to be responsive to the needs of individuals and take account of learner differences. Two categories of learner differences for which there is some map related evidence in the literature are now discussed: gender and special educational needs.

Gender differences

There is a broad consensus that males generally perform better than females on tasks requiring 'spatial ability', that is the ability to generate, represent, transform and recall spatial information (Maccoby and Jacklin, 1974; Linn and Petersen, 1985). However, this single term encompasses a number of qualitatively different abilities (Halpern, 1992). These include: spatial perception (such as being able to draw the water level in a tilted glass), mental rotation (imagining how objects appear when rotated in 2D or 3D space), spatial visualisation (detecting an embedded figure) and spatial problem solving (recalling a geometric figure and matching it to a pattern). Because spatial ability is thus so complex many reports of gender differences are contradictory.

Nevertheless, males and females are generally said to differ in the way they recall spatial information and the strategy they use to navigate (see, for example, Miller and Santoni, 1986). Reference was made in Chapter 5 to two types of environmental knowledge: route knowledge (i.e. of landmarks and the 'corridor' connections between them as defined by egocentric directions such as 'right', 'left', and straight ahead) and configurational knowledge (i.e. a coordinated Euclidean representation in which spatial characteristics are defined by cardinal directions and metric distances). In recalling spatial information and in wayfinding, females appear to emphasise landmarks and the use of an egocentric frame of reference whereas males appear to use cardinal directions and metric distance information more. Males also appear to have an advantage in learning new routes. Gender differences generally seem to arise in map using and spatial orientation tasks that are 'difficult', i.e. high in cognitive demand or requiring a high memory load (Coluccia and Louse, 2004). For example, in a study where 6- to 11-year-olds were required to make a map of an unfamiliar real-world environment (Matthews, 1987) the children were first 'primed' by following a route on which features of the environment were pointed out. For half the children this introduction to the area they had to map was interrupted by a half-hour break. Boys and girls in the 'uninterrupted' group performed similarly on the map test but boys from the 'interrupted' group made higher scoring maps. The implication seems to be that boys were able to hold spatial relationships in memory for longer.

Boys' knowledge of their home locality tends to be more extensive than girls, as a result of their wider home range (described in Chapter 6) and the maps they make are generally more detailed, with more route information, more accurate representation of spatial relationships and stronger hierarchical structure. Girls appear more likely than boys to make maps using pictorial forms (Matthews, 1984a) and this tendency may persist through to young adulthood (Kumler and Buttenfield, 1996). Boys may also have an advantage in relation to small scale maps as there is some suggestion of gender differences in relation to children's knowledge of distant places. Boys, for example, appear to perform better when tested on world geography knowledge (Liben, 1995), a finding supported by similar evidence (summarised in Dabbs *et al.*, 1997) from older students.

There have, however, been very few studies specifically designed to explore gender differences in children's ability to *read* maps. Where evidence exists it generally shows an advantage to the boys. In a broad skills test on an Ordnance Survey 1:50,000 map for 16-year-olds, Boardman and Towner (1979) found that boys outperformed girls in all sections of the test, involving interpretation of relief, working with cross sections, matching the orientation of a photograph to the map, identifying a route from a written description and drawing inferences from map evidence. When written study materials also include maps, all students appear to achieve higher test scores but it is the boys' scores that improve more (Gilmartin and Patton, 1984).

More recent, controlled studies of older students suggest that males and females may adopt different strategies when reading topographic maps. Males appear to perform better on tasks involving terrain visualisation (the ability to form a 3D mental representation from a contour map). However, not all tasks involving contour maps, require terrain visualisation skills (Lanca, 1998) and females may use verbal strategies to achieve equal success in some circumstances. When matching a cross section to a contour map, for example, females may remember the slope elements sequentially rather than envisioning a three-dimensional image of the land surface. If this diversity of strategies also exists for school students, it suggests the need for teaching approaches that are also diverse (by providing both hardware and virtual landscape modelling opportunities *and* support in building landscape vocabulary).

It is quite likely that boys and girls come to school with different levels of environmental experience as well as other biases in aptitude which may have a bearing on their map learning. However, there is little evidence that such initial advantages or disadvantages persist after appropriate teaching and plenty of evidence that both sexes appear to have room for improvement. Girls may indeed approach maps with less confidence, not least because of expectations based on stereotypes and this situation may not improve as map activities become increasingly computer based. Some girls may need to be encouraged to see map using and map making as appropriate to their gender. Teachers need to create opportunities for enthusiastic engagement with maps in a 'safe' environment where it's acceptable to ask questions if you don't understand and where 'difficult' mapping tasks (for example those requiring spatial information to be held in memory) are broken down into smaller, discrete steps. Such a strategy for building confidence and promoting learning is, however, as applicable to boys as it is to girls.

Maps and special users

Among young map users who have special needs, perhaps most attention has been paid to those who are blind and visually impaired. Tactile mapping is now beginning to play a significant role in inclusive education (Tatham, 2003). Two methods of making tactile maps dominate among the maps available (Rowell and Ungar, 2003a). These are maps made using thermoform (by vacuum forming a heated plastic sheet over a raised surface 'master') and the use of micro-capsule paper (in which tiny capsules containing alcohol embedded in the paper are made to expand under the carbon used in printing or drawing on the paper's surface by exposure to infra-red rays). Other methods include the use of mixed media (by making maps from *collage* materials such as sandpaper, cloth and string) and a new inkjet technology which now promises rapid production of maps with fine, easily discriminated tactile features (McCallum *et al.*, 2003). Internet based tactile and audio-tactile maps are now also being developed (Siekierska and Müller, 2003 and the *Mapping for the Visually Impaired* project: see Appendix), which can be accessed in multiple ways such as: downloading Braille and/or text maps for printing on micro-capsule paper; using an electronic touch tablet to provide audio information (e.g. the sound of splashing water when the finger scans sea); and using a haptic mouse which vibrates or provides differential resistance as the cursor is moved across the screen.

Significant progress has been made in recent years in understanding the potential of tactile maps for supporting visually impaired children's ability to estimate directions (Ungar *et al.*, 1994), locate themselves on the map (Ungar *et al.*, 1996) and make judgements about distances (Ungar *et al.*, 1997). Research has also considered the effectiveness of alternative tactile reading strategies (such as using one or two hands and one or more than one finger) and how these may vary for individuals in different contexts (Perkins and Gardiner, 2003). A current initiative in research and development in tactile mapping is the preparation of a taxonomically structured archive of tactile map symbols that can be accessed and searched online by remote users (Rowell and Ungar, 2003b). This potentially offers significant support for teachers making tactile maps for visually impaired children. Up to date developments in relation to maps for blind and visually impaired children can be found on the INTACT website (see Appendix).

In some of the few case studies of visually impaired children's practical map use in the field, Gardiner and Perkins (2003) describe children's exploration of a route using a map as well as their efforts to make their own maps using a selection of symbols for the thermoform process. This work suggests that visually impaired children are able to use tactile maps in similar ways to sighted children and offers potentially fruitful directions for further research. In a previous study, Gardiner and Perkins (1996) described the design of a tactile map for a single child with visual impairment enabling her to explore and appreciate a small area of countryside.

A wider range of cartographic support for children with special educational needs largely awaits exploration. Where research has been reported it indicates interesting possibilities. Working with a single student with emotional and behavioural difficulties, for example, Tischer (2002) reported that use of GIS could foster increased time on task, greater focus on the topic in hand and the promotion of coping strategies when faced with frustration. Tischer called on GIS professionals to support schools through their ability to offer stimulating and challenging activities that can be customised to the needs of individuals.

The next three chapters describe appropriate teaching approaches based on the evidence for children's learning described earlier in this book. Suggested student activities are provided in three age bands, although individual development will vary substantially within each phase and curriculum content will need to be harmonised with that provided in other subjects (for example, coordinate skills are generally also introduced in mathematics). As Catling notes, an outline programme such as this is only a guide or starting point for planning: 'The child, not the guide, should be the focus of planned activities' (1996: 104). The programme I am suggesting is a demanding one (with activities that are intended to challenge learners in each age group) and in most curriculum frameworks as currently configured there is unlikely to be time for all the strands. I am attempting to propose an ambitious programme based on evidence for children's thinking which I hope will provide helpful ideas for the present but will also serve as a manifesto for future curriculum change.

10 Practical map activities: up to age 7

For children up to the age of about 7 years there should be a strong emphasis on practical activities that establish prerequisite concepts for map understanding. This includes direct experience of their local environment (and indirect experience of more distant ones), language development and representational play. Children should, for example, be able to identify and name common features in the natural and built environment. They should have safe opportunities to do this through first hand observation as well as through use of photographs and models. They should be able to use locational language to describe topological relationships such as 'next to' and 'opposite'. Representational play using blocks and models will be a key element of children's experience in order to develop the perspective of a 'view from above'. Tasks will include matching, sorting and completing sets. Maps in this phase should have simple outlines with strong key lines, require limited reading ability and will include large scale plans of the classroom and school.

From a very early age children are aware that there exist lands of ice and snow, deserts and jungles, that people in other parts of the world have clothes and homes that are different to their own, and they bring these impressions of life elsewhere to their interpretation of atlas maps and the globe. Preparation for small scale map use in this phase therefore includes providing children with accurate images of other environments and ways of life through photographs and videotape and supporting their use of accurate descriptive language.

Direct and indirect environmental experience

In this phase children learn to orientate themselves in their surroundings. They play games (such as 'Simon Says') in which they follow directional instructions ('Turn left', 'Raise your right hand') and recognise that 'your left' is 'my right'. They follow and give directions for moving around the school using terms such as 'right', 'left', 'forward' and 'back'. They learn, for example, that in corridors you have to 'keep left' and that movement in some parts of the building is 'one way'. They describe the location of objects and features around them, in terms that are absolute (such as 'in front of', 'behind', 'near', 'next to', 'opposite') as well as relative ('nearer than' and 'further than'). Relative distances can be estimated in the classroom using a fixed length of string ('my table is further from the door than the book cupboard') and distances around the school can be compared by counting paces. Once these direction and distance relationships have been established from their own perspective they have to be transferred to the perspective of someone else. The relative location of objects in pictures and photographs can be described ('What is in front of the boy in the picture? What is to the left of the girl? Who is nearest the door?').

A model TV camera can be made from a cardboard box and moved to different positions in the classroom for practice in describing what the camera 'sees' (e.g. what's on the left or right of the picture) from each position.

In addition to direction and distance, young children also learn about scale through practical activity. Different sized objects such as items of doll's house furniture or model people and cars are sorted into matching sets for play and some items are discarded as they are 'too big' or 'too small' for others. Nested hierarchies can be directly experienced through stacking toys and Russian nesting dolls. Scale and nested hierarchies can also be approached through stories (such as *Goldilocks and the Three Bears*) and songs (*There was an old woman who swallowed a fly . . .*).

Children at this age also need experience of representations. They should have opportunities to talk about the similarities and differences between a real person and a picture of a person, a real house and a model house. They should be able to identify the meanings of everyday symbols: what red means when it is shown as a traffic light and what it means when it is shown on a tap. They should become familiar with some common universal signs in buildings (such as a green running figure for a fire exit) and on the street (such as a green cross for a pharmacy). They should begin to recognise the meaning of road signs that use pictograms (children for a school or playground; an elephant for a zoo; an aeroplane for sudden aircraft noise).

Symbols represent categories and the objects in each category may not look alike. In the UK, for example, a post box can be a free standing pillar-like structure or a small box mounted on a post or a large box set flush into a wall. Yet all of these manifestations of 'a place where you post letters' may be represented on a map by the same symbol (say, an envelope). Children need experience, therefore, of classifying phenomena in order to understand that different instantiations can be represented by a single symbol. Sorting photographs (for example of supermarkets, swimming pools, telephone boxes) and grouping them with a single representing symbol (such as a shopping trolley, swimmer or telephone handset) is a good way to do this. Pictures of local shops can also be categorised into, for example, those selling food and drink, clothing and footwear or books and stationery.

Perspective and the 'view from above' can be practised by observing familiar items from a number of viewpoints. This can be done with geometric solids (a sphere looks the same from the 'top' as from the 'side' whereas a cylinder doesn't) or everyday objects (a mug, teapot or shoe). In some classrooms, tools and utensils are stored so that the item matches a painted 'footprint' when placed on a table top or a 'shadow' when hung on a hook on the wall: another useful way of reinforcing outline shape. Small toys, geometric solids and familiar items can be placed on an overhead projector (but hidden from view) so that children have to guess the object from its 'footprint' projected on the screen.

As preparation for understanding small scale maps children need to see photographs and videotape of life in other parts of the world. They need their attention drawn to similarities and differences in relation to climate, plants, animals and how people live. Images seen early in childhood are extremely durable so pictures need to be positive and up-to-date. Extra care should be taken to avoid pejorative language (such as 'mud huts'). Teachers need to be sensitive to the fine distinction between national imagery that has become emblematic (such as windmills, Lederhosen and kilts) and unhelpful stereotypes ('Eskimos live in igloos'). Countries and place names should be referred to with precision. Although most children of this age have heard of 'Africa' (see Chapter 8) they generally have little knowledge of either its constituent countries or its great ecological variety.

Much map learning at this age is especially effective if it's based on home as this will probably be the area best known to the child. Teachers have an important role therefore in suggesting ways in which parents can best support their children's learning by, for example, talking about where they live and planning local trips with the help of a map.

Learning with models, photographs and large scale plans

Children's early understanding of representations of the three-dimensional world comes through using three-dimensional materials. A popular way of doing this is to arrange blocks or model buildings to make representations of small scale spaces (such as an imaginary community) and make up stories about the people who live there and what happens to them. The blocks can be used as tools for thinking about location – where is the 'best place' for particular buildings? What possibilities are offered by it being here rather than there? Construction can be made on large sheets of paper and toy vehicles 'driven' through the model on roads drawn between the blocks with discussion taking place about features that are passed to the left and right. Model layouts, especially in the early stages, can be large (perhaps several metres square) and children encouraged to extend their thinking about the represented environment to include elements that stretch their imagination (an airport, building site, railway terminal, dock or industrial area). Some of these elements (such as a zoo, theme park or farm) can generate further models (with a consequent change in scale). Models of real, known places can be put to work in a different way. A model of the classroom, for example, can be used to represent the location of a 'reward' in the real classroom (DeLoache, 1991). Similarly, a model of the school can be used to determine a route that can then be walked as a treasure hunt.

A more malleable modelling medium, such as sand or clay, is especially useful for representing landforms. In this phase the shape of simple landforms such as hills, valleys, islands and lakes are appropriate learning targets. For many children in urban areas, hills are directly experienced only as a gradient 'up' or 'down' between rows of buildings. The 'three-dimensionality' of hills may not be appreciated in the way that is more apparent when they are seen from a distance in the countryside. Modelling helps, therefore, to extend experience and allow consideration of when and how to apply descriptive terms such as steep and gentle.

Many common landscape concepts are rather elusive. The distinction between hills and mountains, for example, is only partially determined by height (and even then it's relative height, above the surrounding land, that's more significant than absolute height, measured in, say, metres above sea level). Steepness of slope, land cover and land use also help to define the difference. Children can appreciate this subtlety by sorting photographs (e.g. postcards) of hills and mountains and progressively refining their understanding by talking about those pictures which are difficult to classify.

Playbases (see Figure 10.1 and Appendix) are particularly good starting points for map-like representations in this phase as they are robust, extendable and offer many opportunities for imaginative play. It may be advantageous if children start with 'oblique' versions of these before progressing to those where features are shown in 'plan' (Liben and Yekel, 1996). Playbases are very popular items of equipment in early years classrooms but far less commonly used for *structured* learning. A typical map playbase activity might involve children working in pairs: one giving directional instructions ('turn left', 'go straight on', 'take the second right') to another who 'drives' a model vehicle between one location and another. Possible scenarios include provision of emergency services (directing

Figure 10.1 Oblique view playbase with model vehicles. Map playbase by Sport and Playbase Ltd.

an ambulance to an accident involves working out the quickest route between two places and evaluating alternative short cuts) and delivering goods (directing a delivery van to a number of addresses involves working out the shortest route between a series of locations). To start with, both children can sit at the same side of the playbase, so that they share the same orientation. Later, the direction-giver sits opposite so that directions (left and right) have to be mentally reversed for the 'driver' to follow. Later, children can change the instructions from those using relative directions (left, right) to cardinal directions (north, south) and observe that these stay constant irrespective of where the players sit around the playbase.

The first 'real' maps used in this phase are likely to be teacher-made large scale plans of the classroom and the school. These can be 'set' (aligned so that they are oriented to match the referent space) and used to find the location of a hidden object: X marks where the prize is hidden, perhaps under one of a number of upturned buckets marked on a plan of the playground. In a more complex activity each child marks the location of his/her seat on a duplicated plan of the classroom. The plans are then collected, randomised and redistributed. Each child then makes his/her way to the seat location marked on the new map.

The theme of using a map to find a specified location can be extended to children's own representations. Each child hides a unique object (such as a numbered cloakroom tag or a coin with a unique date) in the school grounds and makes a map to show where it is hidden. The maps can include annotations (such as the number of steps to take from an unambiguous landmark) and should have the number or date of the hidden object so the 'finder' can tell when the right one is found. After the exercise, children then discuss what makes a good map. The activity is repeated with children now using their agreed 'rules for good map making'. Mapping skill at this stage is still fragile but the principles can be extended to plans of their own bedrooms, homes and as much of the neighbourhood as they know. There are many ways to make a map and the emphasis in this phase should be on developing confidence and enlarging representational possibilities, not narrowing options.

This especially applies to understanding how symbols work. A large plan of the school can be used to experiment with representing information: for example colouring class-rooms, offices and play spaces according to a key; sticking pictograms on the plan showing favourite or least liked places and drawing routes from the classroom to familiar destina-tions such as the assembly hall and playground. Some information can be shown on a plan in three dimensions, such as counters piled up on areas representing classrooms and offices to show the number of people in each (established by means of a survey of the school). Room plans can be used to think about alternative arrangements of furniture (perhaps using teacher-made scale cut outs representing tables and chairs). Symbols can also be added to copies of maps from children's fiction (e.g. A.A. Milne's *Winnie the Pooh*, Roald Dahl's *Fantastic Mr Fox*) and the maps annotated to show the progress of characters as the story unfolds. More demands are made on children generating their own maps to illustrate stories but good starting points include simple narratives such as *Hansel and Gretel*, *Red Riding Hood*, etc. where the action is limited in space to simple journeys between a single starting point and a single destination.

Learning with 'real' maps can be supported through the use of 'map like' games and puzzles such as board games and mazes, many of which mark out spatial relations between points, lines and areas. Variations on Blades and Spencer's (1989a, 1994) coordinate test materials (described in Chapter 4) can be made to identify squares on a grid by simple 'grid references' using colours and shapes.

Learning with atlases and globes

In this phase, children enjoy browsing with simple picture maps and atlases, including electronic atlases with animated pictures and sound. They can talk about what the pictures show and describe similarities and differences between where they live and other parts of the world. Talk with an adult should focus both on what the pictures *show* (for example, an unfamiliar animal) and what they *stand for* (to show that this is where you can find these animals).

Children can also talk about the globe as a model of the Earth and point to approximately where they live. They can identify land masses and water bodies and match the shapes of continents on the globe with those on a world map. They can play 'catch' with an inflatable globe and say which continent is under each hand. 'Snap' cards with outlines of countries or continents are easy to make, as are cards for the 'memory game' (or pelmanism, in which you turn up and collect matching pairs of cards) and 'happy families' (in which, perhaps, you collect the set of seven continents or a set of countries within each continent 'family'). 'Lotto' cards and boards can similarly be based on the world map. 'Dominoes' can also be made whereby a country shape outline has to be matched to its written name on another domino. All these activities can help to reinforce shape recognition and naming (including spelling and pronunciation) of countries and continents.

Children in this phase should also be familiar with a map outline of their home region or country and be able to point to approximately where they live. They should be able to say their address and recognise some of the elements of that address on the map. An outline map is a convenient way of recording places that children in the class have been to and talking about places that are 'nearer' and 'further'. Destinations and journeys on the map can be annotated according to mode of transport and how long the journey took. An outline map can also be used in conjunction with simple symbol weather forecast maps (is there a sun or cloud symbol near to where we live?). Map displays like this also offer opportunities for developing map literacy – labels should be differentiated according to type of geographical feature. For example, the country name might be in one colour, the names of settlements in another and physical features in a third. This helps children understand that names on maps include different categories of place.

The next chapter describes how these early foundations are followed through into the middle and later primary years.

11 Practical map activities: age 7 to 11

This phase contains perhaps the greatest range of children's development and most opportunities for promoting understanding of maps yet much map related teaching is still likely to be by non-specialist teachers. Activities in this phase are characterised by increasing abstraction in children's use of language and their developing ability to describe patterns, generalise and classify as well as gradually being able to adopt other perspectives. Activities will still be rooted in practical tasks in relation to the immediate environment (such as making increasingly accurate measurements and comparing distances) but there will be a shift in scale to encompass the wider locality. As children's knowledge of their home area expands so will their use of maps at scales of, for example 1:25,000 and 1:50,000. Parents continue to play a key role in providing for their children first hand experience of a widening area based on home as well as helping them interpret its representation in map form. Key resources in this phase include maps and plans of theme parks and shopping centres, maps on postcards and maps of the school catchment area and the home region. Three-dimensional support for learning in the form of models and plastic moulded relief maps will still be necessary. Children's awareness of the wider world expands rapidly during this phase and they also encounter small scale maps (at country and continent scale) and make increasing use of atlases. Although most maps made by children are likely to be in hard copy, they should increasingly be able to use simple electronic tools with digital maps. Children also develop in this phase a beginning sense of the social purposes of maps. They understand that maps are particularly important for some groups of people (such as lorry drivers, estate agents and travel agents), that the maps themselves will vary according to the users' needs and that the information shown on maps is selective. They understand that maps generally show permanent features (such as roads, buildings and woodland), not ephemeral ones (such as smoke, people and parked cars).

The next two sections identify some important aspects of map numeracy and literacy which form useful prerequisite knowledge and skills for map reading, map using and map making.

Developing map numeracy

In this phase children continue to orientate themselves to their surroundings. They may be able to use left and right with consistent accuracy in relation to themselves but have difficulty when considering a perspective other than their own. Figure 11.1 shows an exercise intended to practise taking another perspective. Having established left and right in relation to your own feet you are required to 'think yourself into the picture' and colour the left boots of the children on the climbing frame red and the right boots green.

Figure 11.1 'Colour the left boots red and the right boots green'. An exercise from Wiegand, P., *Oxford Junior Map Skills*, copyright © 1998, Oxford University Press, reproduced by permission of Oxford University Press.

This is a useful prerequisite for describing a route on a map from another person's perspective (or your own route without having to align the map to the environment).

Children also learn to orientate themselves to cardinal directions by using a compass to identify first four, then eight, then sixteen directions. There are two important components to understanding compass directions. One is to recognise where the points are in relation to each other (as though on a clock face with north at 12 o'clock, east at three o'clock, etc.). The second (crucial, but less commonly taught) is to understand that these directions have a constant relationship with the Earth. Many children in this phase can answer simple directional questions in relation to a map (A is west of B, especially if north is at the 'top' of the map) but far fewer understand how to use a compass to identify the direction of places in the locality, how to align a map correspondingly and then draw inferences about direction using the map in conjunction with the environment it represents. Remembering directions of the compass card is usually accomplished by simple mnemonics. Understanding azimuth (i.e. directional bearing) can be supported by real world observation. For example, children can observe where the sun rises and sets and note the movement of the sun's shadow from a stick or post at different times of day. Although this latter activity is a prerequisite for understanding the movement of the Earth in relation to the sun, it can also be used simply to practise cardinal directions in describing the direction of shadows. Children can also discuss how the position of the sun affects our everyday lives. Which classrooms have the sun in the morning and which have it in the afternoon? Which way do gardeners prefer a garden to face? Does the orientation of a house affect its market value? Why do lichen and moss grow more on the north facing sides of trees? Why are Christian churches mostly aligned east–west and in which direction is Mecca? Children also need to understand directional reciprocals (if you're travelling westwards you're coming from the east) and that a westerly wind blows *from* the west. In preparation for understanding bearings children at this stage can also practise turning left and right through 90°, 180°, 270° and 360° using the terms 'quarter turn', 'half turn', ' three quarter turn' and 'whole turn', respectively.

Map scale is the ratio between distance in the real world and distance on the map. At this stage, therefore, children need to have a developing sense of standard distances. They achieve this by estimating, then measuring, using (for real world scale units) measuring tapes and trundle wheels and (for hard copy map scale units) rulers. For digital maps, children will need to learn to use a distance measuring device (usually incorporating a window showing real world distance units between points on the map indicated by mouse clicks). Throughout this phase they should be able to make measurements in the real world as well as on the map with increasing accuracy. They should also relate larger distance units to their knowledge of the locality (for example, know that it is about 1 kilometre from the school to the library, 5 kilometres to the town centre). For small scale maps, a *comparitor* (a map of a known place presented at the same scale as the place being studied) is useful, but only if children really have a clear understanding of the size of that known place. Figure 11.2 shows a comparitor as part of a map made by a teacher for British children studying Australia. Typical preparation for using this map might include a discussion of the approximate straight line distance between the extremes of Great Britain (in round figures, about 1,000km) and how long it would take to travel between John O'Groats at the far north and Land's End at the far south-west by air (perhaps two hours?), road (perhaps two days?) or on foot (for someone extremely fit, perhaps a month?). To counter the common misconception by children that a journey round the world is 'millions' of miles, children can use a globe in conjunction with a list of flight times from their home country to distant places or work out how many times the family car has been 'round the world'. Scale concepts can be further developed by sorting pictures and plans at different sizes (the enlargements and reductions can be made with a photocopier) into matching sets. Children can enlarge and reduce their own pictures by using squared paper and transferring a simple outline image square by square to a larger or smaller scale. A 'join the dots' puzzle can also be solved at both large and small scales. It is important that the elusive terminology of scale is frequently reinforced: the enlargement is at a larger scale.

In this phase children increasingly come across the need for a means of specifying location. An understanding of grids and coordinates is required for traditional games such as 'battleships' but children in this phase are also often becoming interested in board games such as chess which uses a rather different type of notation. The horizontal rows on the chessboard are called ranks and the vertical rows are called files. Files are named after the piece that stands on them (on the first rank) at the beginning of the game. The sports pages of newspapers also generally carry 'maps' of the positions of named players in

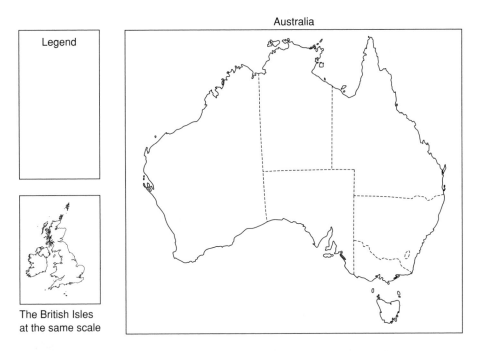

Figure 11.2 A teacher-produced map of Australia showing a British Isles scale comparitor.

football teams at the start of a match – yet another system of describing and recording location.

Developing map literacy

At age 7–11, children need to build up more targeted literacy skills that will be applied to map reading and map making. Maps at all scales yield very large numbers of words. Physically sorting a number of representative map labels into (for example) settlements, rivers and mountains, or continents, countries and capitals, is one way of helping children become more confident about what these categories mean. Practice is usually also needed in saying and spelling unfamiliar place names and identifying patterns can help. For example, residential areas often have themed street names (the Woodlands housing estate may have an Oak Close, Ash Drive, Elm Way, etc.). Some basic toponymy (the study of place names) can also support learning. Place names tell us a great deal about the physical geography of a locality, its culture and history and the people connected with it. Swansea, for example, comes from Sweyn's ey (island) whilst its Welsh name Abertawe means mouth of the river Tawe. Seeing patterns in names with similar derivations (e.g. Orkney, **Aber**ystwyth) helps make new words more manageable. Identifying the suffix '-cester' (which, like '-caster' and '-chester' means a Roman town or fort) helps with learning to spell Gloucester and Leicester. Using atlas maps involves being able to talk about countries and there are patterns in the way many country names make adjectives. We say Australi**an** and Americ**an** but Banglades**hi** and Oma**ni**; Span**ish** and Pol**ish** but Chin**ese** and Japan**ese**. Some country adjectives follow no pattern at all (Dutch, Greek and French). Identifying families of country adjectives is a further way of building confidence with unfamiliar words.

Typeface provides important clues to the meaning of labels on maps: **YORK** is likely to refer to the unitary authority, **York** only to the city. **Thame** is probably the town, *Thame* the river. If children can decode the typeface (for example, understand that administrative areas are in upper case, settlements in upper and lower and physical features in italics) they have a good chance of understanding what the words on maps mean. Familiarity with abbreviations is also important prerequisite knowledge for map reading. There are a surprising number of these commonly found on street maps (e.g. Rd., St., Ave., Ln., Dr., Terr., Pk., Wy., Cl., Pde) and topographic maps (e.g. R., Mt., Is., Pen., Fm., Ho., Ch., PH., PO, WC).

Small scale maps in particular demand prior understanding of some abstract concepts. These include the notion of a country (perhaps explained at this level as a 'land with its own people and its own laws'?) and a capital city (children may like to consider why this is not always the largest settlement). Macro-environments (for example desert, tropical rain forest, savannah, tundra, ice cap) and large scale landforms (peninsula, mountain range, cape) will also need to be explored through pictures and videotape as these are common 'atlas words'.

Children's ability to give and follow directions can be improved by having an enhanced wayfinding vocabulary. This includes distinguishing between, for example, a cross roads and a T junction and understanding the difference between taking the left turn and the left fork. Greater precision in the use of wayfinding language can be practised in relation to frequent journeys in the locality (such as the journey from home to school).

The use of streetfinder and atlas index pages will make demands on children's facility with alphabetical order. This is a progressive skill. It's easier, for example, to sort Cardiff, Birmingham and Dublin into alphabetical order than it is to sort Kingston, Kingstown, Kingston-upon-Hull and King's Lynn. More general language development also continues to be a significant goal in this phase, involving more abstract concepts than the concrete ones characteristic of earlier years. Children will, for example, progress from using *shop* to *shopping centre* or *mall*; from *factory* to *industrial estate*; from *house* to *residential area*. Physical landscape concepts are similarly extended, refined and increased in scale from, say, *river* to *tributary* and *drainage basin*; *mountain* to *mountain range*. The meta language of maps and globes such as *legend (key), scale bar, grid, title, sphere* and *hemisphere* are also learned so that the parts of maps and how they 'work' can be talked about.

Learning with large scale maps

Some specific map skills can be reinforced in this phase by targeted activities. For example, Figure 11.3 illustrates a simple exercise aimed to develop a more secure understanding of plan. Each building has to be matched to its footprint. The artwork in this illustration (fairly easily prepared without specialist drawing skill) was based on pictures and plans from estate agents' literature and holiday cottage brochures. The 'view from above' can also be developed through use of simple cut out templates in order to plan room layouts (such as those provided by some companies that supply fitted kitchens, bathrooms and bedrooms). Plan can be reinforced too by a problem solving approach: where is the best place in the classroom for a new electricity socket or another computer; how could the tables be reorganised so that we can work in smaller groups? At a smaller scale, children could map the fire exit routes for each class or solve a corridor congestion problem by considering alternative routes around the school. Alternatively, consideration of some environmental issue might be appropriate: where is there most litter in the school grounds

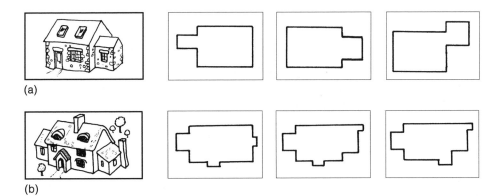

Figure 11.3 'Match the building to the correct plan'. Exercises from Wiegand, P., *Oxford Junior Map Skills*, copyright © 1998, Oxford University Press, reproduced by permission of Oxford University Press.

and where could additional bins be most advantageously placed? Point, line and area features can also be identified on an aerial photograph of the school and familiar routes between known points traced. Comparisons can be made too between the way aerial photographs and maps represent places by, for example, naming two things that are shown on the photograph but not the map, and vice versa.

In thinking about plan, the need for a reference framework will soon become apparent. On a map of the school, for example, places can be located in relation to each other using compass directions (e.g. 'the playground is north of the main building'). An alphanumeric grid code can be used to locate grid squares ('our classroom is at B3'). Comparisons are made between distances on the map using a fixed length rule and between areas using a template. At first these comparisons are relative (longer/shorter than; bigger/smaller than). Later, a measuring strip and template marked in 'real world' units (e.g. metres) is used to measure to the nearest unit. Later still, 'map scale' units (e.g. centimetres) can be measured on the map and converted using the linear scale into 'real world' units (e.g. metres). Map distances should be measured on both conventional and digital maps first as straight line distances and later as actual distance. Direction, distance and grid information can be used in conjunction with each other for more elaborate treasure hunts under safe supervision, involving finding the way to several locations in order to find the next clue.

In this phase, a great deal of work can be based on a large scale map, perhaps at 1:10,000, of the locality. For example, the map can be aligned with a compass to its correct orientation. Point, line and area features are identified and described in relation to the school and in relation to each other. Places are located on the map using four, then six figure grid references. Directions are given and routes followed between places on the map by children working in pairs. As the children will have some knowledge of the mapped locality these routes can be selected and described as though tailored to the needs of specific users, for example: a route from the church to the High Street for an elderly couple; from the school to the post office for a wheelchair user; from the station to the Town Hall for a tourist. In describing routes, children are prompted to use cardinal directions and approximate distances, to use appropriate vocabulary to describe junctions and features en route. Direction givers must speak clearly, provide instructions with precision (take the second left, then first on the right, then left at the T junction) and check for understanding. Landmarks are essential to check you're going the right way. But what makes a good landmark? The best ones are those that are clearly visible, distinctive, permanent and unambiguous.

Point, line and area information can be added to the map. For example, if the map shows the school's catchment area, each child can mark his/her home on the map with an adhesive dot. What does the pattern of children's homes look like and how can it be described? For example: 'most of the class live south of the school', 'no one lives west of the railway line'. Children then draw (perhaps on a copy of the map) their own route to school. Addresses and postcodes can be compared and common elements of these 'zoned' on the map. Using a measuring strip based on the map scale each child can measure straight line distance from home to school and (with string) the actual distance travelled. Real world actual distances can then be calculated from the linear scale. The results can be shown on a graph with a single axis and the children who live nearest to, or furthest from, the school identified. But how does each child come to school? Coloured symbols for those walking, travelling by bus, car, etc. can be used for each home location on the map and the resulting pattern examined. The bus routes can be identified and marked. Does that help explain part of the overall pattern of modes of transport? Does it explain the shape of the catchment area? Concentric circles representing, say, each successive half kilometre radius from school can be drawn and the number of children using each mode of transport counted in each concentric circle. And how long does it take to come to school? Children's journeys can be graphed on two axes – distance and time taken in order to test hypotheses such as whether the children who live furthest from school will take longer to travel.

Projects like this consolidate key elements of map skill such as using symbols, finding location, orienting the map, using directions, using scale and finding distances. By gradually widening the scope to include maps at a scale of, say, 1:25,000 and 1:50,000 children ought to recognise many cartographic conventions (e.g. the standard symbol sets used on national maps) as their knowledge of their surroundings increases.

Map activities should not be restricted to formal maps from national mapping organisations, however. Stories with maps remain popular at this age (classics include A.A. Milne's *Winnie the Pooh*, Robert Louis Stevenson's *Treasure Island*, J.R.R. Tolkien's *The Hobbit* but there are many more).

Map making

There are a number of approaches to map making in this phase. Small spaces such as a bedroom or classroom can be modelled in a cardboard box with appropriate dimensions. Larger spaces such as the school and its grounds can be modelled with blocks. With a digital camera, it is relatively easy for teachers (and children) to produce step-by-step instructions for making a model of a particular space. Following instructions for building a model with Lego is especially helpful as it requires children to count 'along' and 'up' the grid of pegs on a rectangular base board in order to construct the model with accuracy.

Deep, clear plastic storage bins are invaluable for modelling and mapping landforms. A number of complementary strategies are helpful. Children can create a model landscape in the storage bin using sand and other natural materials or small model components. A sheet of clear, rigid plastic or plexiglass is positioned over the top of the model so that it can be viewed from above (see Figure 7.3). The model can then be mapped using felt tip pens on overhead projector acetate and colours used to record different categories of feature, for example building outlines in red and trees in green. Another way of mapping the model layout is to use a quadrat frame (divided into squares, of the sort used by botanists to record plant species) to identify the location of each feature so that its position can be transferred to a grid drawn to the same size. The same equipment can be used to engage children in a problem-solving approach to relief mapping. Children can consider alternative forms of relief representation, such as hill pictures and hachures, before some attention is paid to how contours work. For this, structured learning support will probably be necessary. A common approach is to use storage bins with modelling clay and water. A height scale is drawn up the side of the bin and a clay model hill is created inside it. Water is poured into the bin and at each height level the 'shore' is marked on the model (drawn with a waterproof felt tip pen or scratched with a point). Looking down through the plexiglass 'lid', the contours are then drawn on a sheet of acetate. Typical starting points are egg-shaped hills (so that a distinction can be noticed between a steeper and a gentler slope and therefore between closer and more widely spaced contours). The materials can, and should, however, be exploited for landforms where the contour patterns are far less obvious: such as valley forms, plateaux and coastal cliffs. The notion of mapping land height can be applied to the area around the school if it is sited on sloping land. Colour a map with the school in the centre to show those places that are higher than the school and those that are lower: the resultant map should show two layer colours separated by a single contour passing through the school.

This phase of development is a time when children's 'worlds' are expanding rapidly. Their own maps of the neighbourhood can indicate their favourite places and places they dislike; places that are good for quietly talking and places that are good for vigorous games. Local mapping can run hand in hand with increasing environmental awareness, observation of pattern, shape, texture and detail as well as learning to express preferences for some places over others. The cartographic teaching emphasis should be on points, lines, areas and labels. This forms a convenient checklist for prompting children: what's at this point? How do you get from here to there? What's the name of this area? These maps will probably be drawn freehand using pencil and paper or by using a simple software mapping tool (for example *Local Studies* by Soft Teach Educational (see Appendix). The example in Plate 6 illustrates an early step towards understanding the map as a GISystem. Using this tool children come to appreciate that spatial data (such as the picture and text relating to the old bridge) can be stored then interrogated by interaction with the map. Simple mapping tools such as these will also enable children to create their own symbol systems so that they can be introduced to the most appropriate use of visual variables (e.g. size, hue, shape) in order to represent a distribution (such as a selection of leisure destinations). Children can design map symbols for familiar features (such as a cinema, ice rink, football stadium, etc.) and talk about what makes good symbol design. An underemphasised aspect of map making in this phase is designing maps for particular users. This helps to reinforce the notion that maps are selective in what they show and that map makers exercise choice over the form of representation. Suitable target user categories for a map of a local shopping centre might include elderly people using public transport, teenagers on bicycles and young families with a car. Collaborative map making is especially effective as children have to articulate the reasoning behind their representations. Whether maps are drawn freehand or with computer software, children in this phase ought to be able to self-check their own maps to ensure that they have included appropriate map information (National Geography Standards, 1994). This should include: a title, which may specify thematic content as well as the location of the place mapped (for example, *A map to show types of shops in Millbridge*); orientation (a North pointer); date (so the user can assess whether there are likely to have been changes since the map was made); author (who made the decisions about the way the data was represented); scale (shown in a way that is meaningful to the user); legend (with items appropriately grouped in the key); and the source of the data (for example, collected by field observation). For larger maps a grid with an index might be appropriate. Some of these items (such as author and source) form an important introduction to the notion of metadata in GIScience.

Learning with atlases and globes

In this phase, children should be able to use a globe and small scale maps to access key locational knowledge. This includes being able to identify the country in which they live, the continents and selected countries in each (e.g. the largest and the most populous in each continent) as well as key global reference points: the poles, polar circles, tropics, equator and prime meridian. They should be able to identify the northern and southern hemispheres on a globe and be able to classify places according to their location in each hemisphere. They should be able to use a globe to estimate relative distances between places (e.g. that London and New York are further apart than London and Paris) and to use a length of string representing the circumference of the Earth to estimate distances between home and far distant places (e.g. if the length of string represents 25,000 miles and the distance from London to San Francisco is about one fifth of the length of string, then the distance from London to San Francisco is about 5,000 miles). They should be able to compare relative country areas (e.g. that the USA is larger than the UK) using a comparator map (i.e. one which shows a familiar area such as the home country at the same scale). Whilst using the globe it may be helpful to visit concepts such as vertical directions in relation to the Earth's surface (i.e., *up* as away from the globe and *down* as towards it. Small dolls can be used to illustrate this, based on the research methodology used by Nussbaum (1985, see Chapter 8). Children should also have some understanding that day and night are a consequence of the Earth's rotation and that times vary around the world. When using a globe it is helpful always to rotate it in the correct direction (west to east). There are a large number of internet sites that show an animated Earth graphic – but many rotate it in the opposite direction!

Children should also use the globe and small scale maps to ascertain basic spatial properties of their own country and others. This includes relative location (Scotland is north of England) and location within a spatial hierarchy (Wales is part of Great Britain which is part of the United Kingdom which is part of Europe). Absolute location can be investigated on a globe and in an atlas by using locational terms such as 'tropical' and 'equatorial' and finding out the nearest intersection of the meridians and parallels marked on the map. At this stage only whole numbers of degrees of latitude and longitude are probably considered and perhaps rounded to the nearest 10 or 20 degrees. Other spatial properties children can identify at this stage from globe and atlas include whether a country is landlocked and the names of neighbouring countries.

Directed atlas browsing in this phase is to be much encouraged. Appropriate prompts include: find where you live (on several maps at different scales); find a place you've been to on holiday; find a place you've never been to but would like to visit. Regular access to an atlas prompts children to look up places associated with their (rapidly increasing) interests: sporting events, natural disasters, where things are made and where famous people come from. 'Lexical' skills (looking up where places are) using an alphanumeric grid code should become increasingly proficient. Children enjoy playing 'Guess the country'. In this, pairs of players sit opposite, each having an atlas. One partner chooses a country on an agreed map and the other has to guess it in the smallest number of questions. The first player can only answer yes or no. Examples of good questions are: is it in the northern hemisphere? Is it equatorial? Does it have a coastline?

Teaching with atlases (conventional and electronic) in this phase requires some regular routines to check for understanding. Here are some examples of systematic questioning intended to help children focus on what small scale maps show:

- What is the title of this map? What place does the map show?
- What do the colours mean on the map?
- Point to the area represented by this map on the globe.
- Name the towns in square B3 (to clarify pronunciation).
- Is country X bigger or smaller than our country?
- How long might it take us to get there?
- How far is it from Y to Z on the map? How long might that take to travel?
- Name country X's neighbours.
- What is the capital of country X (assuming the legend identifies capital cities)?
- What is the name of the mountain range in the west?
- Look at the symbols in the legend for different town sizes. What towns in our country are about the same size?
- What do these words in the legend mean: precipitation, inhabitants, ecosystems.

Atlases are effective when used in conjunction with displays on topics of interest to children. Imagine, for example, a large outline wall map of the world used as the basis for a display of (for example) coins, stamps, postcards, animals, menus, recipes, sports teams, flags, airlines, where cars are made, famous buildings, songs, stories, earthquakes, explorers, round the world adventurers and 'record breaking' locations (such as the highest, lowest, deepest, coldest, windiest, snowiest, wettest, driest, richest, poorest, etc. places). Suppose the map was constructed like an advent calendar so that each day a flap was lifted on the map to find picture surprises? Suppose it was a *collage* map where fabrics and other materials represented landscapes and environments (sandpaper for deserts, green felt for tropical rain forest?). Suppose we coloured places that children in the class, or people we know, had visited – or places we would most like to visit? Is there a pattern to those places? What do they have in common? What about the places no one has visited?

By the end of primary school, children should be able to identify some simple relationships and patterns on small scale maps. This includes simple map interpretation and hypothesis testing. For example, after studying a settlement located on a river children might investigate using map evidence whether it is true that *all* settlements are located on rivers. They should also be able to make simple summaries of distributions. For example, after studying a map of world population they should be able to state that most people in the world live on low coastal land.

The next chapter follows these primary school map learning gains through into secondary school.

12 Practical map activities: age 11 to 14

This phase is generally characterised by systematic map teaching, undertaken largely by geography subject specialists. Maps should begin to be used at this age as a means of promoting higher order thinking skills and students should continue to develop their ability to describe patterns, generalise and classify as well as beginning to apply analytical strategies to what maps show. Teaching objectives include increasing precision in the use of geographical terminology and the meta language of maps (describing, for example, *types* of maps such as topographic and thematic, as well as *parts* of maps such as ways of expressing scale (linear, representative fraction and written statement) and north (magnetic, grid and true)). Measurements, in the real world and on the map, should become more accurate and the range of maps encountered should become more comprehensive. Key resources include national large scale mapping (e.g. from the Ordnance Survey) at the most popular scales, a selection of specialist maps (such as those showing geology and land use), street maps, world atlases, road atlases and a selection of foreign and historical maps. Students are likely to access cartographic resources as diverse as the London Underground diagram, tourist maps, maps in newspapers, weather maps and digital elevation models. Satellite maps and aerial photographs are also used as evidence in conjunction with maps. Although at the time of writing the majority of school students have relatively little exposure to GISystems, this is the phase which will soon, it is hoped, see the beginning of more widespread and systematic instruction in GIS skills as part of school students' curriculum entitlement in GIScience.

Map numeracy

In this phase school students continue to match key metrics with their own direct experience with increasing accuracy (knowing that it is, for example, 10km from the school to the station, that the highest point of their town is 105m above sea level, that the average temperature for where they live is 17°C in summer and that the average annual rainfall is 750mm). They should understand that a hectare is $10,000m^2$ and that 100 hectares is $1km^2$ and be able to make rough estimates of these areas in relation to places they know. They should also know the approximate dimensions of the planet (that the equatorial circumference of the Earth is approximately 25,000 miles or 40,000km) and be able to make reasonable estimates of large distances around the Earth using a globe as a guide.

Activities to support understanding of the Earth as a whole include using string to demonstrate great circle routes on a globe, describing the route with reference to the places traversed and then transferring details of the route to a world map. In this phase too, students ought to be able to use a handheld GPS receiver to identify the latitude and longitude of their position. They can then relate these values to meridians and parallels on atlas maps and should be able to identify locations using latitude and longitude coordinates as well as an alphanumeric grid code. Using a compass and a globe for reference they can orient themselves towards the poles and the equator and point towards a selection of named parts of the world in both hemispheres. They can estimate the latitude and longitude of a selection of world cities using a globe and a map and attempt to predict what sort of landscape, vegetation and human activity would be likely at various points on the Earth's surface. These predictions can then be compared with images on the Degree Confluence Project website (see Appendix). The goal of this project is to visit each place on Earth where whole numbered lines of longitude and latitude meet and to take photographs at each location. This creates a sample of 64,442 places, of which 14,027 are on land. The website provides a growing (and fascinating) database of visual images and 'travellers' tales' for each location.

In the early secondary years, school students should be able to understand basic relationships between the Earth's rotation, time and length of day, such as knowing that the Earth rotates west to east (and be able to demonstrate its movement with a globe). They should be able to generate statements such that (e.g.) people in the USA rise several hours later than people in Europe. The internet provides a useful means of indirectly experiencing changing time zones around the world, for example through accessing webcams that show daylight and weather conditions in real time for other global locations. Many airlines now provide real time online flight information so that individual flights can be tracked with the opportunity of monitoring the time at the departure point, arrival point and local time for each time zone the aeroplane flies over. An atlas time zone map can be used to compute the time in, say, New York or Tokyo for a given time in London.

Students should also understand the difference between True North (the direction to the North Pole, aligned with meridians of longitude), Magnetic North (to which a compass needle points) and Grid North (aligned with the map's rectilinear grid lines). They should also be able to 'set' a map. This is done either by using a compass (by turning the map until the compass needle is aligned with magnetic north) or by reference to a landmark (by locating your position on the map, identifying a prominent landmark and turning the map until a line from your position through the landmark on the map is pointing to the actual landmark in the field). They should understand three figure bearings (for example, north-east as 045°) and have some appreciation of how and why bearings are used in everyday life (for example that runways are numbered according to the first two digits of their bearing so that pilots can always orientate themselves to approach an aerodrome in the right direction).

In this phase too, prior understanding of gradient is required for map reading. Gradient is calculated as difference in height divided by distance on the ground (both parts of the fraction must be expressed in the same units) and expressed either in the form of a ratio (e.g. 1 in 5) or, increasingly on road signs and maps, as a percentage (e.g. 20 per cent). For these figures to have meaning they need to be related to students' direct experience (knowing that a local hill has a gradient of, for example, 1 in 6).

Grid references are generally widely taught in this phase but often as a technique with little contextual understanding of how the grid actually works. In the UK the National Grid has a point of origin to the west of the Isles of Scilly. 'Eastings' provide information about how far any location is east of the point of origin and 'northings' indicate how far north. The country is divided into 100km × 100km blocks, each identified by letters. Each block is further divided into 1km × 1km squares. A unique grid reference to one of these squares on, say, a map at 1:50,000 scale consists of the letters followed by the easting and northing that intersect at the south-western corner of the square (the so called 'four figure grid reference'). For a more accurate (six figure) reference the 1km square is divided into a further imaginary 100 squares and tenths added to both eastings and northings. Few secondary school students recognise that the technique they know for 'doing' grid references actually identifies a location as being distance east and north from a known point and that the numbers on the grid lines relate (depending on the scale of the map) to multiples of metres. Many, if not most, grasp the basic principle of using grid references but there are two common difficulties. One is confusion over terminology (as, for example, eastings are observed to run north–south), the other is remembering whether eastings or northings are given first. It is common for teachers to use the mnemonic 'along the corridor and up the stairs' to indicate that you read eastings *along* the base of the map and then *up* the (right) hand edge. In my view this seems to imply that top and left numbered edges of the grid have no value and leads to confusion if grid references are required for a folded map where only the top left corner can be seen. It also inadequately reinforces the concept of measured distance east and north from a known point of origin so it may be more helpful to focus attention on the eastings and northings themselves (perhaps through an alternative mnemonic: *E* comes before *N* in the alphabet).

Map literacy

School students' understanding of place names should develop further in this phase. On a map, language is used to refer to what features are *called* (mountain, river) as well as what they are *named* (Helvellyn, Thames). Generic topographic labels (such as *valley*) can also vary regionally as, for example in Wensley*dale*, the *Vale* of York, *Glen* Mor and *Strath*spey. Understanding word endings (for example, that -thwaite, -thorp(e) and -ness mean, respectively, forest clearing, farm and headland as part of Viking settlement names) can raise interest and support learning of spellings and pronunciation. Enriched understanding can also come from recognising that places have lent their names to products (for example, Tweed, Jersey, Cardigan) and that place names have been exported to other countries (there is a Lincoln in Argentina, Canada, New Zealand and the USA). At this point in their school experience, students are generally learning other languages and atlas maps provide teaching opportunities through identification of topographic vocabulary, for example (in Spanish): bahia (bay); costa (coast); isla (island); laguna (lagoon); pico (summit); rio (river); etc.

Students should be able to appreciate in increasing detail the diversity of the Earth's physical and human systems and use appropriate vocabulary. This includes being able to describe locations (e.g. polar, tropical, inland, peripheral), distributions (clustered, dispersed), landforms (e.g. spur, cuesta, incised meander, river bluff, plateau) and geomorphological patterns (e.g., for drainage: radial, dendritic, parallel, trellised). This phase is also charac- terised by greater accuracy in environmental description (e.g. savannah, semi-desert, rain shadow). Students in this phase are able to work with maps more analytically because they understand the difference between geographical terms (such as settlement *form* and *func- tion*) as well as the rubric of tasks they are set (for example, the difference between *describe* and *explain*). They become more proficient in describing relative locations, giving and following directions, talking about distances and areas and are able to use terms such as 'small scale' and 'large scale' with increasing accuracy. In this phase, the meta-language of maps (choropleth, inset, generalisation, projection) and aerial photographs (oblique, aerial) should also develop. Students understand that atlas maps generally have a *locator* (showing where the main map is in relation to a larger area of the Earth's surface) and a *comparator* (showing how the area of the main map compares to an area better known to the reader).

Maps can be used as the starting point for independent writing in a variety of *genres* including narrative, poetry and plays. Writing provides an opportunity for synthesis of information from cartographic sources, for example writing an account of the economy or quality of life experienced in a region from map evidence alone, or in conjunction with other sources. There are opportunities for writing fiction (mystery, romance, thriller, horror, sci-fi, fantasy) as well as non-fiction (description, explanation, history). Developing a map based fictional narrative is excellent practice in map reading. Could the robber see the bank from the station? Did the getaway car have to go uphill or downhill? Maps especially provide stimulus material for writing promotional literature such as a tourist brochure, guidebook or visitor website. Other ideas starting with maps include: writing extracts from a film script set in the map area; the diary of a resident; a letter to an MP protesting about proposed house building in the green belt; and creating a tabloid newspaper front page about a proposed by-pass or airport extension.

Developing map and atlas skills

In this phase, students need to learn the systematic skills of map reading and map use such as finding location, measuring distance and direction, interpreting relief, etc. with increasing accuracy. They become familiar with most of the conventional symbols used on national topographic mapping and understand that these symbols are not scale representations of the referent (for example, that a road width on a large scale topographic map is not actually proportional to how wide the road actually is). They also engage with cartographic representation of more abstract phenomena such as population density, average food consumption, wealth and water deficiency.

Students' exposure to a range of cartographic styles and functions should increase and include practical everyday map use. For example, they should be able to give directions using a road atlas and use distance markers on the map to calculate cumulative distances between places. They should begin to be competent in the use of rail and bus maps (including transformed maps), timetables and distance charts to plan journeys and compare itineraries. They should also be able to draw conclusions from cartograms (for example, on a world population cartogram, where size of countries is shown proportional not to area but their population, identify countries that have a small area and large population). They should have experience of using world maps with contrasting projections, centred on different parts of the world and comparing these with a globe. They should have a broad understanding of the limitations and properties of some common projections (for example that on a polar projection, every distance away from the South Pole is north).

In addition to interpreting contour patterns for concave and convex slopes and individual geomorphological features, students should be able to visualise the relief of larger tracts of land. They may be helped in this by making a 3D model of the neighbourhood or wider region. A traditional way of doing this is to trace and cut layers of card corresponding to key contours then superimpose these to build a layer model, smoothing the steps with a modelling medium. Such hardware models can now be complemented with digital elevation models that can be manipulated on screen. Students should be able to draw freehand contour sketch maps of idealised landform types (e.g. cliff, drumlin, cuesta and plateau) although many students will need to revisit 3D models as learning support for some landforms that are more difficult to visualise such as hanging valleys and truncated and interlocking spurs. They should be proficient in drawing cross sections across maps at a scale of, say, 1:25,000 or 1:50,000. This is usually done by placing the edge of a piece of paper along the line of a section on the map, marking on the paper where the contours cut its edge and marking every line with the height of the contour. The paper edge is then placed along a pre-prepared base line on graph paper, an appropriate vertical scale selected (usually considerably exaggerated in relation to the horizontal scale), perpendiculars measured to the appropriate height and the marks joined up. This graphical technique enables students to assess intervisibility (whether one point on the map can be seen from another): a critical military skill but one which also has important implications for landscape planning.

Students in this phase continue to make associations between what they learn about the world's physical and human systems and their expression in map form. They identify patterns of similarity and difference. They learn how to use map evidence logically to describe and analyse physical landscapes (for example river patterns, glaciated and limestone land-scapes) and human features (such as land use, settlement patterns and communications). They may do this by relating map information to aerial photographs or satellite images as well as by comparing maps at different scales or those made at different dates. Map evidence can be used to identify regions (e.g. using a world population density map, draw lines around areas that are densely and areas that are sparsely populated) and classify forms (e.g. using a large scale topographic map, classify settlements into linear, dispersed or nucleated types). Maps can be used to make locational recommendations (e.g. the best site for a new factory, shopping mall or sports centre) or to draw inferences (e.g. suggest the history of settlement in a region through the use of place name information).

Students' own map making will continue to develop in this phase with an enhanced appreciation of the use of visual variables and symbol design. Activities might include constructing a set of symbols for use on tourist maps (for example to show locations for swimming, fishing, boating, horse riding, tennis, museums, theatres, etc.) in which pictograms are enclosed in themed geometric shapes (such as squares for cultural activities, circles for water-based activities etc.). These can be drawn, reduced with a photocopier, tested with peers and modified as necessary to give the clearest and most unambiguous symbols possible. Maps should also be designed for different users. For example, a local business might require two forms of map giving directions to its premises: one for the public visiting a showroom (indicating public transport routes and car parking) and another for lorry drivers bringing deliveries (indicating trunk routes and avoiding tight turns). Other forms of mapping include converting information from text to map and making a single summary (précis) map from other, multiple, map sources. A suitable challenge might be to make an annotated map for sailors of Ellen MacArthur's 2005 record-breaking round-the-world voyage. Using diary and photographic evidence from the internet students would mark and label significant winds (westerlies, doldrums, south-east trades) and difficult choices to be made (such as whether to sail further south to take advantage of a shorter route but running the risk of encountering icebergs). Students' maps should contain (as appropriate) the following: a map *title*, the map's *orientation* (e.g. a North pointer), *date*, name of the *author* (who made the decisions about the way the data was represented), map *scale* (shown in a way that is meaningful to the user), a *legend* (or key), an *index*, a *grid* and the *source* of the data used (National Geography Standards, 1994).

By the end of this phase, students should begin to be able to evaluate maps and express their preferences in an informed way as a result of their own map making. They should be able to examine maps critically, taking into account the date and what may have taken place since the map was made. Evaluating map quality and assessing the degree to which a map meets stated needs is not a skill that has traditionally been taught but one which is increasingly important. The enormous numbers of maps that are available online makes it essential that school students are empowered to make an appropriate selection for a particular purpose (such as illustrating a project report, wayfinding or using the map as a source of evidence). A suitable activity might be to select five maps of the same place or on a similar theme from the internet and rank them for quality against a list of criteria.

Learning to use GISystems

Reference was made in the last chapter to *Local Studies* as a simple digital mapping tool popular in primary schools. For secondary school, *AEGIS 3* (see Appendix) is an educational GISystem constructed specifically for classroom use which assembles maps, data, text and multimedia boxes in the form of standard A4 sized interactive worksheets with which students can explore data, solve problems and then readily print. Learning is thus situated in the context of a familiar 'page' format although with standard GIS functionality (for example, vector maps can be drawn or imported at any scale and in a variety of formats and then edited and data displayed). Plate 11 shows a partly completed exemplar worksheet with which students are exploring changes in the economic geography of Italy.

Whatever software is being used it is likely that early learning in GIS will need to be monitored against some key basic skills. These include being able to zoom in and out of the map area, pan in order to slide into view those parts of the map area 'off screen', add labels to features (and change the font size of labels), sort tables in ascending and descending order and select individual records from a table so that they can be identified on the map. Students should be able to make a map for a specified purpose by selecting and adding data, selecting the most appropriate symbology and displaying and printing the map together with the peripheral information a reader needs in order to be able to interpret it (e.g. a title, scale, legend, etc.). Other basic skills include understanding (for example) the operation of the Windows environment and how to save a project. Later, students will learn to operate wizards and drop down dialog boxes in order to fulfil particular display and analytical functions. This might include looking for spatial associations between datasets such as assessing the extent to which one phenomenon is found within a certain distance of another. In the case of the *ArcView* project in Figure 8.5, for example, students could use an enquiry function to calculate the proportion of all earthquakes found within 100 miles of a plate boundary. They can then further refine the query to explore the relationship between the plate boundaries, earthquake magnitude and earthquake depth.

A growing knowledge and experience base will enable teachers to identify where 'bugs' in learning GIScience can occur. In relation to *ArcView*, for example, it is critical for students to understand that themes in the legend (or 'table of contents') are arranged in layers in the same order as they are presented in the map (or 'view'). Themes at the bottom of the list may, therefore, be hidden by those on top. It is also important to appreciate the difference between a theme being 'on' or 'off' and 'active' or 'inactive'. In Plate 2a the themes that are 'ticked' are *on*, i.e. they are potentially visible on the map. The theme which shows the age of buildings by colour is *active*, i.e. it appears 'raised' in the list. This means that information can be obtained about it and actions carried out on it using the tool buttons. Many students fail at the outset to internalise this important difference, which can interrupt the pace of their work and damage their confidence. Another learning bug is failing to understand directionality of data. Does it suggest a better quality of life, for example, to have more doctors per thousand head of the population, or fewer? If the Human Development Index is high does that mean that the level of development is better or worse?

Once students have understood the basic operation of the system they are using they will probably embark on a structured series of curriculum-specific assignments. There are models of these in *Mapping Our World* (Malone, *et al.*, 2002) and *Community Geography* (English and Feaster, 2003). It is important to bear in mind, however, that the purpose of teaching GIScience is to develop spatial reasoning. It's not simply about teaching technical skills, although these are necessary in order to further the aim of higher order thinking. It's about teaching problem solving in contexts as authentic as possible. It's also about helping students to understand the nature of cartographic representation so that they can look with greater criticality at the maps made by others because they have experience of representing data cartographically for themselves.

Beyond age 14

By the middle and later years of secondary schooling, it is anticipated that students will move towards more independent use of maps and GIS as part of geographical enquiry and community projects. Through their own map making they should appreciate that reclassification of data (for example changing the number of classes in the choropleth maps in Plate 9) can affect the map's appearance and therefore begin to understand the nature of subjectivity and bias in cartographic representations, recognising that maps can be used to persuade and misinform. They should be able to select appropriate maps to meet their requirements, for example being able to choose (from a small selection) an appropriate world map to show the extent of Arctic permafrost (a polar projection) or major world ecosystems (an equal area projection). They should increasingly be able to 'decentre', understanding that from space the world has no 'right way up' and that map makers can place any direction they like at the 'top' of the map. This is accompanied by the recognition that many statements we commonly make about the Earth (for example that the North Pole is 'the top of the world' or that Australia is 'down under') are erroneous. Young adults should also appreciate the potential bias in individuals' mental maps, for example that a free recall sketch map of the world drawn by someone in the UK may be quite different from that drawn by someone in Australia.

In this phase it is appropriate for students to be taught to use and interpret maps at multiple scales to analyse associations and patterns, make inferences and predict. They should begin to synthesise data from multiple map sources and use map based evidence to solve problems and make decisions. Appropriate activities include collecting georeferenced environmental data using a GPS receiver, transferring the data points to a spatial database, representing the data in map form and analysing the findings. Young adults should also engage with more advanced wayfinding skills. For example, under suitable supervision and within a safe environment they should have the opportunity to plan a day's walk, of a length appropriate to their age and the terrain, using a large scale topographic map. This activity could include predicting from the map what would be seen *en route* as well as identifying gradients, calculating travel time and evaluating alternative paths (such as a shorter, steeper route compared with a longer one following contours). They should also be able to use route planning software (e.g. *Mappy*, see Appendix) to plan an itinerary with cumulative time and distance information and evaluate the route recommended using other sources such as a road map. Alternative routes, for example avoiding motorways or incorporating scenic sectors, can be considered.

Students should begin to make judgements about the provenance of data by examining metadata files. This involves generating questions about who collected the data and when as well as making an assessment of its reliability. They should use presentation software to display the results of their work. They should have some understanding of the social and economic significance of maps and GIScience, perhaps by experience of seeing how maps and GIS are used in the workplace (e.g. as part of a visit to the local planning department, public service organisation or commercial company).

At the end of Chapter 9 it was suggested that the map activities proposed in this chapter and the two previous ones would be demanding. They are. But if we agree that maps are important and are serious about providing a rigorous programme that will support children and young people's higher order thinking, it is difficult to see what might be omitted. The next chapter examines a neglected aspect of teaching with maps and outlines some of the ways in which teachers can promote good cartographic practice through the maps they make for students.

13 Making better maps for children

Most of this book has been concerned with the evidence for children's ability to read, interpret and use maps. This chapter considers the implications of that evidence for teachers (and others) who need to prepare maps for classroom use. Although much of the guidance offered below is applicable to maps made by hand, the assumption has been made that teachers will increasingly want to prepare maps using any of an increasing number of software applications for drawing, desktop publishing and map making. The main focus will therefore be on teachers using their computer to produce maps that can be printed and copied for students. Reference to specific software has, however, been avoided and the general principles apply equally to maps drawn by hand. Although there is a substantial difference between the needs of, say, 5-, 10- and 15-year-olds, relatively little specific support exists on how to design maps for children and much has to be extrapolated from principles established for adults. Children's own views suggest that they value clarity above all and in particular high contrast, large type and a clear visual hierarchy. They want detail, but they want it clearly structured so that it has strong visual impact (Bartz, 1967b).

Putting maps on the page

Page orientation is largely dependent on the shape of the area to be mapped: Argentina is 'portrait', whereas Turkey is 'landscape'. Landscape format has often been preferred as this is said (Sandford, 1980b) to better match children's page scanning patterns. Whatever the page orientation, there are significant advantages in putting a clear frame around the map area. Frames help to separate the map from its peripheral tools such as scale and legend information. If these tools are to be effective they need to be prominent and, if possible, presented in a predictable place on the page. Framing is a well-established teaching tradition and there is a strong belief among many teachers that maps *must* have frames. An alternative to framing, 'bleeding' maps off the page edge, has been claimed to reinforce the notion of continuity of the Earth's surface (e.g. Klawe, 1965; Sandford, 1980b) but this thought may only occur to children if it's pointed out to them. 'Free floating' maps (i.e. presenting countries as land areas only, unframed, on a 'non-sea' background) can be effective for making comparisons when maps are repeated side by side and this makes economical use of space. This approach to page design can, however, be misleading as islands and other non-contiguous areas can appear to 'belong' to an adjacent map.

Figure 13.1 illustrates these contrasting approaches using the United Kingdom as an example. Map 13.1a shows a 'floating' map of the UK. Omitting geographical context (i.e. the Republic of Ireland and France) makes this a poor choice for younger users who

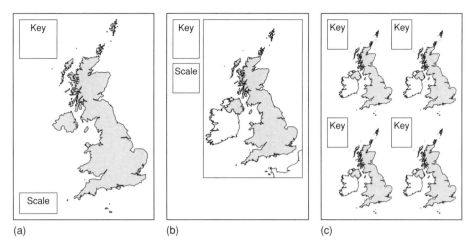

(a)   (b)   (c)

Figure 13.1 Some alternative page layouts for the maps of the United Kingdom.

may perceive Northern Ireland to be an island and the British Isles to be located very far from the mainland of Europe. In Figure 13.1b, the map frame acts as a 'window' on the Earth's surface, enabling the UK to be visualised in its correct geographical context. It is probably more helpful to banish scale and legend information from this window so that, if an alphanumeric grid is provided, column and row 'sight lines' across the map are uninterrupted. Notice that moving scale and legend information outside the frame reduces the map scale. Figure 13.1c illustrates an economical repeat pattern commonly used in atlases for climate or statistical data. The maps 'float' in order to maximise scale but, although the position of the legends helps to separate one map from another, there remains the possibility that some young readers will fail to perceive where one map ends and another begins.

For most children, the dominant visual form on a small scale map is the coastline and therefore sheet lines of land-locked areas should be extended to the coast where it is reasonable to do so in order to help 'fix' the mapped area in the context of recognisable coastline shape (Sandford, 1980a). Effective land and sea differentiation on the map is important for figure–ground discrimination. This is illustrated in Figure 13.2a which shows a coastline, but it is not immediately clear whether the central feature is a south-east–north-west oriented strait or an isthmus. For most British adults the figure–ground puzzle is speedily resolved when the map is reoriented with north at the top (Figure 13.2b) as the shape of south-east England is unmistakeable. Having less experience of viewing the 'bigger picture' of Great Britain, children may not recognise south-east England as part of the whole and will therefore generally find a *locator* helpful in order to place the map area in its wider context. This is likely to be most effective when the viewing area of the map is related to an outline of a whole country or a continent. If the target area of the map is very large, a globe locator can be used but the extent to which this will be helpful depends on children's understanding of the configuration of the Earth's land masses. Bartz (1967a), for example, found that although some children understood that on a globe locator showing Africa, America was 'round the other side', many others did not. Further support for learning, especially for younger children, can be provided by explicitly keying land and sea areas to a legend (e.g. Figure 13.2c). Most support in figure–ground discrimination in this example is probably given when colour (for example, green and blue) is used but

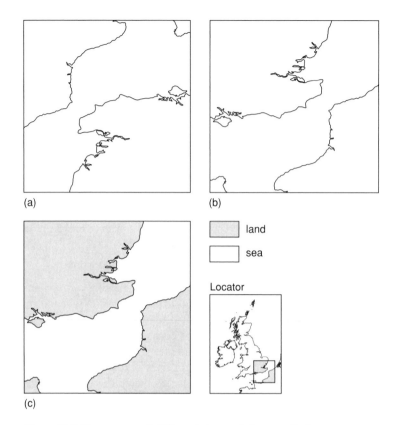

Figure 13.2 Figure–ground differentiation and the use of a locator.

when working in black and white only, the use of 'water lining' (drawing lines parallel to the coastline which decrease in thickness seawards) have been shown to be more effective than a simple line representing the coast or the use of solid black and white fills to distinguish land and/or sea (Head, 1972). Land/sea discrimination can also be supported by the way type is used. A common cartographic convention is to use horizontal lettering on the land area and curved lettering on the sea.

In order to make more effective use of page space, remote or peripheral regions are often shown as insets (for example, on maps of Scotland, the Shetland Islands may be represented on a 'map within a map' further south than their true geographical location). There is some evidence, however, that insets may not be well understood by children (Bartz, 1965) and their use should probably be avoided where possible. Many American schoolchildren appear to have thought that Alaska was an island to the southwest of California as this was the common position of an Alaskan inset, often at a smaller scale, on maps of the coterminous USA before the Alaskan State legislature's request to publishers in January 1990 to place it in its correct geographical context (Holmes, 1992).

Map titles should obviously be comprehensible to young map users. Geography educators have generally preferred concrete titles (*British Isles: a map to show roads and railways*) to more abstract ones (*British Isles: communications*) but the choice depends on the age and experience of users. *Factories* or *Where Things are Made* might be appropriate for age 9, *Manufacturing Industry* for age 13. Titles can often provide more effective focus and raise interest in the map content when they are expressed as questions. Compare, for example, the effect of a rather bland title such as *A Map to Show Nuclear Power Stations* with one that makes a personal appeal to the reader: *How Far do You Live from a Nuclear Power Station?*

Graticules and grids

Much geographical knowledge embedded in the map graticule of meridians and parallels appears sadly to have been lost to school education, at least in the UK. The meridians of longitude, for example, provide information about time (one degree of longitude = 4 minutes, 15 degrees = 1 hour, 360 degrees = 24 hours) and the parallels of latitude provide information about length of day. The graticule also gives clues as to the shape of the Earth and scale of the map. Maps for school commonly have an alphanumeric grid code instead of a graticule. Although these are arbitrary, they may be easier for younger students to use than latitude and longitude coordinates. A common compromise is to embed an alphanumeric code in the 'columns' and 'rows' formed by the meridians and parallels. This can work well where the meridians and parallels are approximately vertical and horizontal (for example on a map of Africa) but can cause difficulties in high latitudes where the meridians bunch together, making use of the grid challenging because the columns change (sometimes substantially) in width across the map. Figure 13.3a illustrates the potential confusion that can occur in labelling alphanumeric grids, especially at the corners of the map frame. If the letters and numbers that form the code are too large they will intrude on map information. If they are too small they will be lost in the map detail. Figure 13.3b shows an attempt to provide additional support for younger users by fixing the letters and numbers more securely to the map frame and making the row and column directionality more explicit by 'pointers'.

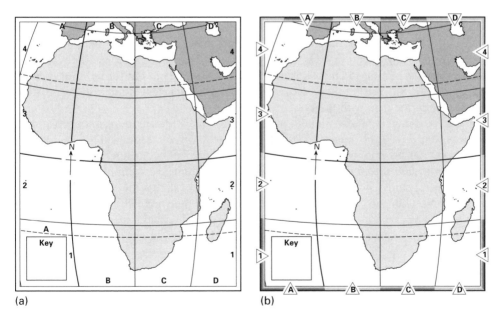

(a)   (b)

Figure 13.3 Supporting students' use of coordinates. Figure 13.3b adapted from the *Oxford Primary Atlas*, copyright © 2004 Oxford University Press, reproduced by permission of Oxford University Press.

Showing scale information

Children often assume that if maps fill the same size pages (such as an A4 sized worksheet) the areas they represent must all be at the same scale (Bartz, 1965). Scale information should, therefore, be highly conspicuous on the page and preferably in a predictable place. Unfamiliar terms (e.g. statute miles) should be avoided. It seems likely that children's understanding of scale is better supported when round values are used in the representative fraction (such as 1:1,000,000) or scale statement (One centimetre on the map represents 100 kilometres on the ground). Graphic scales that have numbered distances *above* the scale bar rather than below are better for measuring with a ruler or straight edge as the numbers are not obscured (see Figure 7.1). It may be unhelpful to put a scale bar on a world map as the scale is generally only true for the equator and the presence of a graphic scale can encourage children to measure non-equatorial distances inappropriately.

For large scale maps, scale may be effectively shown by reference to distances the reader knows. A map of an unfamiliar locality might, for example, have a line annotated as being the same distance as from school to a familiar location (*This distance is the same as from the school to the swimming baths*). For small scale maps a comparator is necessary (see Figure 11.2).

How much detail to show?

Students and teachers often consider maps for school to be 'too cluttered, too crowded, too cramped, too complicated and too confusing' (Keller *et al.*, 1995: 417). There is an interesting cartographic relationship, however, between impact (which implies less detail) and information (which implies more detail) but also a paradox involving young readers. The more information there is on the map, the more difficult it is to locate the name you are looking for but the more likely that, once located, the name will make a more secure connection between the map and places that you know in the real world. Children searching a simplified map that only has large cities marked will not find the smaller town or suburb in which they live – so finding it on a more detailed map may be worth the additional effort. Sandford argues for more towns to be marked but for fewer of them to be named (1978), creating the impression of higher settlement density in some areas but not cluttering the map with unnecessary text.

Maps for younger children should generally show single distributions of concrete phenomena (e.g. a map showing the location of castles). With increasing age, more complex symbology can be employed, for example a dot map to show livestock so that one dot represents 10,000 sheep. Older children will be able to interpret multiple relationships in symbology (such as circles on seaports drawn proportionally to the volume of tonnage handled and subdivided into imports and exports). The potential difficulty of interpreting relationships between more abstract phenomena (e.g. a choropleth map showing receipts from tourism as a percentage of gross national product) should not be underestimated.

Symbology and legends

A major design goal in developing maps for children is to provide age-appropriate support for the detection, discrimination, identification and interpretation of symbols (Keates, 1996). Symbols can be detected more easily if they have bold keylines and there are clearly recognisable differences between visual variables such as hue and shape. Children are said

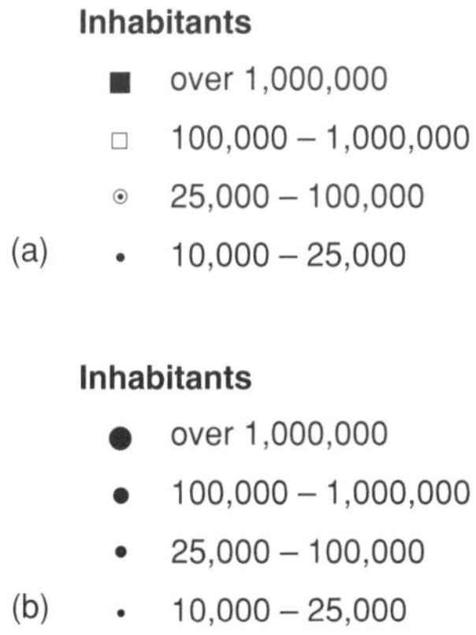

Inhabitants

■   over 1,000,000

□   100,000 – 1,000,000

◉   25,000 – 100,000

(a)   •   10,000 – 25,000

Inhabitants

●   over 1,000,000

●   100,000 – 1,000,000

•   25,000 – 100,000

(b)   •   10,000 – 25,000

Figure 13.4 Contrasting hierarchies of settlement symbols.

to prefer bright colours with strong contrast (Sorrell, 1974) and there are classroom advantages in using colours that can be simply named and are thus easily referred to (e.g. yellow and red rather than cream and beige). The visibility of point symbols for young map users can be enhanced by use of two colours (e.g. a yellow fill within a black outline) that provide strong contrast across a wide range of background hues (Potash, 1977).

Discrimination of symbols can be supported by exaggeration of differences between points, lines and areas. For example, as children's perception of size differences is often limited, point symbols for towns may need, additionally, to be differentiated by shape and fill (Figure 13.4a as compared with 13.4b). Discrimination between thematic point symbols appears to work best when there is a combination of pictographic elements within a geometric frame so that the pictogram interior carries meaning and the geometric frame supports the user's ability to locate the symbol amongst others (Forrest and Castner, 1985). Pictorial symbols may also need to be age-appropriate. In a children's atlas of Bulgaria (a country where tobacco production is high and many people smoke) an image of a pipe, instead of a cigarette, was used to represent tobacco cultivation. The pipe image (see Plate 10), although perhaps less obvious as a symbol, was judged by the editor as less likely to promote smoking among children than that of a cigarette (Bandrova, 2003). Bandrova also describes how some picture symbols in her atlas were constructed so that they combine several elements in order to clarify what was being represented, for example the addition of a saw blade to the image of a tree in order to increase the likelihood of the symbol being interpreted as timber (not forestry) and the addition of a 'dry dock' to the image of a ship in order to suggest shipbuilding and repairing (not a port). Readers who are not Bulgarian speakers may like to put themselves in the position of a student with reading difficulties and assess the extent to which the other symbols in the legend illustrated in Plate 10 are self explanatory.

Some symbol interpretation may be supported by additional text support in the legend. Children may assume, for example, on a political map (where, say, five colours are used arbitrarily to distinguish countries) that countries sharing a colour have something in common. In this situation a legend note (e.g. *Colours only show where one country ends and another begins*) is useful. Other legend support can be provided by visual images. For example, land height categories (mountains, moors and uplands, hills, low land) can be illustrated by photographs surrounding the map that are 'tagged' with the relevant land

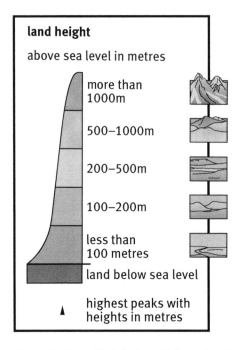

Figure 13.5 Land height legend from the *Oxford Primary Atlas*, copyright © 2004 Oxford University Press, reproduced by permission of Oxford University Press.

height colour. In Figure 13.5 additional support in the form of pictograms has been added to the land height legend in order to reinforce the association between land height colour and topography. Where numerical values are identified in the legend (such as *Land below 100m* or *Temperatures over 30°C*) these can be complemented by descriptive category labels (such as *low land* and *hot places*).

Supporting map reading through type

The legibility of type on maps has been investigated in a number of studies but generally with inconclusive results. Much discussion has focused on font, such as whether type is easier to read if it has serifs (slight projections finishing off the strokes of printed letters, as in **T**, compared to the sans serif **T**). Bartz (1970b) found little variation in the time adolescents took to find place names when all the labels on the map were set in the same style (e.g. all in a serif, or sans serif, or bold, or condensed, face), nor when all names were set in capitals or in upper and lower case. She concluded that none of the fonts used was superior and that 'cartographers can feel relatively free to make choices from a relatively wide spectrum of available type' (1970b: 107). By contrast, in tests with Australian and English children, Gerber (1982) found that fastest search times were achieved using a map on which names were shown in the sans serif typeface Univers with the largest settlements shown in bold condensed type (this typeface was also most preferred by young users). Sandford (1978) also suggests that a sans serif typeface is more effective, although with undergraduates Phillips *et al.* (1975) found that search times were generally faster with maps using Times New Roman (which uses serifs) and that bold was no more legible than

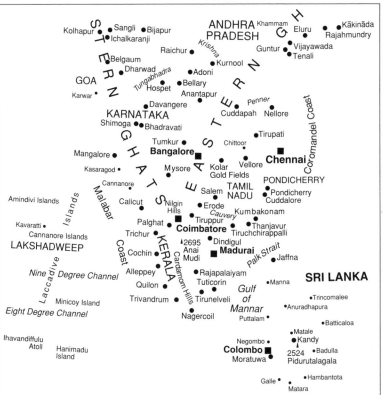

Figure 13.6 Sample of school atlas type from the *Oxford Student Atlas*, copyright © 2002 Oxford University Press, reproduced by permission of Oxford University Press.

medium weight type. Names set in upper case are generally said to be more difficult to read than names set in lower case with an initial capital. Lower case is considered easier because the ascenders and descenders of letters help word recognition by forming a recognisable silhouette. Another issue, often raised by teachers, is whether the letter **A** in lower case should be 'open' (a) or 'closed' (ɑ). Many books for younger children use the closed form yet this is easily confused with the letter o when, as is often the case with maps, the type is small. The position of map features (such as settlements or administrative areas) within a hierarchy (e.g. city, town, village) is generally indicated by size of type. It has been suggested (Miller, 1982) that young children find it difficult to discriminate between more than three or four sizes of type.

As empirical evidence is inconclusive, professional map designers tend to rely principally on experience and informed judgement about what is effective. Thus the *Junior Atlas of Alberta* (Wonders, 1980) made use of Century School Book for page title, questions, statements and text and Univers for the map face and for graphics. Figure 13.6 shows a selection of type used in the *Oxford Student Atlas* in which settlements and administrative areas are shown in Univers and physical features in Photina.

Readability of type is significantly enhanced when the map user has some expectation of the typographic appearance of the name searched for. When scanning for place names,

Figure 13.7 Background affects legibility of type.

readers make use of the first letters of each word in deciding whether to 'reject' and move on to the next word or 'examine further'. The use of differentiated typeface enables readers to reject 'non-relevant' words more efficiently but only if they have some understanding of the typographical 'code' that gives clues to word meaning. This can be provided through the legend entries, for example:

AUSTRALIA Countries are shown in letters like this
Melbourne Cities are shown in letters like this

Readability is also affected by the amount of visual contrast between type and the background on which it appears. To increase legibility, use of type over intense colours or dark shaded areas should be avoided, as should intercutting of type (one place name cutting through another) and the coincidence of vertical lines such as railways, boundaries and grid lines with the vertical elements of each letter's form. Note that long labels may be spread over several background colours resulting in key symbols and/or letters becoming lost, especially for insecure readers (see Figure 13.7). Lead lines (lines joining text to features), used sparingly, can also support legibility.

The *positioning* of labels on the map profoundly affects children's interpretation of them. Some well established principles of type placement (Imhof, 1975) are particularly significant for children. Name labels should be clearly associated visually with the features to which they belong. The established convention is that type is placed horizontally on large scale maps and parallel with lines of latitude on small scale maps. However, for very young children it is probably preferable that type is positioned horizontally regardless of scale as this conforms more to their expectations of how words are written. Where possible it is best to position the name to the right of, and slightly above, the symbol so that the symbol is 'read' first, followed by the label as in position 1 in Figure 13.8a. Where this cannot be achieved because of other map detail, positions 2–6 may be appropriate, although not all are equally good. In positions 7 and 8 the town stamp may become unhelpfully visually 'incorporated' into the text, making the label less legible. Figure 13.8b illustrates the need for careful spacing of type to avoid misinterpretation of 'double-barrelled' place names by young readers.

Linear features such as rivers should have their names placed along the line (horizontally where possible) but the letters should not be too widely spaced. The name should not be cut by the linear symbol itself (as in Figure 13.9a). Labelling above the line is preferable to below, as there are potentially fewer descenders than ascenders in the Roman alphabet to interfere with the linework, but the label must not be too close to the line (Figure 13.9b). Type should also be positioned so that competing linear symbols do not intervene (Figure 13.9c).

Labels for area features such as countries, mountain ranges, oceans and physical regions should be placed within the area to which they refer (whether this is defined on the map

(a)

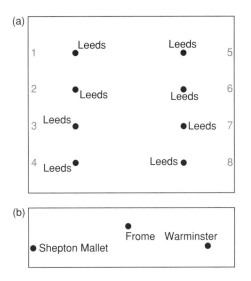

(b)

Figure 13.8 Some contrasting positions of type for point symbols (after Imhof, 1975).

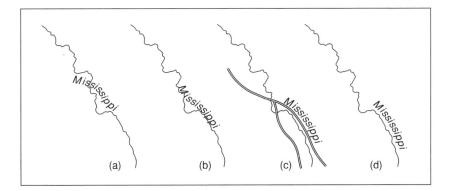

Figure 13.9 Some contrasting positions of type for linear symbols (after Imhof, 1975).

or not) so that they comfortably fill the area. This makes the extent of the area clear. Areas often overlap, in which case the hierarchy can be shown by size and boldness of type. There is a strong case for labelling areas more compactly than Imhof (1975) recommends as children are less able to accommodate to different letter spacing than adults. Where possible, type should be aligned left to right. Figure 13.10 illustrates poor (a) and better (b) practice in relation to labelling the British Isles. Where space is tight the use of abbreviations (with the full form available in an explanatory note) is preferable to using a numerical key as letters provide more of a clue to the full form of the word than numbers.

Labelling geographical names

Geographical names may have many different forms (Kadmon, 2000). *Endonyms* are the names by which places are known in the local language, for example, Praha, not Prague.

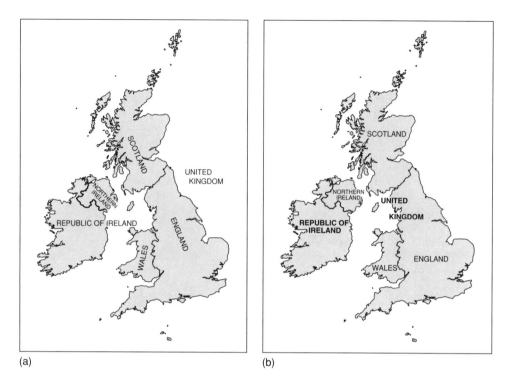

(a)   (b)

Figure 13.10 Some contrasting positions of type for areas.

In multi-lingual societies alternative versions (*allonyms*) are often in use (e.g. Bruxelles and Brussel). But people living outside the local language area may be more familiar with place names as they are commonly known in their own language (*exonyms*). Thus English speakers will recognise Warsaw (not Warszawa) and French speakers Londres (not London). The United Nations, through its Group of Experts on Geographical Names (UNGEGN) promotes the use of standardised names in order to reduce confusion and this may seem an obvious strategy to adopt when naming places. Young users, however, need to connect their everyday, non-standardised, experiences with the words they read on the map. It is, as Sandford (1990) says, unnecessarily complicated to use the standardised name of Baile Atha Cliath for the city most non-Irish speakers know as Dublin. Similarly, few young people will recognise al-Qahirah as Cairo. However, the place name strategy adopted will probably vary according to the age of the target readership. Consider the following German towns and cities and their anglicised equivalents.

German	Anglicised
Hameln	Hamelin
Hannover	Hanover
Braunschweig	Brunswick
München	Munich
Nürnberg	Nuremberg
Köln	Cologne

Three strategies are possible in labelling these towns and cities on the map: all German (with the merit of avoiding ethnocentrism and supporting the language skills of those students who may be learning German); all anglicised (with the merit of using forms that may be more familiar to young readers); or a mixture of each. It could, for example, be argued that the first three (smaller) towns should be presented in their standardised form as the anglicised versions are largely historical, although this is unlikely to help the teacher and children who are, in another lesson, reading Robert Browning's *The Pied Piper of Hamelin* ('Hamelin Town's in Brunswick/By famous Hanover city . . .'). Loyalty to the anglicised forms of the last three cities may be more difficult to dislodge and avoids reading difficulties that might arise with young readers unfamiliar with the umlaut. Yet for older readers we might expect to see both versions – either as Cologne (Köln), or Köln (Cologne). The choice also depends on prevailing attitudes, which may change over time. In the UK, there was a significant trend towards reducing ethnocentrism in geography education in the 1970s and 1980s and the greater use of endonyms in atlases and school books. The advent of the National Curriculum, however, from 1991 seems to have been accompanied by a reversion to greater emphasis on English exonyms. It goes without saying, of course, that place names should be up-to-date (thus Mumbai, not Bombay; Chennai, not Madras).

This chapter has provided guidance on how maps may best be prepared for young readers, taking into account available evidence and good cartographic practice. The final chapter draws some conclusions about learning and teaching with maps.

14 Conclusion

This book has attempted to draw together the evidence for children and young people's thinking with maps and to use it as a basis for generating appropriate learning activities. The discussion has been presented in the context of fundamental changes that have taken place in the art, science and technology of cartography. There remain, however, a number of significant paradoxes and unresolved issues in relation to learning and teaching with maps. Maps are increasingly important in the real world yet the status of map learning in school seems even less secure now than in the past. Maps in the workplace are increasingly digital yet, despite massive investment in school hardware and teacher training in ICT, the take-up of digital cartography in education has been limited. Perhaps the most significant adult use of a map is to find the way, yet this is a skill not generally taught at school. Conversely, some school mapping tasks appear to have little practical utility for the world of work. Small scale maps, because of their greater generalisation, can be regarded as significantly more challenging for learners yet teachers generally assume that they are unproblematic in the classroom. The role of visual variables in determining how maps represent information is generally not recognised by teachers, yet this is a key understanding that children need in order to make their own maps, particularly when selecting from the wide range of options available to them in mapping software. Geography teachers, despite being under considerable pressure from competing curriculum areas, have not appeared to capitalise on the enormous potential of GIS: one of their subject's most distinctive 'unique selling points'.

Teachers, researchers, curriculum developers, cartographers and geographic information scientists need to respond to the challenges presented by these paradoxes. We need a clearer view of children's learning with maps and spatial information so that we can identify where the 'bugs' in learning are likely to occur and how we can best plan for effective teaching. We know that map learning starts early, but that it is not as well developed in infancy as some have suggested. In each phase of education, children's conceptual grasp will be partial. Learning is likely to be more effective where teachers are able to identify 'what comes next' in relation to cartographic concepts and skills and match this to children's cognitive development. In constructing a more robust map pedagogy, however, we need a better understanding of which concepts and tasks are more difficult than others. Some 'top level' features of map learning can reasonably be predicted. Projective and Euclidean spatial relationships, for example, are likely to be mastered after topological ones and correspondences between elements on the map and those in the real world are more likely to be identified when the map is aligned with the environment it represents than when it is not. Other aspects of children's interactions with maps are less well established. For example, we know relatively little about children's understanding of how information is represented on small scale maps, of how visual variables operate or of the interrelationship between map scale and generalisation.

We need more evidence for 'what works' at the level of detailed teaching strategy. In particular, we need to identify progression in learning and teaching in relation to new technological tools. How, for example, can we most advantageously deploy the potential of digital elevation models in helping children understand landforms and their representation on maps? How does being able to reposition symbols when using software to make a map of the neighbourhood sharpen children's appreciation of spatial relationships in the locality? What are the steps by which teachers can reliably scaffold students' learning of how to represent and interpret information using GIS functions? We also need a revision of our map related curricula. This includes reconceptualising some traditional topics as well as filling gaps that have now become evident in the typical school curriculum. For example, practice in using grid references is now surely more appropriately set in the broader context of multiple approaches to identifying location, including searching digital maps by postcode and using a handheld GPS receiver to establish geographical coordinates. Measuring distance using a straight edge on a paper map is a skill that now needs to be complemented by using a distance (and area) measuring tool on a digital map. As well as understanding what the symbols mean, children need to be able to interpret the typographical code of map text. Proliferation of cartographic resources implies that map 'reading' by children now needs to be supplemented by an understanding of the appropriate criteria by which to select a map for a specified purpose and evaluate it.

Professional cartographers and GI scientists will have a role to play in implementing these changes by promoting a better understanding of how maps work and disseminating good practice in making maps for children. But stronger collaboration between educators and cartographers would be welcome. Atlas editors, for example, need to be more alert to potential misconceptions by young users, such as their misinterpretation of legend information or insensitivity to the limitations of an equatorial scale. Teacher involvement in the development of map materials and trialling in schools would help ensure that educational cartographic products are age-appropriate. A more effective dialogue between teachers and software developers will be required before we can make significant improvements to the mapping software currently available for educational use.

There are some significant practical challenges to be overcome. How, for example, are we to teach wayfinding with maps in real world environments whilst having due regard to the health and safety of students off site? The 'local' nature of learning with large scale maps, especially for young children, means that teachers cannot rely on published textbook materials, so how can we best support non-specialist teachers in primary schools to develop their own schemes of work and cartographic resources based on the catchment area of their school? There are significant resource implications for the purchase of maps, aerial photographs, atlases and globes. This is especially true of GIS software and associated costs of training teachers how to use it.

There are, however, grounds for optimism. A new generation of teachers, skilled in ICT and experienced in GIS, is entering the profession. Interactive whiteboards are rapidly appearing in classrooms offering enormous potential for enhanced map learning. The availability of online maps and mapping tools is increasing rapidly. National mapping organisations are making digital and hard copy maps available at no or low cost to schools. And maps continue to be popular with children. They maintain their appeal as an intriguing form of communication that offers children opportunities for systematic learning as well as for imagination and fantasy. Map reading and interpretation, at whatever level, are readily seen by children as skills worth having.

We can be confident that maps are going to become ever more significant in the workplace and in recreational activity. The response from schools has to be to position cartography and geo-information science in the curriculum more securely so that children and young people are properly equipped for a world increasingly dependent on maps.

Appendix

Websites of organisations and resources referred to in the text
(All accessed 13 May 2005)

AEGIS 3 (The Advisory Unit: Computers in Education)
  http://www.advisory-unit.org.uk/aegis3.html

Cartography and Children Commission of the International Cartographic Association
  http://lazarus.elte.hu/ccc/ccc.htm

Degree Confluence Project
  http://www.confluence.org/

ESRI (Schools and Libraries)
  http://www.esri.com/industries/k-12/

ESRI Canada (Schools and Libraries)
  http://k12.esricanada.com/index.html

ESRI UK (Schools)
  http://www.esriuk.com/solutions/schools/intro.asp

International Cartographic Association
  http://www.icaci.org/

INTACT
  http://www.surrey.ac.uk/~pss1su/intact/

Local Studies (Soft Teach)
  http://www.soft-teach.co.uk/

Mapping for the Visually Impaired
  http://tactile.nrcan.gc.ca/

Mappy
  http://www.mappy.com/

Mapquest
  http://www.mapquest.com/

Multimap
  http://www.multimap.com/

National Atlas of the United States
  http://nationalatlas.gov/

Ordnance Survey (Education)
   http://www.ordnancesurvey.co.uk/oswebsite/education/

Orton Family Foundation
   http://www.orton.org/programs/mapping/

Oxford Student Atlas
   http://www.oup.co.uk/oxed/secondary/geography/atlases/

Sport and Playbase Ltd
   http://www.sportandplaybase.co.uk/home_page.htm

Textease (Softease)
   http://www.softease.com/textease.htm

United States Geological Survey (USGS) (Education)
   http://www.usgs.gov/education/

Wildgoose (*Getmapping* aerial photography at educational prices)
   http://www.wgoose.co.uk/

Bibliography

Acredolo, L. (1976) 'Frames of reference used by children for orientation in unfamiliar spaces', in G. Moore and R. Golledge (eds) *Environmental Knowing: Theories, Research and Methods*, Stroudsburg, PA: Dowden, Hutchinson and Ross.

Anderson, J.M. (1996) 'What does that little black rectangle mean? Designing maps for the young elementary school child', in C.H. Wood and C.P. Keller (eds) *Cartographic Design: Theoretical and Practical Perspectives*, Chichester: Wiley.

Axia, G., Bremner, J.G., Deluca, P. and Andreason, G. (1998) 'Children drawing Europe: the effects of nationality, age and teaching', *British Journal of Developmental Psychology*, 16: 423–37.

Baker, T.R. and Bednarz, S.W. (2003) 'Lessons learned from reviewing research in GIS education', *Journal of Geography*, 102: 231–3.

Baker, T.R. and White, S.H. (2003) 'The effects of GIS on students' attitudes, self-efficacy and achievement in middle school science classrooms', *Journal of Geography*, 102: 243–54.

Balchin, W.G. and Coleman, A.M. (1973) 'Graphicacy should be the fourth ace in the pack', in J. Bale, N. Graves and R. Walford (eds) *Perspectives in Geographical Education*, Edinburgh: Oliver & Boyd.

Bandrova, T. (2003) 'Atlas Rodinoznanie', *International Research in Geographical and Environmental Education*, 12: 354–8.

Bartz, B.S. (1965) 'Map design for children', unpublished report, Field Enterprises Educational Corporation.

—— (1967a) 'Evaluation of two-color political maps in the World Book', unpublished report, Field Enterprises Educational Corporation.

—— (1967b) 'What about Illinois? Or, children and a reference map', unpublished report, Field Enterprises Educational Corporation.

—— (1970a) 'Maps in the classroom', *Journal of Geography*, 69: 18–24.

—— (1970b) 'Experimental use of the search task in an analysis of type legibility in cartography', *The Cartographic Journal*, 7: 103–12.

—— (1971) 'Designing maps for children', in H.W. Castner and G. McGrath (eds) *Map Design and the Map User*, Cartographica Monograph No. 2 (Papers from the Symposium on the Influence of the Map User on Map Design), Kingston, Canada, September 1970.

Bednarz, S.W. and Audet, R.H. (1999) 'The status of GIS technology in teacher preparation programs', *Journal of Geography*, 98: 60–7.

Bertin, J. (1983) *Semiology of Graphics*, Madison, WI: University of Wisconsin Press.

Biel, A. and Torell, G. (1979) 'The mapped environment: cognitive aspects of children's drawings', *Man–Environment Systems*, 9: 187–94.

Black, J. (1997) *Maps and History*, Newhaven, CT: Yale University Press.

Blades, M. (1990) 'The reliability of data collected from sketch maps', *Journal of Environmental Psychology*, 10: 327–39.

—— (1991a) 'The development of the abilities required to understand spatial representations', in D.M. Mark and A.V. Frank (eds) *Cognitive and Linguistic Aspects of Geographic Space*, Dordrecht: Kluwer Academic Press.

—— (1997) 'Research paradigms and methodologies for investigating children's wayfinding', in N. Foreman and R. Gillett (eds) *Handbook of Spatial Research Paradigms and Methodologies. Volume 1: Spatial Cognition in the Child and Adult*, Hove: Psychology Press.

Blades, M. and Medlicott, L. (1992) 'Developmental differences in the ability to give route directions from a map', *Journal of Environmental Psychology*, 12: 175–85.

Blades, M. and Spencer, C.P. (1986a) 'Map use by young children', *Geography*, 71: 47–52.

—— (1986b) 'Map use in the environment and educating children to use maps', *Environmental Education and Information*, 5: 187–204.

—— (1987a) The use of maps by 4–6 year old children in a large-scale maze, *British Journal of Developmental Psychology*, 5: 19–24.

—— (1987b) 'How do people use maps to navigate through the world?', *Cartographica*, 24: 64–75.

—— (1989a) 'Young children's ability to use coordinate references', *Journal of Genetic Psychology*, 150: 5–18.

—— (1989b) 'Children's wayfinding and map using abilities', *Scientific Journal of Orienteering*, 5: 48–60.

—— (1990) 'The development of 3–6 year olds' map using ability: the relative importance of landmarks and map alignment', *Journal of Genetic Psychology*, 151: 181–94.

—— (1994) 'The development of children's ability to use spatial representations', *Advances in Child Development and Behavior*, 25: 157–97.

Blades, M., Blaut, J.M., Darvizeh, Z., Elguea, S., Sowden, S., Soni, D. *et al.* (1998) 'A cross-cultural study of young children's mapping abilities', *Transactions of the Institute of British Geographers*, 23: 269–77.

Blades, M., Spencer, C., Plester, B. and Desmond, K. (2003) 'Young children's recognition and representation of urban landscapes, in G. Allen (ed.) *Human Spatial Memory: Remembering Where*, Mahwah, NJ: Lawrence Erlbaum.

Blaut, J.M. (1991) 'Natural mapping', *Transactions of the Institute of British Geographers*, 16: 55–74.

Blaut, J.M., McCleary, G.S. and Blaut, A.S. (1970) 'Environmental mapping in young children', *Environment and Behavior*, 2: 335–49.

Blaut, J.M. and Stea, D. (1971) 'Studies of geographic learning', *Annals of the Association of American Geographers*, 61: 387–93.

—— (1974) 'Mapping at the age of three', *Journal of Geography*, 73: 5–9.

Bloom, B.S. (ed.) (1956) *Taxonomy of Educational Objectives: The Classification of Educational Goals: Handbook 1, Cognitive Domain*, New York: Longman.

Bluestein, N. and Acredolo, L.P. (1979) 'Developmental changes in map reading skills', *Child Development*, 50: 691–7.

Boardman, D. (1974) 'Objectives and constraints on geographical fieldwork', *Journal of Curriculum Studies*, 6: 158–66.

—— (1983) *Graphicacy and Geography Teaching*, London: Croom Helm.

—— (1988) 'The impact of a curriculum project: geography for the young school leaver', *Educational Review* Occasional Publication 14. Birmingham: University of Birmingham.

—— (1989) 'The development of graphicacy: children's understanding of maps', *Geography*, 74: 321–31.

Boardman, D. and Towner, E. (1979) *Reading Ordnance Survey Maps: Some Problems of Graphicacy*. Birmingham: Teaching Research Unit, Department of Curriculum Studies, Faculty of Education, University of Birmingham.

Brewster, S. and Blades, M. (1989) 'Which way to go? Children's ability to give directions in the environment and from maps', *Environmental Education and Information*, 8: 141–56.

Bruner, J.S. (1966) *Towards a Theory of Instruction*, New York: W.W. Norton.

Buttenfield, B. and McMaster, R. (1991) *Map Generalisation*, Harlow: Longman.

Castner, H.W. (1987) 'Education through mapping: a new role for the school atlas?', *Cartographica*, 24: 82–100.

—— (1990) *Seeking New Horizons: A Perceptual Approach to Geographic Education*, Montreal and Kingston: McGill-Queen's University Press.

—— (1997) 'Modifying our view of geography in light of research in spatial development', in R.G. Boehm and J.F. Petersen (eds) *The First Assessment: Research in Geographic Education*, San Marcos, TX: Gilbert Grosvenor Center for Geographic Education.

Castner, H.W. and Wheate, R. (1979) 'Re-assessing the role played by shaded relief in topographic scale maps', *The Cartographic Journal*, 16: 77–85.

Catling, S. (1978) 'The child's spatial conception and geographic education', *Journal of Geography*, 77: 24–8.

—— (1979) 'Maps and cognitive maps: the young child's perception', *Geography*, 64: 288–96.

—— (1981) 'Using maps and aerial photographs', in D. Mills (ed.) *Geographical Work in Primary and Middle Schools*, Sheffield: The Geographical Association.

—— (1992) *Mapstart*, 2nd edn, Books 1–3, Harlow: Collins-Longman.

—— (1996) 'Technical interest in curriculum development: a programme of map skills', in M. Williams (ed.) *Understanding Geographical and Environmental Education: The Role of Research*, London: Cassell.

—— (1998) 'Children as mapmakers', in S. Scoffham (ed.) *Primary Sources: Research Findings in Primary Geography*, Sheffield: The Geographical Association.

Catling, S. and Martin, F. (eds) (2004) *Researching Primary Geography*, London: Register of Research in Primary Geography.

Coluccia, E. and Louse, G. (2004) 'Gender differences in spatial orientation: a review', *Journal of Environmental Psychology*, 24(3): 329–40.

Dabbs, J.M., Chang, E-Lee, Strong, R.A. and Milun, R. (1997) 'Spatial ability, navigation strategy and geographic knowledge among men and women', *Evolution and Human Behavior*, 19: 89–98.

Daggs, D.G. (1986) 'Pyramid of places: children's understanding of geographic hierarchy', unpublished M.S. thesis, State College, PA, Pennsylvania State University.

Dale, P.F. (1971) 'Children's reactions to maps and aerial photographs', *Area*, 3: 170–7.

Dalke, D.E. (1998) 'Charting the development of representational skills: when do children know that maps can lead and mislead?', *Cognitive Development*, 13: 53–72.

DeLoache, J.S. (1987) 'Rapid change in the symbolic functioning of young children', *Science*, 238: 1556–7.

—— (1989) 'The development of representation in young children', in H.W. Reese (ed.) *Advances in Child Development and Behavior*, San Diego, CA: Academic Press.

—— (1991) 'Young children's understanding of models', in R. Fivush and J. Hudson (eds) *Knowing and Remembering in Young Children*, New York: Cambridge University Press.

—— (1995) 'Early understanding and use of symbols: the model model', *Current Directions in Psychological Science*, 4: 109–13.

DeLoache, J.S., Kolstad, V. and Anderson K.N. (1991) 'Physical similarity and young children's understanding of scale models', *Child Development*, 62: 111–26.

DeLoache, J.S., Miller, K., Rosengren, K. and Bryant, N. (1997) 'The credible shrinking room: very young children's performance with symbolic and non-symbolic relations', *Psychological Science*, 8: 303–13.

DeLucia, A.A. and Hiller, D.W. (1982) 'Natural legend design for thematic maps', *The Cartographic Journal*, 19: 46–52.

Dove, J.E., Everett, L.A. and Preece, P.F.W. (1999) 'Exploring a hydrological concept through children's drawings', *International Journal of Science Education*, 21: 485–97.

Dow, G. and Pick, H. (1992) 'Young children's use of models and photographs as spatial representations', *Cognitive Development*, 7: 351–63.

Downs, R.M. (1985) 'The representation of space: its development in children and in cartography', in R. Cohen (ed.) *The Development of Spatial Cognition*, Hillsdale, NJ: Lawrence Erlbaum.

Downs, R.M., Liben, L.S. and Daggs, D.G. (1988) 'On education and geographers: the role of cognitive development theory in geographic education', *Annals of the Association of American Geographers*, 78: 680–700.

Downs, R.M. and Siegel, A.W. (1981) 'On mapping researchers mapping children mapping space', in L. Liben, A.H. Patterson and N. Newcombe (eds) *Spatial Representation and Behavior Across the Lifespan*, New York: Academic Press.

Dupre, A. and O'Neil-Gilbert, M. (1985) 'Town and country children's macro-space cognitive representation: a comparative study', *Children's Environments Quarterly*, 2: 27–33.

Elg, M. (2003) 'The cartography of a school atlas', poster presented at the 21st International Cartographic Conference, International Cartographic Association, 10–16 August, Durban.

English, K.Z. and Feaster, L.S. (2003) *Community Geography: GIS in Action*, Redlands, CA: ESRI Press.

Fairbairn, D.J. (1993) 'On the nature of cartographic text', *The Cartographic Journal*, 30: 104–11.

Filippakopoulou, V.P. (2002) 'Comparing children's sketch maps of the British Isles and Greece', in Proceedings of the 1st Ibero-Latin American Symposium on Cartography and Children, 7–10 August, Rio de Janeiro.

Flavell, J.H., Green, F.L. and Flavell, E.R. (1985) 'The road not taken: understanding the implications of initial uncertainty in evaluating spatial directions', *Developmental Psychology*, 21: 207–16.

Forrest, D. and Castner, H.W. (1985) 'The design and perception of point symbols for tourist maps', *The Cartographic Journal*, 22: 11–19.

Freundschuh, S. (1990) 'Can young children use maps to navigate?', *Cartographica*, 27: 54–66.

Gagné, R.M. (1965) *The Conditions of Learning*, New York: Holt, Rinehart, Winston.

Gardiner, A. and Perkins, C. (1996) 'Teaching touch on the towpath: a tactile map for a visit to the countryside', *The Cartographic Journal*, 33: 111–18.

—— (2003) '"Here is the beech tree!" Understanding tactile maps in the field', *The Cartographic Journal*, 40: 277–82.

Gerber, R. (1981) 'Young children's understanding of the elements of maps', *Teaching Geography*, 6: 128–33.

—— (1982) 'An international study of children's perception and understanding of type used on atlas maps', *The Cartographic Journal*, 19: 115–21.

—— (1984) 'Factors affecting the competence and performance in cartographic language for children at the concrete level of map reasoning', *Cartography*, 13: 205–13.

—— (1992) 'Is mapping in schools reflecting developments in cartography and geographical information?', in M. Naish (ed.) *Geography and Education: National and International Perspectives*, London: University of London Institute of Education.

Gerber, R. and Kwan, T. (1994) 'A phenomenographical approach to the study of pre-adolescents' use of maps in a wayfinding exercise in a suburban environment', *Journal of Environmental Psychology*, 14: 265–80.

Gilmartin, P.P. and Patton, J.C. (1984) 'Comparing the sexes on spatial abilities: map use skills', *Annals of the Association of American Geographers*, 74: 605–19.

Golbeck, S.L., Rand, M. and Soundy, C. (1986) 'Constructing a model of a large scale space with the space in view: effects on preschoolers of guidance and cognitive restructuring', *Merrill-Palmer Quarterly*, 32: 187–203.

Golledge, R.G. (ed.) (1999) *Wayfinding Behavior: Cognitive Mapping and Other Spatial Processes*, Baltimore, MD: Johns Hopkins Press.

Golledge, R.G., Pellegrino, J.W., Gale, N. and Doherty, S. (1991) 'Acquisition and integration of route knowledge', *National Geographical Journal of India*, 37: 130–46.

Golledge, R.G., Smith, T.R., Pellegrino, J.W., Doherty, S. and Marshall, S.P. (1985) 'A conceptual model and empirical analysis of children's acquisition of spatial knowledge', *Journal of Environmental Psychology*, 5: 125–52.

Griffin, M.M. (1995) 'You can't get there from here: situated learning, transfer and map skills', *Contemporary Educational Psychology*, 20: 650–87.

Halpern, D.F. (1992) *Sex Differences in Cognitive Abilities*, Hillsdale, NJ: Lawrence Erlbaum.

Hart, R.A. (1979) *Children's Experience of Place*, New York: Ilvington.

Hart, R.A. and Moore, G.T. (1973) 'The development of spatial cognition: a review', in R.M. Downs and D. Stea (eds) *Image and Environment: Cognitive Mapping and Spatial Behavior*, Chicago, IL: Aldine.

Harvey, M. (2000) *The Island of Lost Maps*, New York: Random House.

Harwood, D. and Jackson, P. (1993) ' "Why did they build this hill so steep?": problems of assessing primary children's understanding of physical landscape features in the context of the UK National Curriculum', *International Research on Geographical and Environmental Education*, 2: 64–79.

Harwood, D. and McShane, J. (1996) 'Young children's understanding of nested hierarchies of place relationships', *International Research on Geographical and Environmental Education*, 5: 3–29.

Harwood, D. and Rawlings, K. (2001) 'Assessing young children's freehand sketch maps of the world', *International Research in Geographical and Environmental Education*, 10: 20–45.

Harwood, D. and Usher, M. (1999) 'Assessing progression in young children's map skills', *International Research in Geographical and Environmental Education*, 8: 222–38.

Head, C.G. (1972) 'Land–water differentiation in black and white cartography', *Canadian Cartographer*, 9: 25–38.

Holmes, N. (1992) *Pictorial Maps*, London: The Herbert Press.

Huttenlocher, J., Newcombe, N. and Sandberg, E.H. (1994) 'The coding of spatial location in young children', *Cognitive Psychology*, 27: 115–48.

Huttenlocher, J., Newcombe, N. and Vasilyeva, M. (1999) 'Spatial scaling in young children', *Psychological Science* 10: 393–7.

Huttenlocher, J. and Presson C.C. (1979) 'The coding and transformation of spatial information', *Cognitive Psychology*, 11: 375–94.

Imhof, E. (1975) 'Positioning names on maps', *The American Cartographer*, 2: 128–44.

Incorporated Association of Assistant Masters in Secondary Schools (IAAM) (1954) *The Teaching of Geography*, 3rd edn, London: George Philip.

Innes, L. (2003) 'Maths for map users', Proceedings of the 21st International Cartographic Conference, International Cartographic Association, 10–16 August, Durban.

ICA (International Cartographic Association) (2003) *A Strategic Plan.* <http://www.icaci.org/> (accessed 13 May 2005).

Jahoda, G. (1963) 'The development of children's ideas about country and nationality', *British Journal of Educational Psychology*, 33: 47–60.

Joshi, M.S., MacLean, M. and Carter, W. (1999) 'Children's journey to school: spatial skills, knowledge and perception of the environment', *British Journal of Developmental Psychology*, 17: 125–39.

Kadmon, N. (2000) *Toponymy*, New York: Vantage Press.

Kastens, K.A., Kaplan, D. and Christie-Blick, K. (2001) 'Development and evaluation of a technology supported map skills curriculum', *Journal of Geoscience Education*, 49: 249–66.

Keates, J.S. (1989) *Cartographic Design and Map Production*, 2nd edn, Harlow: Longman.

—— (1996) *Understanding Maps*, 2nd edn, Harlow: Longman.

Keiper, T.A. (1999) 'GIS for elementary students: an inquiry into a new approach to learning geography', *Journal of Geography*, 98: 47–59.

Keller, C.P., Hocking, D. and Wood, C.J.B. (1995) 'Planning the next generation of regional atlases: input from educators', *Journal of Geography*, 94: 412–18.

Kerski, J. (2001) 'A national assessment of GIS in American high schools', *International Research in Geographical and Environmental Education*, 10: 72–87.

—— (2003) 'The implementation and effectiveness of geographic information systems technology and methods in secondary education', *Journal of Geography*, 102: 128–37.

Kitchin, R. and Blades, M. (2002) *The Cognition of Geographic Space*, London: I.B. Taurus.

Klawe, J.J. (1965) 'The limits of editorial freedom in school atlases', *International Yearbook of Cartography*, London: George Philip.

Klett, F.R. and Alpaugh, D. (1976) 'Environmental learning and large scale environments', in G.T. Moore and R.G. Golledge (eds) *Environmental Knowing*, Stroudsberg, PA: Dowden, Hutchinson and Ross.

Knapp, C. (2003) *Making Community Connections*, Redlands, CA: ESRI Press.

Kraak, M-J. (2001) 'Web maps and atlases', in M-J. Kraak and A. Brown, *Web Cartography*, London: Taylor and Francis.

Kraak, M-J. and Ormeling, F.J. (1996) *Cartography: Visualisation of Spatial Data*, Harlow: Addison-Wesley-Longman.

Kulhavy, R.W., Lee, J.B. and Caterino, L.C. (1985) 'Conjoint retention of maps and related discourse', *Contemporary Educational Psychology*, 10: 28–37.

Kulhavy, R.W., Stock, W.A., Verdi, M.P., Rittschof, K.A. and Saveyne, W. (1994) 'Why maps improve memory for text: the influence of structural information on working memory operations', *European Journal of Cognitive Psychology*, 5: 375–92.

Kumler, M.P. and Buttenfield, B.P. (1996) 'Gender differences in map reading abilities: What do we know? What can we do?', in C.H. Wood and C.P. Keller (eds) *Cartographic Design: Theoretical and Practical Perspectives*, Chichester: Wiley.

Kwan, T. (1999) 'Pre-teenage children's vernacular perception and experience of maps in Hong Kong', *International Research in Geographical and Environmental Education*, 8: 5–25.

Lambert, S. and Wiegand, P. (1990) 'The beginnings of international understanding', *The New Era in Education*, 71: 90–3.

Lanca, M. (1998) 'Three-dimensional representation of contour maps', *Contemporary Educational Psychology*, 23: 22–41.

Landau, B. (1986) 'Early map use as an unlearned ability', *Cognition*, 22: 201–23.

Laurendeau, M. and Pinard, A. (1970) *The Development of the Concept of Space in the Child*, New York: International Universities Press.

Lawrence, V. (2003) 'Cartography and the information economy', paper presented at the 21st International Cartographic Conference, International Cartographic Association, 10–16 August, Durban.

Leinhardt, G., Stainton, C. and Bausmith, J.M. (1998) 'Constructing maps collaboratively', *Journal of Geography*, 97: 19–30.

Liben, L. (1981) 'Spatial representation and behavior: multiple perspectives', in L.S. Liben, A.H. Patterson, and N. Newcombe (eds) *Spatial Representation and Behavior across the Life Span*, New York: Academic Press.

—— (1995) 'Psychology meets geography: exploring the gender gap in the national Geography Bee', *Psychological Science Agenda*, January/February: 8–9.

—— (1997) 'Children's understanding of spatial representations of place: mapping the methodological landscape', in N. Foreman and R. Gillett (eds) *A Handbook of Spatial Research Paradigms and Methodologies*, Hove: Psychology Press.

—— (2002) 'Spatial development in childhood: where are we now?', in U. Goswami (ed.) *Blackwell Handbook of Childhood Cognitive Development*, Oxford: Blackwell.

Liben, L. and Downs, R. (1989) 'Understanding maps as symbols: the development of map concepts in children', in H. Reese (ed.) *Advances in Child Development*, New York: Academic Press.

—— (1991) 'The role of graphic representations in understanding the world', in R.M. Downs, L.S. Liben and D.S. Palermo (eds) *Visions of Aesthetics, the Environment and Development: the Legacy of Joachim F. Wohlwill*, Hillsdale, NJ: Lawrence Erlbaum Associates.

—— (1992) 'Developing an understanding of graphic representation in children and adults: the case of GEO-graphics', *Cognitive Development*, 7: 331–49.

—— (1993) 'Understanding person–space–map relations: cartographic and developmental perspectives', *Developmental Psychology*, 29: 739–52.

—— (1994) 'Fostering geographic literacy from early childhood: the contributions of interdisciplinary research', *Journal of Applied Developmental Psychology*, 15: 549–69.

—— (1997) 'Can-ism and can't-ianism: a straw child', *Annals of the Association of American Geographers*, 87: 159–67.

—— (2001) 'Geography for young children: maps as tools for learning environments', in S.L. Golbeck (ed.) *Psychological Perspectives on Early Childhood Education*, Mahwah, NJ: Lawrence Erlbaum Associates.

Liben, L., Kastens, K.A. and Stevenson, L.M. (2002) 'Real-world knowledge through real-world maps: a developmental guide for navigating the educational terrain', *Developmental Review*, 22: 267–322.

Liben, L., Moore, M. and Golbeck, S. (1982) 'Preschoolers' knowledge of their classroom environment: evidence from small-scale and life-size spatial tasks', *Child Development*, 53: 1275–84.

Liben, L. and Yekel, C.A. (1996) 'Preschoolers' understanding of plan and oblique maps: the role of geometric and representational correspondence', *Child Development*, 67: 2780–96.

Linn, M.C. and Petersen, A.C. (1985) 'Emergence and characterisation of gender differences in spatial abilities: a meta analysis', *Child Development*, 56: 1479–98.

Linn, S.E. (1997) 'The effectiveness of interactive maps in the classroom: a selected example in studying Africa', *Journal of Geography*, 96: 164–70.

Lynch, K. (1960) *The Image of the* City, Cambridge, MA: MIT Press.

McCallum, D., Rowell, J. and Ungar, S. (2003) 'Producing tactile maps using new inkjet technology: an introduction', *The Cartographic Journal*, 40: 294–8.

Maccoby, E.E. and Jacklin, C.N. (1974) *The Psychology of Sex Differences*, Stanford, CA: Stanford University Press.

MacEachren, A.M. (1995) *How Maps Work*, New York: Guilford Press.

McNamara, T.P. (1986) 'Mental representations of spatial relations', *Cognitive Psychology*, 18: 87–121.

Malone, L., Palmer, A.M. and Voigt, C.L. (2002) *Mapping Our World*, Redlands, CA: ESRI Press.

—— (2003) *Community Geography: GIS in Action. Teacher's Guide*, Redlands, CA: ESRI Press.

Matthews, M.H. (1980) 'The mental maps of children: images of Coventry's city centre', *Geography*, 65: 169–79.

—— (1984a) 'Cognitive mapping abilities of young boys and girls', *Geography*, 69: 327–36.

—— (1984b) 'Environmental cognition of young children: images of journey to school and home area', *Transactions of the Institute of British Geographers*, 9: 89–105.

—— (1985b) 'Young children's representation of the environment: a comparison of techniques', *Journal of Environmental Psychology*, 5: 261–78.

—— (1987) 'Sex differences in spatial competence: the ability of young children to map "primed" unfamiliar environments', *Educational Psychology*, 7: 77–90.

—— (1992) *Making Sense of Place: Children's Understanding of Large-scale Environments*, Hemel Hempstead: Harvester Wheatsheaf.

—— (1995) 'Culture, environmental experience and environmental awareness: making sense of young Kenyan children's views of place', *Geographical Journal*, 161: 285–95.

Miller, J.W. (1982) 'Improving the design of classroom maps: experimental comparison of alternative formats', *Journal of Geography*, 81: 51–5.

Miller, L.K. and Santoni, V. (1986) 'Sex differences in spatial abilities: strategic and experiential correlates', *Acta Psychologica*, 62: 225–35.

Mitchell, L.S. (1934) *Young Geographers*, New York: John Day (republished 1991, New York: Bank Street College of Education).

Moellering, H. (1980) 'Strategies of real time cartography', *The Cartographic Journal*, 17: 12–15.

Monmonier, M.S. (1981) 'Trends in atlas development', *Cartographica*, 18: 187–213.

—— (1996) *How to Lie with Maps*, 2nd edn, Chicago, IL: University of Chicago Press.

Moore, G.T. (1976) 'Theory and research on the development of environmental knowing', in G.T. Moore and R.G. Golledge (eds) *Environmental Knowing*, Stroudsberg, PA: Dowden, Hutchinson and Ross.

Moore, R.C. (1986) *Childhood's Domain*, Beckenham: Croom Helm.

Muehrcke, P.C. and Muehrcke, J.O. (1974) 'Maps in literature', *Geographical Review*, 64: 317–38.

Muller, J.C. (1985) 'Mental maps at a global scale', *Cartographica*, 22: 51–9.

National Geographic Society (2001) *Path Toward World Literacy: A Standards Based Guide to K-12 Geography*, San Marcos, TX: Gilbert M. Grosvenor Center for Geographic Education.

National Geography Standards (1994) *Geography for Life*, Washington, DC: National Geographic Research and Exploration.

Nebel, J. (1984) 'German children's perception of France', in H. Haubrich (ed.) *Perception of People and Places through Media*, Freiburg: Pädagogische Hochschule.

Nelson, B.D., Aron, R.H. and Francek, M.A. (1992) 'Clarification of selected misconceptions in physical geography', *Journal of Geography*, 91: 76–80.

Newcombe, N.S. (1989) 'Development of spatial perspective taking', in H.W. Reese (ed.) *Advances in Child Development and Behavior*, vol. 22, New York: Academic Press.

Newcombe, N.S. and Huttenlocher, J. (1992) 'Children's early ability to solve perspective taking problems', *Developmental Psychology*, 28: 635–43.

—— (2000) *Making Space: The Development of Spatial Representation and Reasoning*, London: The MIT Press.

Newcombe, N.S., Huttenlocher, J., Drummey, A.B. and Wiley, J.G. (1998) 'The development of spatial location coding: place learning and dead reckoning in the second and third years', *Cognitive Development*, 13: 185–200.

Nussbaum, J. (1985) 'The Earth as a cosmic body', in R. Driver, E. Guesne and A. Tiberghien (eds) *Children's Ideas in Science*, Milton Keynes: Open University Press.

Ottosson, T. (1987) *Map Reading and Wayfinding*, Göteborg Studies in Educational Studies, 65, Gothenburg: Acta Universitatis Gothoburgensis.

Overjørdet, A.H. (1984) 'Children's views of the world during an international media covered conflict', in H. Haubrich (ed.) *Perception of People and Places through Media*, Freiburg: Pädagogische Hochschule.

Owen, D. (2003) 'Collaborative electronic map creation in a UK 5–11 primary school: children's representation of local space and the role of peer and teacher scaffolding in this process', Proceedings of the 21st International Cartographic Conference, International Cartographic Association, 10–16 August, Durban.

Paivio, A. (1986) *Mental Representations: A Dual Coding Approach*, New York: Oxford University Press.

Passini, E. (2003) Paper presented at the Cartography and Children Commission of the International Cartographic Association Conference, 8–9 August, Cape Town.

Patton, J.C. and Crawford, P.V. (1978) 'The perception of hypsometric colours', *The Cartographic Journal*, 15: 115–27.

Perkins, C. and Gardiner, A. (2003) 'Real world map strategies', *The Cartographic Journal*, 40: 265–8.

Petchenik, B.B. (1985) 'Facts or values: basic methodological issues in research for educational mapping', *Cartographica*, 22: 20–42.

Phillips, R.J. (1979) 'An experiment with contour lines', *The Cartographic Journal*, 16: 72–6.

Phillips, R.J., de Lucia, A. and Skelton, N. (1975) 'Some objective tests of the legibility of relief maps', *The Cartographic Journal*, 12: 39–46.

Piaget, J. and Inhelder, B. (1956) *The Child's Conception of Space*, London: Routledge.

Piaget, J., Inhelder, B. and Szeminska, A. (1960) *The Child's Conception of Geometry*, London: Routledge and Kegan Paul.

Piaget, J. and Weil, A. (1951) 'The development in children of the idea of homeland and of relations with other countries', *Institute of Social Science Bulletin*, 3: 561–78.

Piché, D. (1981) 'The spontaneous geography of the urban child', in D.T. Herbert and R.J. Johnston (eds) *Geography and the Urban Environment: Progress in Research and Applications*, vol. 4, Chichester: John Wiley.

Pilkington, R.M. (1999) *Analysing Educational Discourse: The DISCOUNT Scheme*. Technical Report No. 99/2, Leeds: University of Leeds Computer Based Learning Unit.

Plester, B., Blades, M. and Spencer, C. (2003) 'Children's understanding of aerial photographs', *Children's Geographies*, 1: 281–93.

Postigo, Y. and Pozo, J.I. (1998) 'The learning of a geographical map by experts and novices', *Educational Psychology*, 18: 65–80.

Potash, L.M. (1977) 'Design of maps and map related research', *Human Factors*, 19: 139–50.

Potash, L.M., Farrell, J.P. and Jeffrey, T. (1978) 'A technique for assessing map relief legibility', *The Cartographic Journal*, 15: 28–35.

Potter, R.B. (1985) 'The development of spatial cognitive maps among Barbadian children', *Journal of Social Psychology*, 125: 675–7.

Provin, R.W. (1977) 'The perception of numerousness on dot maps', *American Cartographer*, 4: 111–25.

Pufall, P.B. (1975) 'Egocentrism in spatial thinking: it depends on your point of view', *Developmental Psychology*, 11: 297–303.

Pufall, P.B. and Shaw, R.E. (1973) 'Analysis of the development of children's spatial reference systems', *Cognitive Psychology*, 5: 151–75.

Radziszewska, B. and Rogoff, B. (1991) 'Children's guided participation in planning imaginary errands with skilled adult or peer partners', *Developmental Psychology*, 24: 840–8.

Rittschof, K.A., Kulhavy, R.W., Stock, W.A., Verdi, M.P. and Hatcher, J. (1993) 'Thematic maps and text: an analysis of "what happened there?"', *Cartographica*, 30: 87–93.

Rittschoff, K.A., Stock, W.A., Kulhavy, R.W., Verdi, M.P. and Doran, J.P. (1994) 'Thematic maps improve memory for facts and inferences: a test of the stimulus order hypothesis', *Contemporary Educational Psychology*, 19: 129–42.

Rosser, R.A. (1983) 'The emergence of spatial perspective taking: an information processing alternative to egocentrism', *Child Development*, 54: 660–8.

Rowell, J. and Ungar, S. (2003a) 'The world of touch: results of an international survey of tactile maps and symbols', *The Cartographic Journal*, 40: 259–64.

—— (2003b) 'A taxonomy for tactile symbols: creating a useable database for tactile map designers', *The Cartographic Journal*, 40: 273–6.

Rumelhart, D.E. and Norman, D.A. (1985) 'Representation of knowledge', in A.M. Aitkenhead and J.M. Slack (eds) *Issues in Cognitive Modeling*, Hillsdale, NJ: Lawrence Erlbaum Associates.

Saarinen, T.F. (1973) 'Student views of the world', in R.M. Downs and D. Stea (eds) *Image and Environment*, Chicago, IL: Aldine.

—— (1999) 'The Eurocentric nature of mental maps of the world', *Research in Geographic Education*, 1: 136–78.

Sandberg, E.H. and Huttenlocher, J. (2001) 'Advanced spatial skills and advance planning: components of 6-year-olds' navigational map use', *Journal of Cognition and Development*, 2: 51–70.

Sandford, H.A. (1972) 'Perceptual problems', in N. Graves (ed.) *New Movements in the Teaching and Learning of Geography*, London: Temple Smith.

—— (1978) 'Taking a fresh look at atlases', *Teaching Geography*, 4: 62–5.

—— (1979) 'Things maps don't tell us', *Geography*, 64: 297–302.

—— (1980a) 'Directed and free search of the school atlas map', *The Cartographic Journal*, 17: 83–92.

—— (1980b) 'Map design for children', *Bulletin of the Society of University Cartographers*, 14: 39–48.

—— (1981) 'Towns on maps', *The Cartographic Journal*, 18: 120–7.

—— (1985) 'The future of the school pupils' desk atlas', *The Cartographic Journal*, 22: 3–10.

—— (1986) 'Atlases and atlas mapwork', in D. Boardman (ed.) *Handbook for Geography Teachers*, Sheffield: The Geographical Association.

—— (1990) 'The geographical name in modern school atlases: a study of the reasons for the persistence of exonyms despite the worldwide adoption of standardised names', *The Cartographic Journal*, 27: 137–41.

Scholnick, E.K., Fein, G.G. and Campbell, P.F. (1990) 'Changing predictors of map use in wayfinding', *Developmental Psychology*, 26: 188–93.

Schwartz, N.H. (1997) 'Human information processing of maps: a report to the geographic community', in R.G. Boehm and J.F. Petersen (eds) *The First Assessment: Research in Geographic Education*, San Marcos, TX: Gilbert M. Grosvenor Center for Geographic Education.

Shevelan, C., Craddock, S., Spencer, C. and Blades, M. (2002) 'Learn to look down', *Primary Geographer*, 47: 30–1.

Shiffrin, R.M. and Atkinson, R.C. (1969) 'Storage and retrieval processes in long term memory', *Psychological Review*, 76: 179–93.

Siegel, A.W., Herman, J.F., Allen, G.L. and Kirasic, K.C. (1979) 'The development of cognitive maps in large and small scale spaces', *Child Development*, 50: 582–5.

Siegel, A.W. and Schadler, M. (1977) 'The development of young children's spatial representations of their classrooms', *Child Development*, 48: 388–94.

Siekierska, E. and Müller, A. (2003) 'Tactile and audio-tactile maps within the Canadian "Government On-Line" program', *The Cartographic Journal*, 40: 299–304.

Smith, G. (1999) 'Changing fieldwork objectives and constraints in secondary schools in England', *International Research in Geographical and Environmental Education*, 8: 181–9.

Sneider, C. and Pulos, S. (1983) 'Children's cosmologies: understanding the Earth's shape and gravity', *Science Education*, 67: 205–21.

Somerville, S.C. and Bryant, P.E. (1985) 'Young children's use of spatial coordinates', *Child Development*, 56: 604–13.

Sorrel, P. (1974) 'Map design – with the young in mind', *The Cartographic Journal*, 11: 82–90.

Sowden, S., Stea, D., Blades, M., Spencer, C. and Blaut, J. (1996) 'Mapping abilities of four year old children in York, England', *Journal of Geography*, 95: 107–11.

Spencer, C.P., Blades, M. and Morsley, K. (1989) *The Child in the Physical Environment*, Chichester: John Wiley.

Spencer, C., Harrison, N. and Darvizeh, Z. (1980) 'The development of iconic mapping ability in young children', *International Journal of Early Childhood*, 12: 57–64.

Spencer, D. and Lloyd, J. (1974) *A Child's Eye View of Small Heath, Birmingham*. Research Memorandum 34, Birmingham: University of Birmingham.

Stevens, A. and Coupe, P. (1978) 'Distortions in judged spatial relations', *Cognitive Psychology*, 10: 422–37.

Tatham, A.F. (2003) 'Tactile mapping: today, yesterday and tomorrow', *The Cartographic Journal*, 40: 255–8.

Tischer, L. (2002) Using GIS to Teach Basic Skills to Young Learning Disabled Children. <http://gis.esri.com/library/userconf/proc02/pap0122/p0122.htm> (accessed 13 May, 2005).

Towler, J.O. (1970) 'The elementary school child's concept of reference systems', *Journal of Geography*, 69: 89–93.

Towler, J.O. and Nelson, L.D. (1968) 'The elementary school child's concept of scale', *Journal of Geography*, 67: 24–8.

Trifonoff, K.M. (1995) 'Going beyond location: thematic maps in the early elementary grades', *Journal of Geography*, 94: 368–74.

Tshibalo, A.E. (2003) 'Cooperative learning as a strategy to improve the teaching of mapwork to grade 11 and 12 geography learners', Proceedings of the 21st International Cartographic Conference, International Cartographic Association, 10–16 August, Durban.

Tversky, B. (1981) 'Distortions in memory for maps', *Cognitive Psychology*, 13: 407–33.

Ungar, S., Blades, M. and Spencer, C. (1996) 'The ability of visually impaired children to locate themselves on a tactile map', *Journal of Visual Impairment and Blindness*, Nov–Dec: 526–35.

—— (1997) 'Teaching visually impaired children to make distance judgments from a tactile map', *Journal of Visual Impairment and Blindness*, Mar–Apr: 163–74.

Ungar, S., Blades, M., Spencer, C. and Morsley, K. (1994) 'Can visually impaired children use tactile maps to estimate directions?' *Journal of Visual Impairment and Blindness*, May–June: 221–33.

Uttal, D. (1994) 'Preschoolers' and adults' scale translation and reconstruction of spatial information acquired from maps', *British Journal of Developmental Psychology*, 12: 259–75.

—— (1996) 'Angles and distances: children's and adults' reconstruction and scaling of spatial configurations', *Child Development*, 67: 2763–79.

—— (2000) 'Seeing the big picture: map use and the development of spatial cognition', *Developmental Science*, 3: 247–86.

Uttal, D.H. and Wellman, H.W. (1989) 'Young children's representation of spatial information acquired from maps', *Developmental Psychology*, 25: 128–38.

van der Schee, J., van Dijk, H. and van Westrhenen, H. (1992) 'Geographical procedural knowledge and map skills', in H. Schrettenbrunner and J. van Westrhenen (eds) *Empirical Research and Geography Teaching*, Utrecht and Amsterdam: Koninklijk Nederlands Aardrijkskundig Genootschap and Centrum fur Educatieve Geografie Vrije Universiteit Amsterdam.

van Dijk, H., van der Schee, J., Trimp, H. and van der Zijpp, T. (1994) 'Map skills and geographical knowledge', *International Research in Geographical and Environmental Education*, 3: 68–80.

van Swaaij, L. and Klare, J. (2000) *The Atlas of Experience*, London: Bloomsbury.

Vosniadou, S. and Brewer, W.F. (1992) 'Mental models of the Earth: a study of conceptual change in childhood', *Cognitive Psychology*, 24: 535–85.

Vujakovic, P. (2003) 'Damn or be damned: Arno Peters and the struggle for the "New Cartography"', *The Cartographic Journal*, 40: 61–7.

Vygotsky, L. (1962) *Thought and Language*, Cambridge, MA: MIT Press.

—— (1978) *Mind in Society*, Cambridge, MA: Harvard University Press.

Walsh, S.E. and Martland, J.R. (1993) 'The orientation and navigational skills of young children: an application of two intervention strategies', *Journal of Navigation*, 46: 63–8.

West, B.A. (2003) 'Student attitudes and the impact of GIS on thinking skills and motivation', *Journal of Geography*, 102: 267–74.

Wiegand, P. (1991) 'The known world of the primary school', *Geography*, 76: 143–9.

—— (1995) 'Young children's freehand sketch maps of the world', *International Research in Geographical and Environmental Education*, 4: 19–28.

—— (1998a) 'Children's free recall sketch maps of the world on a spherical surface', *International Research in Geographical and Environmental Education*, 7: 67–83.

—— (1998b) 'Atlases as a teaching resource: findings from a national survey', *Geography*, 83: 1–9.

—— (2002a) 'School students' mental representations of thematic point symbol maps', *The Cartographic Journal*, 39: 125–36.

—— (2002b) 'Analysis of discourse in collaborative cartographic problem solving', *International Research in Geographical and Environmental Education*, 11: 138–58.

—— (2003) 'School students' understanding of choropleth maps: evidence from collaborative mapmaking using GIS', *Journal of Geography*, 102: 234–42.

Wiegand, P. and Stiell, B. (1996a) 'Children's estimations of the sizes of the continents', *Educational Studies*, 22: 57–68.

—— (1996b) 'Lost continents? Children's understanding of the location and orientation of the Earth's land masses', *Educational Studies*, 22: 383–94.

—— (1996c) 'Communication in children's picture atlases', *The Cartographic Journal*, 33: 17–25.

—— (1997a) 'The development of children's sketch maps of the British Isles', *The Cartographic Journal*, 34: 13–21.

—— (1997b) 'Children's relief maps of model landscapes', *British Educational Research Journal*, 23: 179–92.

Winchester, S. (2001) *The Map that Changed the World*, London: Viking.

Winston, B.J. (1984) *Map and Globe Skills: K-8 Teaching Guide*, Macomb, IL: National Council for Geographic Education.

Wonders, L.J. (1980) 'The Junior Atlas of Alberta', *Canadian Geographer*, 24: 306–11.

Wood, D. (1992) *The Power of Maps*, New York: Guilford Press.

Index

abbreviations 61, 110
AEGIS 3 121
aerial photographs 12, 27–9, 50, 120
alphanumeric grid code 36, 111, 114, 117, 127
ArcView 7, 66, 76–7, 121
assessment criteria 46ff
atlases, school 83ff, 104, 106, 114–15

blind map users 13, 98–9
Bloom's taxonomy of educational objectives 94

cardinal directions *see* compass directions
cartograms 119
choropleth maps 65–6, 92, 122
cognitive maps 45
collaborative map making 8, 21, 96, 113
colour on maps 54–5, 60, 65, 113, 125, 128–9
community mapping 8, 95
comparitor map 108–9, 119
compass directions 34, 41, 92, 94–5, 97, 99, 107–8, 111, 117
concentric curriculum 93
configurational knowledge 40
contours 55, 58–9, 59ff, 92, 98, 113, 119, 122
cross sections 97–8, 120
curriculum evaluation 96

data classification 65–6
degree confluence project 117
digital elevation model (DEM) 55–6, 137
digital orthophoto quadrangle (DOQ) 55–6
directionality of data 66
discourse analysis 21, 66
distance 51, 99, 111, 114, 119
dual coding theory 24

Earth, children's conceptions of 67–9, 77–9, 114
Earth, dimensions of 67, 116
economic point symbol maps 23–4, 63–5
Eckert IV projection 74–5

electronic atlases 85–6
ethnocentrism 74
Euclidean spatial relations 15, 17–18, 97, 136

fiction, maps in 104
fiction, map stimulus for 119
figure-ground 125–6

gender differences 97–8
geometric correspondence 29
Geographic Information Systems (GIS) 1, 8–9, 15, 21, 65, 76, 85, 86, 94, 95–6, 113, 116, 121–3, 137
Global Positioning System (GPS) 1, 9, 44, 116, 122, 137
globe 10, 67, 75, 77–9, 92, 100, 104, 108, 114–15, 117
gradient 91, 92, 102, 117, 122
grid references 22, 36, 86, 92, 104, 117–18, 127, 137

hachures 55, 113
hill signs 21, 113
home range 46, 97

imaginary maps 1, 95
information processing 12, 22–5
Internet mapping *see* web cartography
inset maps 53, 126

'journey to school' maps 48–9, 96

key *see* map legend

landmarks 41, 47, 97, 112, 117
landscape concepts 56–7, 102, 110, 112–13
language 37, 56–7, 40–1, 98, 100–1, 106, 109–10, 118–19, 134–5
'lexical' atlas usage 85, 114
Local Studies 50, 113, 121
location finding 30–3, 91, 99, 103–4, 119
location, memory for 80
locator maps 85, 119, 125–6

map alignment 32, 33–4, 44, 103, 107–8
map analysis 91–2
map, children's concept of 29
map coordinates 22, 36, 86, 92, 104, 108–9, 117–18
map evaluation 120–1
map frame 124–5
map games 104
map generalisation 53, 137
map interpretation 91–2, 96, 122, 138
map legend 22, 60–1, 63, 65, 120, 125, 128–30
map projections 10, 15, 74–7, 86, 92, 119
map reading 91–2, 119, 138
map scale 10, 28, 34–6, 51–3, 66, 84–5, 86, 91–2, 101, 106, 108, 111, 120, 125, 128, 137
map symbology 8, 10, 37, 47, 53–5, 63–6, 91–2, 101, 104, 113, 119, 120, 128–30
map text 22, 37, 55, 61–2, 105, 109–10, 128, 130–3
map title 113, 120, 126–7
map use 91, 119, 120
map viewing angle 34
'map-like objects' 26
measurement 36, 51–3, 106, 111, 112, 137
memory 22, 24, 80, 82–3, 97
Mercator projection 74–5
meta-representation 37, 66
meta-language of maps 116, 118
metric spatial relations *see* Euclidean spatial relations
mimetic symbols 63
models 12, 13, 26–7, 28, 34–5, 45, 47–8, 55, 57–9, 93, 102, 113, 119

nativism 12–13
naïve conventional representation 37
navigation *see* wayfinding
nested spatial hierarchy 80–2, 94, 101
normalised data 66

object correspondence 27, 29
oblique Aitoff projection 75
Ordnance Survey 1, 2, 51, 54, 59, 60, 97
orienteering 44
Orton Family Foundation Community Mapping Program 95

Peters' projection 74–5
Piaget, J. 12–19, 47, 48, 80
picture maps 43, 48–9, 62–3, 104
place knowledge 69, 97
place names 37, 56, 101, 105, 109–10, 118–19, 131–2, 133–5

plan view 45, 48–9, 58, 101, 104, 110–11
playbases 102–3
political maps 129
post codes 86, 112, 137
progression 47, 92ff
projective spatial relations 12–18, 136
proportional symbols 65

qualitative symbols 63
quantitative symbols 63

relational correspondence 27, 29
relief interpretation 55–61, 97, 113, 119
relief mapping 55ff
representational correspondence 29
route descriptions 40–2, 103–4, 107, 111–12, 122
route knowledge 97

scaling ability 34–6, 48
sense of place 43, 62, 86
sketch maps (neighbourhood) 45ff, 97
sketch maps (own country) 79–80
sketch maps (world) 69ff, 122
sketch maps (of world, on spherical surface) 77–9
schemata 14, 22–3
spatial hierarchy *see* nested spatial hierarchy
spatial information storage *see* memory
spatial relations 40, 46, 67, 97
special educational needs 98–9
stereotypes 101
street maps 37–8, 109–10
survey knowledge 30
syncretic representation 37

tactile maps 13, 98–9
thematic maps 10, 51, 63ff
time zones 92
Textease 50
topographic maps 10, 51, 92, 98, 122
topological spatial relations 15–18, 136
'three mountains' task 17, 19

United States Geological Survey 51

visual anchors 65
visual variables 10, 22, 120
visually impaired map users 13, 98–9
Vygotsky, L. 12, 20–2

wayfinding 39ff, 122
web cartography 86
Where are we? project 96

eBooks

eBooks – at www.eBookstore.tandf.co.uk

A library at your fingertips!

eBooks are electronic versions of printed books. You can store them on your PC/laptop or browse them online.

They have advantages for anyone needing rapid access to a wide variety of published, copyright information.

eBooks can help your research by enabling you to bookmark chapters, annotate text and use instant searches to find specific words or phrases. Several eBook files would fit on even a small laptop or PDA.

NEW: Save money by eSubscribing: cheap, online access to any eBook for as long as you need it.

Annual subscription packages

We now offer special low-cost bulk subscriptions to packages of eBooks in certain subject areas. These are available to libraries or to individuals.

For more information please contact webmaster.ebooks@tandf.co.uk

We're continually developing the eBook concept, so keep up to date by visiting the website.

www.eBookstore.tandf.co.uk